*Medieval and Renaissance Studies
in honour of Robert Brian Tate*

MEDIEVAL AND RENAISSANCE STUDIES IN HONOUR OF ROBERT BRIAN TATE

Edited by Ian Michael and Richard A. Cardwell

Oxford, The Dolphin Book Co., 1986

The editors and publisher wish to express
their sincere thanks to the following for
the generous financial assistance which has
made the publication of this volume possible:
University of Belfast, University of Nottingham,
Ministério da Educação Instituto de Cultura
e Língua Portuguesa, and the Calouste
Gulbenkian Foundation.

PRINTED IN SPAIN

ISBN: 0-85215-073-3

Depósito legal: V. 67 - 1986   ISBN (España): 84-599-1213-2 (tela)

Artes Gráficas Soler, S. A., Valencia

CONTENTS

FOREWORD

Omne bien instruto, omne de verdad

S E E K I N G to express the essential nature of Spain's leading historian
and philologist, one commentator found his answer in the words of the
fifteenth-century historiographer Fernando del Pulgar. [1] In the case of the
colleague honoured by the present volume, whose connections with Pulgar
are even closer, the link immediately springs to mind:

> Era omne bien instruto en las letras latinas e tenía tan buena memoria que
> pocas cosas se le olvidavan de lo que en la Sacra Escritura avía leído. Era omne
> de verdad e aborrescía tanto mentiras e mentirosos, que ninguno de los tales
> ovo jamás logar cerca dél.

This pen-portrait, from *Claros varones de Castilla,* is of Don Diego Hurtado de Mendoza, the first Duke of Infantado, and not of Robert Brian
Tate. The coincidences, however, are clear, and Fernando del Pulgar
was fortunate in that Hispanism was to provide him in 1971 with a
modern editor who shared his concern for historiography and who was
himself endowed with the retentive memory, the love of truth and the
depth of learning which Pulgar so admired in the Duke of Infantado. These
essays represent a tribute from friends and colleagues to that editor, Brian
Tate, to mark his retirement in 1983 from the Chair of Spanish at the
University of Nottingham.

The one inappropriate note struck by Pulgar's portrait is contained
in the imperfect indicatives which introduce each sentence, for it is very
clear that retirement for Brian Tate has represented a smooth and logical
transition rather than the end of an epoch. He continues as a Fellow
of the British Academy, as a Corresponding Fellow of the Institut d'Estudis Catalans, the Real Academia de la Historia, and the Reial Acadèmia
de Bones Lletres de Barcelona; he is an active and voluble Committee
member of the Asociación Internacional de Hispanistas and the Anglo-
Catalan Society; his Presidential Address delivered to the Association of

---

[1] Yakov Malkiel on Don Ramón Menéndez Pidal, *Romance Philology,* XXIII
(1969-70), 371.

Hispanists of Great Britain and Ireland in 1985 revealed that he has lost nothing of his historical acumen, his powers of persuasion and his ability to transcend the particular; he is still publishing scholarly articles and has been recently engaged in preparing new Spanish editions of Pulgar's *Claros varones de Castilla,* for Taurus, and Don Juan Manuel's *Libro de los estados,* for Castalia.

Brian Tate's academic career has been distinguished. Born in Belfast, Northern Ireland, in 1921, he learned his Spanish at the Royal Belfast Academical Institution, and became an undergraduate at the Queen's University in Belfast in 1939. Nine years later, after a course interrupted for four years by war service in the Far East, he graduated with a First Class Honours Degree in French and Spanish, and was a committed Hispanist. A University post, following a year of postgraduate study in Barcelona, was the next logical step: he was appointed to an Assistant Lectureship in Manchester in 1949, moved to a full lectureship in Queen's University, Belfast, in 1952, and to a Readership in Nottingham in 1956. Although Brian Tate and Nottingham have seemed almost synonymous to Hispanists for the twenty-seven years in which he chaired the Department, and although in that period the Nottingham Department can be seen to have taken much of its distinctive colouring from him, Brian has remained calmly unpretentious, and ever ready to acknowledge his debt to his early mentors. Ignasi González-Llubera and J. W. Rees, who were in charge of the Departments at Belfast and Manchester, respectively, during his apprenticeship there, set a style of scholarship, dedication and honesty which, coupled with a concern for detail and a love of the classics, was to leave its imprint upon a whole generation of British Hispanists, an extended Manchester-Irish family to which Brian has always been proud to belong.

This family, now scattered over all parts of the United Kingdom and Ireland, and spanning three generations, has in no sense been a "school", but rather a collection of individuals with a lively interest in things Hispanic, a healthy respect for one another's work, and a will to cooperate rather than compete in the search for truth. On the evidence of his adaptation of Vilar's *History,* or his entry in the Russell *Companion,* Brian Tate could have been a historian in the traditional mould; his "Adventures in the Sierra" article in Gybbon-Monypenny's *"Libro de buen amor" Studies* illustrates his sensitivity as a literary critic. He has emerged, however, from among his peers as the one who in the course of his career has most determinedly pursued the desire to stand astride the fields of history and literature, to focus his attention on texts generally classed as historical, and to study in them, to quote his own words, "what was written rather than what was written about". In this he has been a creator of fashion rather than a follower: critical reaction to his published work on Fernán Pérez de Guzmán, Fernando del Pulgar and Juan Manuel is eloquent testimony to the validity of the approach.

Like many of his friends, Brian has never subscribed to the notion that scholars should spend all of their lives in libraries, nor that a medievalist should don a chronological blindfold immediately upon completing a reading of *Celestina*. The delight which he takes in the whole European cultural tradition informs both his teaching and his conversation. He has taught widely at Nottingham, on subjects as varied as Cervantes, Camões, Golden Age drama and the modern novel; his love of Catalunya and its language is enduring. His photography is for him an art form as well as an account of his many and varied travels, and it is characteristic that his first major expedition, upon retirement, was along the pilgrim route to Santiago, in the company of his son Marcus, in order to compile a personal visual record of a period of European history about which he cares.

It is always to be expected that one will run into Brian Tate in Spain, but the encounter is as likely to be over a *caña* in a Segovian café as over an autograph manuscript of Alfonso de Palencia in the Escorial. And this is in many ways the measure of the man: the combination of humanity and scholarship, the determination to seek out the truth, and the lively and outgoing interest in the world around him in all its complexity. These have characterized his personal relationships and his scholarly concerns, and make of him a good friend and a respected colleague. To Brian Tate, who, like Diego Hurtado de Mendoza, "todas las cautelas e fictiones aborrescía como cosa contraria a su natural condición", the contributors offer this homage volume, unpretentiously, as a measure of our continuing friendship and professional esteem.

IAN MACPHERSON

University of Durham

CURRICULUM VITÆ ROBERT BRIAN TATE

Born:

Belfast, Northern Ireland, 27 December, 1921.

Education:

Royal Belfast Academical Institution, 1933-39.
Queen's University, Belfast, 1939-41; 1946-48.
B. A. (First Class) in Spanish and French, 1948.
Graduate work with Dr. J. Rubió Balaguer, Barcelona, 1948-49.
M. A. (Belfast), 1949; Ph.D. (Belfast), 1955.

Academic Experience:

Assistant Lecturer in Spanish, University of Manchester, 1949-52.
Lecturer in Spanish, The Queen's University, Belfast, 1952-56.
Reader in Spanish, University of Nottingham, 1956-58.
Professor and Head of Department of Spanish (subsequently of Hispanic Studies), University of Nottingham, 1958-83.
Dean of the Faculty of Arts, University of Nottingham, 1976-79.
Founding committee member and President of Association of Hispanists of Great Britain and Ireland.
Founding committee member, President and committee member of the Anglo-Catalan Society.
Committee member of the Asociación Internacional de Hispanistas.
Founding committee member and Honorary President of the Association of Teachers of Spanish and Portuguese (East Midlands Branch).

Honours:

Corresponding Fellow of the Institut d'Estudis Catalans, Barcelona, 1964.
Corresponding Fellow of the Real Academia de la Historia, Madrid, 1974.
Corresponding Fellow of the Reial Acadèmia de Bones Lletres, Barcelona, 1980.
Fellow of the British Academy, 1980.

PUBLICATIONS

BOOKS

Joan Margarit i Pau, a biographical study, Manchester: University Press, 1954.
Edited with introduction and notes, Fernán Pérez de Guzmán, *Generaciones y semblanzas*, London: Tamesis, 1965.

English translation of Pierre Vilar, *Spain: A Brief History*, Oxford: Pergamon, 1967, 2nd. edn., 1977.

Ensayos sobre la historiografía peninsular del siglo XV, Madrid: Gredos, 1970.

Edited with introduction and notes, Fernando del Pulgar, *Claros varones de Castilla*, Oxford: Clarendon Press, 1971; revised Spanish edn., Madrid: Taurus, 1985.

"The Medieval Kingdoms of the Iberian Peninsula", in P. E. Russell (ed.), *Spain. A Companion to Spanish Studies*, London: Methuen, 1973, pp. 65-105; revised Spanish edn., *Introducción a la cultura hispánica*, I. *Historia, arte, música*, Barcelona: Crítica, 1982, pp. 83-130.

Edited (jointly with I. R. Macpherson) with introduction and notes, Don Juan Manuel, *Libro de los estados*, Oxford: Clarendon Press, 1974; revised Spanish edn., Madrid: Clásicos Castalia, 1986.

El cardenal Joan Margarit, vida i obra, Barcelona: Curial, 1976.

Edited (jointly with A. Yates), *Actes del Tercer Col·loqui Internacional de Llengua i Literatura Catalanes...*, Oxford: Dolphin, 1976.

Edited with introduction and notes, Anon., *Directorio de príncipes*, Exeter Hispanic Texts, Exeter: University, 1977.

Edited (jointly with Rafael Alemany Ferrer) with introduction and notes, Alonso de Palencia, *Epístolas latinas*, Barcelona: Universidad Autónoma, 1982 (1984).

"The *Lusiads* of Camoens and the Legacy of Virgil", in *Virgil in a Cultural Tradition*, Nottingham Monographs in the Humanities (at press).

ARTICLES

"Joan Margarit, Bishop of Gerona", *Speculum*, XXVII (1952), 28-52.

(Jointly with A. Fernández Torregrosa) "Vicent Climent, un valenciano en Inglaterra", *Estudios de Historia Moderna*, VI (1956-59), 3-56.

"The Literary Persona from Díez de Games to Santa Teresa", *Romance Philology*, XIII (1959-60), 298-304.

Introduction to T. S. Eliot, *Quatre Quartets*, versió catalana de Lluís M. Aragó, Palma de Mallorca: Daedalus, 1965.

"Joanot Martorell in England", *Estudis Romànics*, X (1967), 277-81.

"Adventures in the Sierra", in G. B. Gybbon-Monypenny (ed.), *"Libro de buen amor" Studies*, London: Tamesis, 1970, pp. 219-29.

"Don Juan Manuel and his Sources: *Ejemplos* 48, 28, 1", in *Studia Hispanica in honorem R. Lapesa*, 3 vols., Madrid: Gredos, 1972, I, pp. 549-61.

(Jointly with A. M. Mundó) "The *Compendiolum* of Alfonso de Palencia: a humanist treatise on the geography of the Iberian Peninsula", *Journal of Medieval and Renaissance Studies*, 5 (1975), 253-78.

"Who wrote *Don Quixote*?" *Vida Hispánica*, 25 (1977), 5-12.

"Political Allegory in Fifteenth-century Spain: a study of the *Batalla campal de los perros contra los lobos* by Alfonso de Palencia", *Journal of Hispanic Philology*, I (1977), 169-86.

"Don Juan Manuel and the Archbishop of Toledo", in I. R. Macpherson (ed.), *Juan Manuel Studies*, London: Tamesis, 1977, pp. 169-79.

"La geografía humanística y los historiadores españoles del siglo xv", in P.S.N. Russell-Gebbett (ed.), *Belfast Papers in Spanish and Portuguese*, Belfast: Queen's University, 1979, pp. 237-42.

"The Civic Humanism of Alfonso de Palencia", *Renaissance and Modern Studies*, XXIII (1979), 25-44.

Entries in *Dictionary of the Middle Ages*, New York: Scribner, 1980-.

"Margarit i el tema dels gots", in *Actes del Cinquè Col·loqui Internacional de Llengua i Literatura Catalanes...*, Abadia de Montserrat, 1981, pp. 151-68.

"Descripción de un Ms. perdido de las *Crónicas* del canciller Ayala", *Incipit*, I (1981), 81-84.

"Alfonso de Palencia y los preceptos de la historiografía", in *Actas de la III Academia Literaria Renacentista*, Salamanca: Universidad, 1983, pp. 37-51.

"Las *Décadas* de Alfonso de Palencia: un análisis historiográfico", in J. M. Ruiz Veintemilla (ed.), *Estudios dedicados a James Leslie Brooks*, Barcelona: Puvill, 1984, pp. 223-41.

"La sociedad castellana en la obra de Alfonso de Palencia", in *Actas del III Coloquio de Historia Medieval Andaluza*, Jaén, 1984, pp. 5-23.

"El cronista real castellano durante el siglo xv", in *Miscelánea Pedro Sáinz Rodríguez* (at press).

LONGER REVIEWS

Daniel Devoto, *Introducción al estudio de don Juan Manuel y en particular de "El conde Lucanor": una bibliografía* (Valencia, 1972), in *Modern Language Review*, 71 (1976), 671-75.

O. di Camillo, *El humanismo castellano del siglo XV* (Valencia, 1976), in *Modern Language Review*, 73 (1978), 444-47.

R. Boase, *The Troubadour Revival: A Study of Social Change and Traditionalism in Late Medieval Spain* (London, 1978), in *Modern Language Review*, 75 (1980), 211-14.

TABLE OF ABBREVIATIONS

BAE: Biblioteca de Autores Españoles
BHS: *Bulletin of Hispanic Studies*
BN: Biblioteca Nacional [Madrid, unless otherwise stated]
BRAE: *Boletín de la Real Academia Española*
ER: *Estudis Romànics*
EUC: *Estudis Universitaris Catalans*
HID: *Historia Instituciones Documentos*
HR: *Hispanic Review*
JEH: *The Journal of Ecclesiastical History*
JHPh: *Journal of Hispanic Philology*
MLN: *Modern Language Notes*
MLR: *Modern Language Review*
NLH: *New Literary History*
NRFH: *Nueva Revista de Filología Hispánica*
PL: J. P. Migne, *Patrologia Latina*
P&P: *Past and Present*
RABM: *Revista de Archivos, Bibliotecas y Museos*
RFE: *Revista de Filología Española*
RH: *Revue Hispanique*
RHE: *Revue d'Histoire Ecclésiastique*
ZRPh: *Zeitschrift für Romanische Philologie*

LOST LITERATURE IN MEDIEVAL PORTUGUESE

"A s s i m, na nossa história cultural da época, em vez das vastas e sólidas superfícies, só enxergamos, na maioria dos casos, as ilhas isoladas e meio perdidas umas das outras. Temos a impressão de estarmos a ver os pontos mais altos dum continente que se afundou, deixando, apenas, algumas manchas à flor inquieta das águas". [1] Mário Martins's words, written some thirty years ago, refer mainly to religious prose, the field in which he has long been recognized as the leading explorer; but the same could be said of most genres in most medieval literatures. The proportions of lost to surviving works vary from one genre to another, of course: historiography has a far higher survival rate than oral poetry. Yet even in genres where learned authors committed extensive works to parchment, and even towards the end of the Middle Ages, the rate of loss can be surprisingly high: to take but one example, nearly forty Castilian historical works of the Trastámaran dynasty seem to have been lost, some very soon after they were composed. [2]

When we consider the number of works that survive in unique copies, and the variety of perils that beset MSS, it is perhaps surprising that the losses are not even greater. Fires destroyed libraries; the dissolution of monasteries dispersed their MS collections; numerous anecdotes show how little MSS could be valued by the uneducated in the age of print; even when libraries have continued for centuries without major disaster, thefts by readers and librarians have removed many, or even most, medieval MSS (the Biblioteca Colombina is perhaps the worst case); political or religious hostility was often a motive for destruction; when a MS deteriorated, it might be broken up to be used as paste-downs in the binding of other volumes; and this does not exhaust the list of the causes of loss. [3]

---

[1] Mário Martins, *Estudos de literatura medieval,* Braga: Cruz, 1956, p. 94.
[2] See my "La historiografía trastámara: ¿una cuarentena de obras perdidas?", forthcoming in a homage volume for Claudio Sánchez-Albornoz.
[3] For specific instances, see Avelino de Jesús da Costa, *Fragmentos preciosos de códices medievais,* Edições Bracara Augusta, 4 (Braga, 1949), pp. 6-8; Kathleen Hughes, "Where Are the Writings of Early Scotland?", in her *Celtic Britain in the Early Middle Ages: Studies in Scottish and Welsh Sources,* ed. David Dumville,

Since so high a proportion of medieval literature is lost, it is important to form an idea of what has disappeared. One reason is, of course, the hope of recovering lost works. Smith (p. 146) regards this as the chief reason, and it is true that a number of important works thought to have been lost, and others whose existence had not even been suspected, have been found in recent years. Perhaps an even more important reason for the study of lost literature is that, without it, our view of a nation's literary history will certainly be incomplete and will probably be distorted. There are undoubtedly dangers in such an undertaking: incautious assumptions about lost epics, for example, can distort the picture as badly as a refusal to go beyond the extant texts. Nevertheless, the task must be undertaken. Of all the medieval literatures, only Old and Middle English have, as far as I know, been satisfactorily treated from this point of view.[4] For Spain, there is a catalogue covering the pre-vernacular period,[5] but for literature in Castilian and related dialects, in Portuguese and Galician, and in Catalan, the task remains to be done. The same appears to be true of French, Italian, German, and the other vernaculars. This surprised me until I discovered some of the difficulties of the undertaking, by trying to compile a tentative catalogue.[6] It rapidly became clear that only the help of colleagues could make such a catalogue possible. That help was promptly and generously given, and I hope that the catalogue, which now contains well over five hundred items, will soon begin to take a more nearly definitive form. However, it covers only Castilian and related dialects, and there is an obvious need for catalogues for Catalan and Portuguese. The present article, based almost entirely on secondary sources, indicates some of the ground that a Portuguese catalogue should cover, and some of the issues that a study of the lost

---

Studies in Celtic History, 2, Woodbridge: Boydell Press; Totowa, NJ: Rowman & Littlefield, 1980, pp. 1-21; and Colin Smith, "On the 'Lost Literature' of Medieval Spain", in "Guillaume d'Orange" and the "Chanson de geste": Essays Presented to Duncan McMillan, Reading: Univ., 1984, pp. 137-50.

[4] R. M. Wilson, The Lost Literature of Medieval England, 2nd ed., London: Methuen, 1970. There is a similar study for Classical Latin: Henry Bardon, La Littérature latine inconnue, 2 vols., Paris: Klincksieck, 1952-56.

[5] Ursicino Domínguez del Val, "Obras desaparecidas de padres y escritores españoles", in Repertorio de historia de las ciencias eclesiásticas en España, II, Salamanca: Instituto de Historia de la Teología Española, 1971, pp. 11-28.

[6] This was issued privately in mimeographed form, the original catalogue in February 1977 and the fifth (and most recent) supplement in September 1979. I should be happy to supply copies to any interested scholar. It is a pleasure to record that Brian Tate was one of the first and most energetic respondents to my request for additions and corrections to the catalogue.

literature of medieval Portugal raises. I hope that the article may persuade some properly qualified scholar to compile a catalogue.

1. POPULAR LYRIC

The most striking, and yet the most contentious, area of loss is in the traditional oral lyric — predominantly, women's love-song. Some scholars deny that a tradition of oral lyric in the feminine voice lies behind the *cantigas de amigo* of the Galician-Portuguese court poets, and deny even more strongly the existence of a traditional Portuguese lyric actually composed by women. Yet the evidence for the contrary view seems to me to be conclusive. The resemblances between the *cantigas de amigo* and other traditions of love-song in the Iberian Peninsula and around the Mediterranean have been noted by many scholars, and they have been reinforced by James T. Monroe's discovery of a common formulaic system in *cantigas de amigo, kharjas, villancicos* and Old French *refrains*, a system which must have its origin in Vulgar Latin love-song. [7] The similarities between *cantigas de amigo* and Modern Portuguese traditional song provide further powerful evidence. [8] It is of course true that any given *cantiga de amigo* may be mimetic, an invention by a male court poet, but I do not see how the whole tradition can be mimetic: if it is, if there never was an oral tradition of women's love-song, what were the male poets imitating? We can go further: the frequency of parallelistic form with *leixa-pren* in the *cantigas de amigo,* and its scarcity elsewhere in the Peninsula, suggests strongly that the popular lyric tradition of Galicia and Portugal was parallelistic.

To demonstrate the existence of a tradition is one thing; to identify any particular traditional song is another. We may reasonably suppose that behind any parallelistic *cantiga de amigo* we care to select, there lies a traditional song which the court poet has adapted, but supposition is not evidence. When, however, *cantigas de amigo* by two poets are closely related, as is the case with Pero Meogo's "Levou-s'a louçana, levou-s'a velida" and Dinis's "Levantou-s'a velida", the only satisfactory explanations are direct influence and a common source. It may be, as Stephen

---

[7] Monroe, "Formulaic Diction and the Common Origins of Romance Lyric Traditions", *HR,* XLIII (1975), 341-50. More generally, see Carolina Michaëlis de Vasconcellos, *Cancioneiro da Ajuda: edição crítica e commentada.* II. *Investigações bibliográphicas, biográphicas e histórico-litterárias,* Halle: Max Niemeyer, 1904, pp. 836-940.

[8] Firmino Crespo, "A tradição de uma lírica popular portuguesa antes e depois dos trovadores", *Ocidente,* LXXI (1966), 3-17, 98-108, 121-28 and 185-204.

Reckert and Helder Macedo argue, that Dinis borrows and adapts Pero
Meogo's poem, but it is also possible — and even, I think, more likely —
that both poets draw on a popular song which they adapt in different
ways.[9] If the latter hypothesis is correct, the outline and some of the
detail of the song can be reconstructed.

The minstrels, male and female, who sang the poems transmitted to
us by the *cancioneiros* straddle the frontier between the world of popular
traditional song and that of court poetry. Álvaro J. da Costa Pimpão
notes that, although the *jogral* Palha was a contemporary of Marcabru,
and both were at the court of Alfonso VII of Castile and León, we have
no songs of Palha's to compare with those of Marcabru.[10] Pimpão regrets
(pp. 79-80) the loss of a probable "lírica erótica masculina... cantares
dissolutos... de *segréis*". We can, as he says, never know whether such
a tradition existed before and during the period covered by the *cancioneiros,* but it seems likely that it did. It would also be surprising if all
jogralesas confined themselves to singing or accompanying the compositions of male poets. The most striking case is that of Maria Peres Balteira,
Galician by birth and the best-known *juglaresa* of the courts of Fernando III and Alfonso X of Castile.[11] She was the target of *cantigas
d'escárnio e de mal dizer* by a number of poets, especially after she
abandoned her dissolute life and turned to religion.[12] Would such a
woman, who by all accounts was audacious, resourceful and quick-witted,
skilled in the performance of music and poetry, have borne such provoca-
tion in silence, or would she have retaliated with her enemies' own
weapons? No songs of hers, or even references to them, survive; it may
well be that none was written down; but it seems to me highly likely
that such songs existed.

---

[9] Stephen Reckert & Helder Macedo, *Do cancioneiro de amigo,* Documenta
Poética, 3, Lisboa: Assírio & Alvim, 1976, pp. 51-60, 101-04 and 205-13. For a
comparable case of adaptations of a popular song, see Carlos Alvar's study of
La Belle Aëlis, forthcoming in a homage volume for Martín de Riquer.

[10] *História da literatura portuguesa: Idade Média,* 2nd ed., Coimbra: Atlântida,
1959, p. 80.

[11] Ramón Menéndez Pidal, *Poesía juglaresca y orígenes de las literaturas romá-
nicas: problemas de historia literaria y cultural,* revised ed. [of *Poesía juglaresca
y juglares,* 1924], Madrid: Instituto de Estudios Políticos, 1957, pp. 167-69 and 187.

[12] See, for example, Brian Dutton, " 'Lelia doura, edoy lelia doura', an Arabic
Refrain in a Thirteenth-Century Galician Poem?", *BHS,* XLI (1964), 1-9.

2. COURT LYRIC (SECULAR)

Evidence is predictably more plentiful here, though the conclusions to be drawn from it are a matter for argument. I have discussed most of it elsewhere, and it is therefore presented here in summary form. [13]

Two MSS survive from the period of the Galician-Portuguese court lyric: the *Cancioneiro da Ajuda* (containing only *cantigas de amor*) and an individual MS of the *cantigas de amigo* of Martin Codax. All other *cantigas de amigo*, all *cantigas d'escárnio e de mal dizer* and nearly half of the *cantigas de amor* are preserved only in the two *cancioneiros* copied in Italy circa 1500: *Vaticana* and *Colocci-Brancuti* (or *da Biblioteca Nacional*). The fourteenth-century archetype of these two, all intermediate MSS, and most of those preceding the archetype (that is, manuscripts of individual poets other than Martin Codax, and single-genre collections comparable to *Ajuda*) are lost. Every lost *cancioneiro*, every lost single-poet MS, implies the possibility of lost poems; however, since the contents of anthologies and the texts of poems vary less in the Galician-Portuguese MS tradition than in the Castilian *cancioneros*, the number of lost poems is probably smaller than one might have supposed.

The Italian humanist Angelo Colocci compiled a table of contents for a *cancioneiro* closely related to, but slightly more extensive than, the one that bears his name. [14] This shows that a number of poems were lost at a late stage of MS transmission, and they include the entire output of some poets. The poets whose work is known to be lost are: Pero Paez Bazoco (eight poems), Rodrigo Dias dos Cameiros (three), Juano (one), Pero Rodrigues de Palmeira (two), Ayras Soarez (three), and Joam Velaz (one). The same source shows the loss of a poem by Diego Moniz, two of whose other poems are extant, and of six by Joan Soares de Pávia, one of whose poems survives.

References in documents and literary works to *cancioneiros* now presumably lost are fairly plentiful, but almost all are too vague to be useful. [15] In two cases, however, we have clearer information. In 1350 Pedro, Conde de Barcelos, illegitimate son of Dinis, bequeathed his

---

[13] See my "Baena, Santillana, Resende and the Silent Century of Portuguese Court Poetry", *BHS*, LIX (1982), 198-210, where additional bibliographical references are given.

[14] Elsa Gonçalves, "La tavola colocciana: *Autori portughesi*", *Arquivos do Centro Cultural Português*, X (1976), 387-448. See also Michaëlis, pp. 180-83 and 574-79.

[15] They are studied by Michaëlis, pp. 232-75.

Livro das cantigas to Alfonso XI of Castile; this may well have been the archetype of *Vaticana* and *Colocci-Brancuti*. [16] A century later, the Marqués de Santillana described "un grand volumen de cantigas serranas e dezires portugueses e gallegos" that he saw in early youth in the house of his grandmother Mencía de Cisneros. [17] The greater part of the poems were, he says, by Dinis, and "Avía otras de Johan Soarez de Paiva... e de otro Fernand Gonçales de Senabria". Since only one poem by Joan Soares de Pávia is extant, the others that are listed in the *Tavola colocciana* may well have been those that Santillana saw. The *terminus ad quem* for the compilation of the *Cancioneiro de Mencía de Cisneros* cannot, in view of what Santillana says about his age, be much after 1410, but it seems probable that the poets included were all from the period covered by the extant *cancioneiros*.

In the sentence that follows his description of the *Cancioneiro de Mencía de Cisneros* Santillana mentions three poets of the second half of the fourteenth century: Macías, who has extant poems in Galician and in Castilian, and two whose work probably does not survive, Fernand Casquicio and Vasco Peres de Camões. We lack the evidence needed to decide whether they wrote in Galician-Portuguese or belonged to the new Castilianizing tendency, but the former seems on balance more likely. In the first half of the fifteenth century, when Castilian had become the dominant language of court lyric outside Catalonia, Portuguese continued to be used by at least some of the poets writing in Portugal; it is perhaps to this that Garcia de Resende refers in the prologue to his *Cancioneiro geral* when he says "sse as [trovas] que ssam perdidas dos nossos passados se poderam aver..." [18] Some poems do indeed survive from this period, though until recently they were not recognized: they were copied into blank spaces in ancestors of *Vaticana* and *Colocci-Brancuti,* and were therefore accepted as authentic products of the Galician-Portuguese period. [19] Nine poems have now been identified as belonging to the first

---

[16] Michaëlis, pp. 227-31 and 243-54; Giuseppe Tavani, *Poesia del Duecento nella penisola iberica: problemi della lirica galego-portoghese,* Officina Romanica, 12, Roma: Ateneo, 1969, pp. 136-37.

[17] *Letter of the Marquis of Santillana to Don Peter, Constable of Portugal,* ed. Antonio R. Pastor & Edgar R. Prestage, Oxford: Clarendon Press, 1927, p. 77. See Michaëlis, pp. 237-43. *Mencia de Cisneros* is likely to belong to a different tradition from *Vaticana* and *Colocci-Brancuti*: see my "Silent Century", pp. 201-03.

[18] *Cancioneiro geral de Garcia de Resende,* ed. A. J. Gonçalvez Guimarães, I, Coimbra: Univ., 1910, p. 2.

[19] Their true status was established by Giuliano Macchi, "Le poesie di Roy Martinz do Casal", *Cultura Neolatina,* XXVI (1966), 129-57, at pp. 142-46; Lu-

half of the fifteenth century, and their variety and the circumstances of their transmission suggest that there was a substantial and varied body of court poetry in Portuguese at this time. Almost all of it is lost, and if any was collected in *cancioneiros* we know nothing of them. The only information available is that Álvaro Afonso, author of one surviving poem, was a court musician — quite possibly the most eminent one of the century — and it seems likely that in the 1440s he wrote a number of poems influenced by the Castilian traditions of the *Cancionero de Baena.* [20]

The second half of the century is of course covered by Resende's *Cancioneiro geral,* and the likelihood of lost poetry diminishes sharply. Resende can hardly have included every Portuguese court lyric composed in this period, but no specific evidence of lost poems has been discovered. We do, however, have some information about lost *cancioneiros* of this period. When Resende was compiling his *Cancioneiro* he tried to obtain earlier, manuscript, anthologies, and his efforts are reflected in a poem in which he asks his friend Diogo de Melo to bring him from Alcobaça the *Cancioneiro do abade frey Martinho* (now lost). [21]

3. COURT LYRIC (RELIGIOUS)

Duarte Nunes de Leão, in his *Crónica d'El Rei D. Diniz* (Lisboa, 1600), says that the King was "grande trovador... segundo vimos per hum cancioneiro seu, que em Roma se achou, em tempo del rei Dom João III, et per outro que stá na Torre do Tombo, de louvores da Virgem Nossa Senhora". [22] The first MS mentioned is presumably *Vaticana,* though the large number of Dinis's poems in it has led the chronicler to exaggerate (just as Santillana had exaggerated his share of the *Cancioneiro de Mencía de Cisneros*). As to the second, no trace has been found. It is unwise to dismiss Nunes de Leão's statement, as Pimpão does, as a "mais grave

ciana Stegagno Picchio, *A lição do texto: filologia e literatura.* I. *Idade Média,* Colecção Signos, 20, Lisboa: Edições 70, 1979, pp. 111-41; Tavani, *Poesia del Duecento,* pp. 219-33.

[20] Stegagno Picchio, pp. 138-41; Deyermond, "Silent Century", p. 205.

[21] *Cancioneiro geral,* ed. Gonçalvez Guimarães, V (1917), p. 378. On the manuscripts sought by Resende, and other lost *cancioneiros* of the period, see Jole Ruggieri, *Il canzoniere di Resende,* Biblioteca dell'*Archivum Romanicum,* Serie I, 16, Genève: Leo S. Olschki, 1931, p. 8; Andrée Crabbé Rocha, *Garcia de Resende e o "Cancioneiro geral",* Biblioteca Breve, 31, Lisboa: Instituto de Cultura Portuguesa, 1979, pp. 15-16.

[22] Quoted in *Das Liederbuch des Königs Denis von Portugal,* ed. Henry R. Lang, Halle: Max Niemeyer, 1894; repr. Hildesheim: Georg Olms, 1972, p. xxxvii, n. 5.

confusão" simply because he was wrong about *Vaticana*.[23] That error is, as we have seen, understandable, and although what Nunes de Leão saw in the Torre do Tombo may have been a MS of Alfonso X's *Cantigas de Santa Maria* (perhaps one with a wrong attribution), we cannot exclude the possibility that Dinis did indeed compose Marian lyrics. In favour of the supposition is the fact that only every tenth poem of Alfonso's *Cantigas* is a *loor,* while the others are miracle narratives, not easily to be mistaken for *louvores*. It is also worth remembering that no separate MS of Dinis's secular lyrics has survived, and that despite the large number of his extant poems (137), they have reached us only because they were incorporated (at a relatively late stage) in the *cancioneiro* tradition. Since the *cancioneiros* did not include religious verse, a MS of Dinis's Marian lyrics could have been lost, leaving no trace other than Nunes de Leão's memory.

One other Marian lyric, now lost, is mentioned by Álvaro Pais in his mid-fourteenth-century attack on heresies: he denounces Afonso Giraldes de Montemôr, saying "Alii sunt heretici qui dicunt quod Trinitas fuit creata et incarnata in utero virginali, sicut dixit in sua cantillena, quam composuit de Beata Maria, Illefonsus Giraldi de Monte Majori, qui dicitur homo virtutis".[24] The accusation is implausible, but what concerns us now is the evidence for Afonso Giraldes's poem. Giraldes also wrote a religious treatise, which Álvaro Pais denounces at greater length, and he may well be, as Mário Martins argues, the same Afonso Giraldes who wrote a poem on the Battle of the Salado. Of all these works, only a few stanzas of the Salado poem survive.

4. EPIC AND OTHER HEROIC VERSE

The widely-held view that epic in the Iberian Middle Ages was a Castilian genre, in which Portuguese had no part, is increasingly under challenge. António José Saraiva has recently argued for a Galician-Portuguese school of epic *jograis,* with Santiago de Compostela and Coimbra as its centres, and he maintains that there were epics, now lost, on King Ramiro, on Egas Moniz, on the fall of Santarém, and on Afonso Henriques, first king of Portugal, as well as Afonso Giraldes's poem

---

[23] *Idade Média,* p. 130, n. 38.
[24] *Collyrium fidei contra hereses,* quoted by Mário Martins, "Frei Álvaro Pais e o poeta Afonso Geraldes", in his *Estudos de cultura medieval,* II, Braga: Magnificat, 1972, pp. 70-76, at p. 75.

on the Salado.[25] He briefly traces the plots of the first three in historical writings *(Livros de linhagens, Crónica de 1344)*, and deals at length with the *Poema de Afonso Henriques*. Whereas his references to other lost epics are too brief to evaluate, he presents his evidence for a *Poema de Afonso Henriques* in detail and convincingly. He reconstructs parts of the poem from the *4.ª Crónica breve de Santa Cruz de Coimbra*; the MS of this chronicle is of the second half of the fifteenth century, but the relevant text is a fragment of a lost *Crónica de Espanha e Portugal*, probably of the early 1440s.[26] Saraiva has made out his case for the poem's existence; whether he is right to conclude that it was composed in the last quarter of the twelfth century, and that the poet had no clerical background, is less clear, since he does not develop his arguments at any length. He recognizes (pp. 71-74) that the poem might have been composed in Castilian, but his arguments for an original Portuguese text are weighty.

Ten stanzas of Afonso Giraldes's poem on the battle of the Salado are preserved in seventeenth-century chronicles; they come from four sections of the poem. Another four stanzas have just been discovered in MS. The verse-form is that of Rodrigo Yáñez's *Poema de Alfonso XI*, composed in 1348 (quatrains of octosyllables, rhyming abab), and the subject-matter overlaps. The date of Giraldes's poem is unknown (the battle took place in 1340), so the priority as between the Spanish and Portuguese works cannot be established. It is generally assumed that one borrowed from the other, and that Yáñez's poem (and therefore, by extension, Giraldes's) is best classified as a rhymed chronicle. These assumptions must be re-examined in the light of the research of Mercedes Vaquero, who provides strong reasons for believing that the two poems represent — probably independently — a new type of epic that grew up in the first half of the fourteenth century.[27]

---

[25] *A épica medieval portuguesa*, Biblioteca Breve, 29, Lisboa: Instituto de Cultura Portuguesa, 1979.

[26] Diego Catalán Menéndez Pidal, *De Alfonso X al Conde de Barcelos: cuatro estudios sobre el nacimiento de la historiografía en Castilla y Portugal*, Madrid: Gredos & Univ. de Madrid, 1962, pp. 259-75.

[27] "El *Poema de Alfonso XI*: ¿crónica rimada o épica?", unpubl. diss. (Princeton Univ., 1984), pp. 329-34. I am grateful to Dr. Vaquero for communicating to me her discovery of four stanzas. The other ten stanzas are printed by Pimpão, *Idade Média*, pp. 314-16.

5. ROMANCES

Extant texts of Arthurian romances in Portuguese are few, but they are, with one exception, full texts, whereas the more numerous Catalan texts are mostly fragmentary. The one Portuguese fragment, consisting of two folios, was at first thought to be from a *Lancelot* text, but it is — though Lancelot plays a prominent part — from an expanded *Prose Tristan,* and consists of material not found in any other Hispanic *Tristan* text. [28] At least one other Portuguese text may reasonably be supposed to be lost: the first and third branches of the Post-Vulgate *Roman du Graal* exist in Portuguese, but the second, *Merlin,* does not. The extant Portuguese and Castilian Post-Vulgate Arthurian romances seem to descend from a complete *Roman du Graal* translated by João, or Juan, Vivas, circa 1313; the language of Vivas's lost version is unknown, but there are good reasons for thinking that it was Portuguese.

The first sentimental romance, Juan Rodríguez del Padrón's *Siervo libre de amor* (circa 1440), was written in Castilian, though its author was Galician. It was quickly followed by one in Portuguese, the work of Dom Pedro (1429-66), Constable of Portugal and later elected King of the Catalans. Only his Castilian version survives, but we have clear evidence for the Portuguese original in his own words in the dedicatory epistle:

> Et, sy la muy insigne magnificencia vuestra demandare quál fue la causa que a mí movió dexar el materno vulgar, e la seguiente obra en este castellano romance prosseguir, yo responderé que, como la rodante fortuna con su tenebrosa rueda me visitasse, venido en estas partes, me di a esta lengua, más costreñido de la necessidad que de la voluntad. Et traýdo el testo a la desseada fyn, e parte de las glosas en lengua portuguesa acabadas, quise todo trasformar, e lo que restava acabar en este castellano ydioma. [29]

The date of the Portuguese original is probably between 1445 and 1449. After this early start, the sentimental romance seems to have fallen from favour in Portugal, reviving only in the 1540s.

[28] *Fragmento de un "Livro de Tristán" galaico-portugués,* ed. José L. Pensado Tomé, *Cuadernos de Estudios Gallegos,* anejo 14 (Santiago de Compostela: CSIC, 1962). The MS is late fourteenth century. See Harvey L. Sharrer, *A Critical Bibliography of Hispanic Arthurian Material.* I. *Texts: The Prose Romance Cycles,* Research Bibliographies & Checklists, 3, London: Grant & Cutler, 1977, pp. 26-27.

[29] *Obras completas do Condestável Dom Pedro de Portugal,* ed. Luís Adão da Fonseca, Lisboa: Fundação Calouste Gulbenkian, 1975, p. 9 (I have modernized the accentuation and corrected one error). See Elena Gascón Vera, *Don Pedro, Condestable de Portugal,* Madrid: Fundación Universitaria Española, 1979, pp. 75 and 104.

6. HISTORIOGRAPHY

The sixteenth-century historian Cristovão Rodrigues Acenheiro cites a *Crónica gallega* that cannot be identified with any extant text. Diego Catalán has shown that part of its content is incorporated in the *4.ª crónica breve* (see section 4, above), and that it was composed not in Galician but in Portuguese. This lost chronicle, which he calls *Crónica portuguesa de España y Portugal,* derives ultimately from Alfonso X's *Estoria de España,* though it draws also on one of the *Estoria*'s sources, an interpolated version of the *Liber regum.* It was probably composed in 1341-42, and thus precedes the main Portuguese contribution to the Alfonsine historiographic tradition, Pedro de Barcelos's *Crónica geral de Espanha de 1341.* [30]

Alfonso's universal history, the *General estoria,* was translated into Portuguese, at least in part, but only fragments survive. They were discovered in the Torre do Tombo by Avelino de Jesús da Costa during his search for MS leaves used as paste-downs in the bindings of volumes in Portuguese libraries. [31] He located four fragments, quoting briefly from three of them, and concluding that they represented a translation either of the *General estoria* or of the *Historia scholastica* of Petrus Comestor. The generic affinity of these two works makes Costa's doubt understandable, but the problem was solved by Mário Martins, who published three of the fragments in full, with the corresponding passages of *General estoria* part I. [32] Costa's fourth fragment may not be from the same work, but at least one other fragment, that he regards as being from another and unidentified work (p. 22, no. 14), has been shown by Martins to belong to the *General estoria* translation. Since Martins was able to consult only the modern edition of *General estoria* I, it may be that other unidentified fragments will prove to be from later parts of the

---

[30] Catalán, *De Alfonso X al Conde de Barcelos,* pp. 214-88.

[31] *Fragmentos preciosos* (see n. 3, above), p. 19, nos 2-5. I owe to the vigilance and generosity of Ms. Patricia Odber a photocopy of this fundamental but elusive work, rightly praised by Martins, *Estudos de literatura medieval,* p. 93. Costa's researches were carried out in virtually all Portuguese libraries with the curious exception of the Biblioteca Nacional, which refused to co-operate (p. 11). The results were set out in five typescript volumes of reports to the Instituto da Alta Cultura (p. 16); these have, unhappily, remained unpublished.

[32] "A tradução da *General estoria* e da *Formula vitate honestae,* em português", in his *Estudos de literatura medieval,* pp. 93-104, at pp. 94-100.

Alfonsine work. The relation of the Torre do Tombo fragments to a longer *General estoria* fragment in the Escorial, mentioned by Costa and Martins, has yet to be clarified.

7. WISDOM LITERATURE

Two of Costa's paste-down fragments from the Biblioteca Pública, Braga, belong to the Pseudo-Senecan tradition of wisdom literature. He lists them, together with a third of a different kind, as a single fragment of one work (pp. 20-21, no. 9), but they were correctly identified by Martins. [33] One is from the *Liber* (or *Libellus*) *de moribus,* a collection of 145 *sententiae* attributed at first to Seneca and later to the sixth-century São Martinho de Dume; the other is from the *Proverbia Senecae.* The publication of these fragmentary texts would be a useful step in the study of the dauntingly complex body of wisdom texts in medieval Hispanic languages. [34]

The present article offers merely a sample of the material that is available for the study of lost literature in medieval Portuguese, together with an assessment of some of the scholarship in this field. Space does not permit even a bare mention of some lost works that have been studied, and some genres (e.g. drama, hagiography, legal texts, letters) have been entirely omitted. I hope, however, that enough has been said to indicate the urgent need for a full study of this interesting and important aspect of medieval Portuguese literature.

ALAN DEYERMOND

Westfield College, London

---

[33] "A tradução", pp. 100-02 and 103-04. See N. G. Round, "The Mediaeval Reputation of the *Proverbia Senecae*: A Partial Survey Based on Recorded MSS", *Proceedings of the Royal Irish Academy,* 72, section C (1972), no. 5, 103-51.

[34] For a preliminary survey of the material and its textual relationships, see Barry Taylor's article to be published in *La Corónica,* 14 (1985-86). Dr. Taylor is preparing a critical bibliography of this material for Research Bibliographies & Checklists.

LAS TRADUCCIONES DEL CANCILLER AYALA

DESDE Amador de los Ríos, la principal preocupación de los críticos ha consistido en determinar qué traducciones se podían atribuir con toda seguridad al canciller Ayala. Los más antiguos documentos conocidos sobre el tema, o sea las listas establecidas por Fernán Pérez de Guzmán y por el genealogista anónimo, [1] incluyen, con algunas variantes, los siguientes títulos: *Historia troyana*; *De consolatione* de Boecio; *De summo bono* de Isidoro de Sevilla; *Moralia* de San Gregorio; *De casibus* de Boccaccio; *Décadas* de Tito Livio. A los cuales habría que añadir el *Livro de falcoaria* del halconero de Fernando I de Portugal, Pero Menino, que figura prácticamente íntegro en el *Libro de la caza de las aves*. [2]

Se suele considerar como sospechosa la atribución de las tres primeras obras, sea porque no han dejado huellas *(Historia troyana)*, sea porque no consta ningún indicio claro de que fueran de Pero López *(De consolatione* y *De summo bono)*. Tales argumentos parecen efectivamente irrebatibles: los críticos corren un riesgo al cargar en la cuenta de un autor unas obras que carecen de prueba fehaciente en cuanto a su paternidad. Pero se me ocurre que semejante actitud peca quizás, en este caso, de demasiado prudente. No se concibe cómo los dos testigos, contemporáneos del autor, aunque de la generación posterior, hubieran podido incurrir en el error de atribuirle obras que no fueran suyas. Parece indudable que dichas traducciones existían y que, con toda probabilidad, las habían manejado. ¿Por qué poner en duda sus inventarios? No eran tantas las traducciones en época del canciller para que no se supiera a quién se debían las pocas que existían. Tampoco convence el argumento según el que, si las dos listas no coinciden, su testimonio carece de absoluta validez, ya que cada uno de sus autores podía haber omitido un título en una enumeración que transcribía sin duda de memoria. [3]

---

[1] Fernán Pérez de Guzmán, *Generaciones y semblanzas,* ed. R. B. Tate (London: Tamesis Books, 1965), p. 15; *Continuación anónima de la genealogía de los Ayala,* Real Academia de la Historia: Colección Salazar, B 98, fol. 35ᵛ.

[2] Véase M. García, *Obra y personalidad del canciller Ayala* (Madrid: Alhambra, 1982), pp. 207-208.

[3] Sólo Fernán Pérez de Guzmán menciona *De summo bono,* pero también el *Libro de la caça de las aves* y el *Rimado de Palacio.* Dada la notoriedad de esta

Se puede descartar la *Historia troyana,* que, a falta de texto, merece figurar en el catálogo de obras perdidas de A. D. Deyermond. En cuanto a *De consolatione* y a *De summo bono,* sospecho que la ausencia de datos concretos adecuados para confirmar la atribución de su traducción al canciller los ha colocado en situación de desigualdad frente a los otros tres textos. Éstos tienen la ventaja de llevar una firma visible e indiscutible. La de los *Morales* es iconográfica: la ilustración del Ms. Vitrina 17-6 de la Biblioteca Nacional, en la que Pero López aparece arrodillado ante san Gregorio. Los dos personajes quedan identificados por un membrete, y el intercambio verbal que se les presta se refiere justamente a la paternidad de la traducción:

> AYALA: Señor de los peligros guardado en este mundo
>   sea quien te presenta este libro segundo.
> SAN GREGORIO: Dios te guarde amen por la su graçia santa
>   pues que por su seruiçio feziste obra tanta. [4]

Las *Décadas* llevan un prólogo firmado de su traductor. En cuanto a *De casibus,* el continuador de la traducción se ha tomado el trabajo de identificar al que se encargó de verter al castellano las dos terceras partes del texto:

> ... por este poquillo de trabajo que aqui tomo: por tres cosas en esta parte a trabajar me opuse. La primera: la dicha obra por quien fue romançada saber [...] Y quanto a lo primero prosiguiendo mi trabajo: supe en como el muy notable cauallero y muy sabio y muy discreto señor don Pero Lopez de Ayala: señor de Ayala y de Saluatierra chanciller mayor de Castilla de loable memoria: cuya anima Dios perdone: la dicha obra romançara. [5]

Nada semejante para las otras dos obras. Sin embargo, me parece arriesgado negar toda posibilidad de atribución a Pero López. He señalado en otra ocasión cómo la temática de los dos textos concuerda con las preocupaciones manifestadas por el canciller a lo largo de toda su obra. La inspiración gregoriana de *De summo bono,* los estrechos lazos

---

última obra, es evidente que, si el genealogista ha errado, será más por omisión que por exceso.

[4] G. Orduna califica con acierto de "mal dibujo [el] que ilustra la portada del volumen conservado [...] A primera vista se advierte que el que armó esa portada copiaba con mano inhábil un trabajo que debía de tener calidad artística", en "La *collatio* externa de los códices como procedimiento auxiliar para fijar el stemma codicum. Crónicas del canciller Ayala", *Incipit,* II (1982), 36.

[5] Prólogo de Juan Alfonso de Zamora. Cito del *Libro llamado Cayda de Príncipes* (Medina del Campo, MDLII, Biblioteca Nacional, R. 955) y conservo la puntuación del original.

que unían a Isidoro con el santo papa, directamente o a través de su hermano Leandro, a quien los *Moralia* van dedicados, son datos suficientes para justificar que Pero López hubiera manifestado algún interés por la obra isidoriana. Tampoco cabe buscar justificaciones personales para explicar que un texto de tan universal difusión como *De consolatione* de Boecio hubiera podido tentar a un traductor castellano del siglo XIV.

¿Hasta qué punto se puede considerar la ausencia de reivindicación personal de autoría como prueba evidente de que esas traducciones no deben ser atribuidas a Pero López? Si se examinan las obras "firmadas", se observará que este criterio es cuando menos discutible, y que la norma parece ser más bien el anonimato del traductor. En efecto, si Juan Alfonso de Zamora no se hubiera tomado muy a pecho el completar la traducción de *De casibus* e identificar al autor del fragmento existente, ¿qué duda cabe que ignoraríamos hoy que se trataba del canciller, por la sencilla razón de que éste no hizo nada para que se le pudiera conocer? Y no fue sólo porque la dejara sin acabar, ya que circuló así incompleta, como lo demuestra la copia muy cuidada que figura en el Ms. 12733 de la Biblioteca Nacional. [6] Lo mismo se podría decir de los *Morales*, traducción de los *Moralia* de San Gregorio. Salvo en la ilustración ya citada, y que pudo ser obra de un copista posterior, no figura el nombre de Pero López. [7]

De hecho, las *Décadas* constituyen, desde ese punto de vista, un caso excepcional, único. Pero López añade a su traducción un prólogo-dedicatoria dirigido a Enrique III, en el que expone los motivos que le han inducido a llevar a cabo esa tarea. Con todo, no creo que esa iniciativa deba interpretarse como un claro deseo de protagonismo por parte del traductor castellano. En efecto, el texto que Pero López sigue es la traducción francesa de las *Décadas* realizada por Pierre de Bressuire, cuya versión viene encabezada asimismo por un prólogo dirigido al monarca francés Jean le Bon. El canciller no se ha contentado con utilizar el texto de Tito Livio contenido en esa versión francesa sino que ha incluido en

---

[6] Se trata de una copia esmerada con letras de color. Lleva muestras de una lectura atenta, con índices apuntando y llaves en los márgenes. Su texto termina en el sitio señalado por Juan Alfonso de Zamora, en medio de la narración dedicada al rey Artús.

[7] Tampoco consta de que fuera de Pero López en un documento firmado por él, 12 de julio 1405, en el que reconoce guardar en su posesión los tres volúmenes de una traducción en romance de los *Morales*, comp. mi *Obra y personalidad...*, p. 223.

su labor la traducción de los documentos e índices añadidos por Bressuire: un glosario y la dedicatoria. [8] Sea cual sea la razón por la cual Pero López se mostró fiel hasta tal extremo a la obra del monje francés, el hecho es que el texto de su versión llevaba ya una firma, la de Bressuire, y un destinatario, el rey de Francia. La obra de Tito Livio quedaba así demasiado ligada a un ambiente francés y su alcance hubiera sido menor si no se la hubiera "castellanizado" para que inspirara una reflexión eficaz acerca de las debilidades de la política militar de Castilla. Los lectores u oyentes de la traducción de Pero López debían sentirse directamente concernidos por la lección ofrecida por Tito Livio. De ahí la necesidad de referirse claramente a la historia nacional y de promover *disçiplina* y *ordenança*, que son las dos virtudes ilustradas, según Pero López, por los romanos y de las que tanto carecieron los castellanos en circunstancias tan recientes entonces como Aljubarrota. [9] Así se explica mejor, a mi parecer, que el canciller haya firmado su traducción, y no porque se tratara en su caso de una actitud habitual.

Lo dicho hasta ahora me parece suficiente para descartar definitivamente como criterio decisivo de atribución a Pero López de Ayala de tal o cual de sus traducciones la autoproclamada autoría. De la misma manera, la ausencia de firma, por cuanto se trata de la norma en la obra del canciller, tampoco es suficiente para negar que una traducción se deba a él. Para dar cuenta de la dificultad de esas atribuciones, expondré a continuación el caso de *De consolatione*.

El texto más manejado de la traducción al castellano del libro de Boecio [10] viene precedido por dos cartas, una del condestable Ruy López Dávalos y la respuesta no firmada, atribuida al traductor:

> Libro de la Consolaçion natural de Boeçio romano, e comiença una carta de Ruy Lopez Daualos al que lo romançó.

Las palabras del condestable no son del todo claras. Después de aludir a su ignorancia de los escritores de la Antigüedad que "en las sçiençias

---

[8] Véase Pero López de Ayala, *Las Décadas de Tito Livio,* ed. crítica de los Libros I a III, con introducción y notas por Curt J. Wittlin (Barcelona: Puvill, 1983), 2 tomos.

[9] Punto de vista compartido por Curt Wittlin, ed. cit. Las preocupaciones estratégicas encierran también el deseo de "popularizar los preceptos de caballería", según palabras de R. B. Tate en "López de Ayala, ¿historiador humanista?", en sus *Ensayos sobre la historiografía peninsular del siglo XV* (Madrid: Gredos, 1970), pp. 33-54.

[10] Ms. 10220 de la Biblioteca Nacional.

fueron conplidos", quizás más sincera que tópica, ruega a su interlocutor "que trabai[e] en traer a nuestra lengua vulgar la consolaçion del sancto doctor Seuerino", lo cual parece confirmar los términos del título ya citado. Sin embargo, a continuación, afirma haber leído ya la obra, no en su versión original sino "romançad[a] por el ffamoso maestro Nicolas". La fórmula no deja de sorprender tratándose del comentario de Nicolás Treveth que, por razones obvias, el condestable pudo difícilmente haber leído en su versión romance. En su respuesta, el supuesto traductor confirma que se trata efectivamente del comentario del dominico inglés:

E fallando alguna razon que paresca dubdosa en sentençia sera le puesta adiçion de las que *el nonbrado maestro en su letura* ha declarado solo tocante a la letra. [11]

¿Habrá que suponer que el condestable había leído la obra en latín? Es más que dudoso. Por lo menos, no hace ninguna mención de la dificultad para leer el texto en su lengua original. Son otros motivos los que le complican la lectura:

E commo quier que yo he leydo este libro romançado por el ffamoso maestro Nicolas no es de mi entendido ansi como querria. E creo que sea esto por falta de mi ingenio, y aun pienso fazerme algun estoruo estar mesclado el texto con glosas lo qual me trae una grand escuridat. E auria en especial graçia me fuesse por vos declarado en tal manera que mejor lo podiesse entender guardando las palabras con que el actor se rrazona, señalando en la margen lo que vuestro ingenio podiere para que yo syn conpañero el texto pueda entender...

Ruy López se queja, por consiguiente, de la confusión existente en la versión que ha manejado antes de solicitar a su interlocutor y más precisamente de la presencia simultánea del texto de Boecio y de su comentario por Nicolás Treveth.

Así lo ha entendido, al parecer, su corresponsal el cual, después de mencionar algunas dificultades propias de la traducción, le propone varias enmiendas para hacer la lectura más asequible:

... Como sea algunas uezes que por la diuersidat de las lenguas se fallen algunas palauras que non son mudables sin gran daño suyo. contesçiendoles como a las plantas nasçidas en su escogido logar. que mudadas a otro pierden lo mas de su fuerça. y avn a veçes se secan: donde tal diçion fallare. quedara en su propio vocablo (ª) o se trocara por el mas çercano que en nuestro uulgar yo fallare (ᵇ) poniendo de fuera otros en su fauor que al poder mio sostengan su mesma

---

[11] La cursiva es mía.

fuerça (ᶜ). E donde se tocare fiction o ystoria que no sea muy vsada Reduzirse
ha breuemente. no para uuestra enseñança. ca auiendo uos grande notiçia de
muchas leturas mejor podes dezirlo que inclinaruos a lo oyr. Mas seruira a
uuestra memoria que instruyda de cosas diuersas. seyendo de algo oluidada nen-
brarse ha mas de ligero (ᵈ). E fallando alguna Razon que paresca dubdosa en
sentençia. sera le puesta adiçion de las que el nonbrado maestro en su letura ha
declarado solo tocante a la letra...

Este trozo, uno de los más antiguos castellanos que describen con algún
detenimiento el ejercicio de la traducción, ya ha merecido un comentario
de Margherita Morreale, [12] quien interpreta del siguiente modo los recursos técnicos enumerados por el supuesto traductor: (ᵃ), recurre a un
préstamo; (ᵇ), sustitución por una palabra de la lengua receptora; (ᶜ), con
o sin rodeos; (ᵈ), omisión. La realidad parece algo más compleja, por la
sencilla razón que, sabiendo lo que pide Ruy López a su interlocutor,
no tenemos la seguridad de que el trozo trate de traducción o por lo
menos sólo de traducción. Así (ᶜ) podría interpretarse como nota añadida
en margen, bajo forma de glosa o sinónimos; (ᵈ) correspondería más bien
a un resumen, con toda probabilidad colocado en el margen, con el fin
de facilitar la memorización. En cuanto a (ᵃ) y (ᵇ), parecen responder a
la preocupación de un traductor. Sin embargo, muy bien se pueden inter-
pretar como la posibilidad de aplicar a una traducción ya existente criterios distintos de los primitivamente aplicados. Lo cual supone un cotejo
con el texto latín, pero también lo suponen las notas complementarias
que el autor de la carta se proponía añadir.

Las dos cartas referidas pueden, por lo tanto, interpretarse del modo
siguiente. Ruy López disponía ya de una versión castellana del Boecio
con glosas de Nicolás Treveth. La presencia de esas glosas dentro del
texto dificultan la lectura, a la vez que no permiten saber con precisión
qué se debe al autor de *De consolatione*. Además, el comentario de
Treveth no satisface al condestable y merece ser completado. En su respuesta, el corresponsal del condestable se propone revisar la traducción
existente. Para llevar a cabo dicha revisión, procurará separar el texto
de la glosa, añadirá algunas notas complementarias en el margen y reto-
cará la traducción cuando lo juzgue necesario para una mejor compren-
sión del texto, no sin permanecer fiel a la letra del mismo.

Estas consideraciones podrían pasar por exageradamente sutiles si no
fuera por la existencia de otra versión de *De consolatione,* la contenida

---

12 M. Morreale, "Apuntes para la historia de la traducción en la Edad Media",
Revista de literatura, XV, n.º 29-30 (enero-junio 1959).

en el Ms. 174 de la Biblioteca Nacional, que presenta las características propias de la versión primitiva tal como la describe el condestable Ruy López. Al principio, por lo menos, las notas van mezcladas con el texto. Son más extensas que las del Ms. 10220 aunque coinciden con éstas en lo esencial. En este Ms. se leen además algunas notas originales dedicadas principalmente a aclarar el sentido literal de otros tantos vocablos. Todo lo cual parece corresponder a lo contenido en las dos cartas preliminares de la versión más conocida.

La pregunta surge entonces: ¿no será el texto del Ms. 174 el de la versión primera mencionada por el condestable? De ser así, nada impediría que Pero López fuera el autor de esa traducción, señalada como suya conjuntamente por los dos testigos contemporáneos del canciller.

Otro tanto se podría decir de *De summo bono,* que figura sólo en la lista de Fernán Pérez de Guzmán. ¿Quién mejor situado que el propio sobrino de Pero López de Ayala, y además aficionado a las traducciones como lo demuestra el encargo que hizo de la de los *Diálogos* de San Gregorio, para saber con exactitud cuál fue la obra traducida de su tío? Las conclusiones a las que se ha podido llegar respecto a *De consolatione* ponen en tela de juicio la actitud de la crítica, que ha consistido en dudar sistemáticamente frente a las listas antiguas de títulos y en aceptar sólo las pruebas evidentes de autoría que pudieran figurar en los Mss. Pienso que hay que invertir los criterios. Es una hipótesis más probable, y de todos modos más fecunda, la de considerar que Fernán Pérez de Guzmán y el genealogista nos proporcionan una enumeración fidedigna y que cualquier duda en el campo de las atribuciones deberá probarse.

La cuestión de las atribuciones confirma, si fuera aún necesario, la dificultad que resulta para los críticos modernos acometer sin prejuicios el estudio de las traducciones antiguas al castellano. Semejante actitud se explica en gran parte por el desconocimiento en que seguimos de las circunstancias que rodean la composición de las obras de los escritores medievales en general y de las del canciller en particular. Entre otras cosas se resisten a atribuirle una obra que, si se acumulan todos los títulos de las que se le han atribuido, alcanza proporciones considerables. No hay que conceder demasiada importancia al volumen de sus escritos porque muchos de ellos admiten unos recursos de composición un tanto mecánicos. Además, la personalidad política del personaje nos lo hace imaginar constantemente ocupado por sus actividades oficiales, lo cual tiene mucho de visión anacrónica. Por fin ignoramos del todo si se benefició de la ayuda de colaboradores, pero es una hipótesis que no hay que descartar, sobre todo cuando se trata de las traducciones. [13]

Más grave sin duda es lo que esa actitud tiene de dubitativo en cuanto a la capacidad del canciller de componer, en el sentido estricto de la palabra, una obra de conjunto capaz de responder a sus anhelos intelectuales más profundos, y no una *suite* de libros inspirados por las circunstancias o por el azar. Lo que se pone en duda así es nada menos que la *conciencia de Pero López de ser un escritor.* Ésta sólo se puede manifestar en un marco más amplio que tal o cual texto. Y sólo se puede descubrir si se analiza la obra en su conjunto y si en ese conjunto se busca un significado *en sí.* Por lo tanto, no estaría de más intentar establecer una cronología de las traducciones del canciller. Ésta nos permitirá medir mejor el alcance de su proyecto, si es que existió.

Lo más probable es que los *Morales* pertenecen a las obras primerizas del señor de Ayala. Mi opinión es que la vocación literaria del canciller o, mejor dicho, su carrera de escritor, es bastante tardía. La casi totalidad de sus obras fueron escritas a partir del cautiverio de Ovidos (1385), cuando tenía ya cincuenta años cumplidos. Con todo, dado que fue allí donde compuso la mayor parte del *Rimado de Palacio,* incluida, al menos parcialmente, la adaptación de los *Morales,* [14] hay que suponer que la traducción del libro de San Gregorio fue anterior. De las *Décadas,* se sabe por el prólogo que fueron traducidas ya bajo el reinado de Enrique III o sea, con cierta probabilidad, en los últimos diez años de la vida del canciller. [15] *Las caídas de prínçipes* deberían situarse después, si se admite la hipótesis del continuador Juan Alfonso de Zamora para explicar la interrupción de la traducción:

> ... E mucho me marauille obra por el ser començada y no ser acabada. ca otras muy notables obras romanço el & fueron acabadas: assi como el Tito Liuio y los Morales de Job. y otras algunas. E assi fuera esto: saluo por que creo que lo enbargo: o muerte suya al fazer: o ser el libro menguado por do lo romanço: o otro algun inpedimento...

Si no fue la muerte la que interrumpió la traducción, habrá que remontar sin duda a la estancia de Pero López en la Corte lusitana, en 1393, ya que fue allí donde Juan Alfonso de Zamora y Alfonso de Cartagena

---

[13] R. B. Tate, *art. cit.,* 52.
[14] Véase mi *Obra y personalidad...,* pp. 314 y sigs.
[15] Wittlin cree poder fechar la copia del manuscrito de dedicatoria en 23 de marzo de 1401, *op. cit.,* p. 93.

acabaron la traducción. [16] En este caso, *Las caídas de prínçipes* serían contemporáneas de las *Décadas* poco más o menos. *Del soberano bien* y el *Libro de la consolaçión* ocuparían un lugar intermedio.

Desde esta posible cronología, se observa una clara evolución en la elección de obras operada por el traductor. El punto de partida lo constituye la patrística o la tradición cristiana, luego la producción se aparta de la enseñanza exclusivamente religiosa, ya que las dos últimas obras denotan una mayor sensibilidad por las corrientes eruditas contemporáneas. Elegir a Isidoro o a Boecio no supone una gran curiosidad intelectual, ni un gran espíritu novador. Son temas casi obligados. En este caso, la ambición del traductor parece limitarse a facilitar a su lector un acceso directo a unas obras ya ampliamente conocidas por medio de citas y comentarios. No es una preocupación nada desdeñable por cuanto no se satisface de la explotación que se solía hacer de estos textos, y responde a una exigencia mayor de autenticidad. Denota por lo menos cierto interés por la función primordial del oficio de traductor: proporcionar al lector la *materia prima,* aun si la acompaña con notas explicativas.

La elección de las *Décadas* y de *Las caydas* supone mucho más. Se sabe por qué avatares pasó la obra de Tito Livio. [17] El texto, que se hallaba descoyuntado y disperso en diversas bibliotecas monjiles por toda Europa, recobró gran parte de su forma primitiva merced a la diligente erudición de Petrarca, que lo enmendó y completó. Pierre de Bressuire se encargó de verterla al francés en los años 1353-1356. La traducción de Bressuire alcanzó gran notoriedad dentro y fuera de Francia. En la Península, fue sin duda en el reino de Aragón donde suscitó más interés. [18] Pero López no podía ignorar la existencia de esa versión, aunque

---

[16] En *Obra y personalidad...*, pp. 212-214, sugiero que si Zamora y Cartagena acabaron la traducción de *De casibus* en Portugal es porque allí habían hallado la versión inacabada de Pero López, realizada durante su embajada de 1393.

[17] Curt Wittlin, ed. cit., p. 21, n. 4, presenta un corto resumen de la historia del texto de Tito Livio a lo largo de la edad media. Se encontrará una información más completa en G. Billanovitch, "La bibliothèque de Pétrarque et les bibliothèques médiévales de France et de Flandre", en *L'humanisme médiéval dans les littératures romanes du XIIe au XIVe siècle* (Paris: Librairie C. Klincksieck, 1964), pp. 208 y sigs.; también en Ch. Samaran, "Pierre Bersuire, Prieur de Saint-Éloi de Paris (1290?-1362)", en *Histoire littéraire de la France,* XXXIX (Paris: Imprimerie Nationale, 1962).

[18] El infante Juan de Aragón pidió un ejemplar a Carlos V de Francia, 13 de agosto 1380. Hizo una petición similar al duque Juan de Berry en marzo de 1383, a Juan Galeazzo Visconti en marzo de 1386 y a Antonio della Scala de Verona en agosto del mismo año. En 1387, ruega a su hermano Martín que le procure el ejemplar que tenía Pedro III; comp. Wittlin, ed. cit., pp. 45-46.

sólo fuera porque viajaba a menudo a la Corte francesa. Además, tan
grande era la similitud de las situaciones militares de Francia y Castilla,
humillada aquélla en dos ocasiones por los ingleses, [19] y ésta en Aljubarrota por los portugueses, que la enseñanza estratégica que encerraba la
obra de Tito Livio, en opinión de Bressuire, podía ser muy útil también
para los castellanos. Así lo entendió Pero López que optó por imitar al
benedictino francés, dando a conocer la *Historia romana,* ateniéndose,
como ya se ha dicho, a los mismos criterios interpretativos que su modelo. Las motivaciones del canciller son, por consiguiente, muy diferentes
de las que le llevaron a traducir *Moralia, De consolatione* o *De summo
bono.* La finalidad declarada de aquella traducción era la de orientar de
modo inmediato la reflexión de sus contemporáneos —el primero de ellos
el rey— con vistas a una mayor eficacia en el campo militar. Se había
dado un salto cualitativo innegable en la concepción del género, al rela-
cionarlo con las preocupaciones políticas del momento.

La obra de Boccaccio ofrece, al parecer, un carácter menos innova-
dor, por cuanto el tema que desarrolla presenta muchas analogías con
una tradición didáctico-moral de muy lejanas raíces. Sin embargo, su
elección confirma la evolución observada en el caso de las *Décadas.* El
mismo tema había cobrado una nueva actualidad con el asesinato del rey
don Pedro y el cambio dinástico. Las guerras civiles y su culminación en
Montiel constituyeron un verdadero trauma para los contemporáneos de
los acontecimientos. El proyecto de las crónicas del que se encargó Pero
López responde en gran parte a la necesidad de borrar las responsabili-
dades en que la sociedad castellana en su conjunto había incurrido en
aquellas circunstancias trágicas. Pero más que el tema y los ecos que
podía despertar en la memoria de los lectores castellanos de finales del
siglo XIV, es sin duda la notoriedad del autor, Boccaccio, la que decidió
a Pero López a interesarse por la obra. También se había sentido atraído
por la personalidad de Bressuire. El humanismo italiano empezaba a
influenciar las modas culturales en Castilla y en toda la Península. Aun
sin adoptar plenamente las preocupaciones de aquella nueva clase de
intelectuales, los escritores más eminentes de los reinos peninsulares
cedían a la tentación de conocerlos. No es el menor mérito de Pero López

---

[19] En Crécy (1346) y Poitiers (1356), donde las tropas francesas sufrieron
dos descalabros, teniendo la segunda como consecuencia el cautiverio en Inglaterra
del rey Juan el Bueno.

el que haya manifestado, ya muy entrado en años, cierto interés por las corrientes más novadoras de su época.

No hay que ocultarse, sin embargo, que la adhesión del canciller a los nuevos modos de pensar o a las nuevas técnicas humanísticas distaba mucho de ser incondicional, como lo demuestra su obra personal. Existían demasiados impedimentos: la educación recibida, la función política desempeñada, el alejamiento de Castilla de los focos de difusión de la nueva cultura, la edad alcanzada. [20] Pero el mayor de todos concierne la capacidad o, dicho más crudamente, la ignorancia relativa del escritor castellano. Si no se puede achacar a Pero López una falta de curiosidad intelectual, está claro que no poseía los conocimientos suficientes para alcanzar altos niveles de cultura. En particular, no estaba en condiciones de practicar con un mínimo de soltura la literatura latina antigua. Muy significativo resulta que su única aproximación a ese campo la hiciera a través de una traducción francesa. Pero López sabía latín. Creo que las dudas que se han expresado al respecto no se justifican. Quien ha recibido en su infancia una educación religiosa, ha viajado en varias ocasiones como embajador a Aviñón, ha manejado asiduamente los *Moralia* de San Gregorio y emprende una traducción de Boccaccio tenía que poseer una buena práctica en latín. Pero otra cosa era enfrentarse con la prosa de la antigüedad y con la genuina manera de pensar de los antiguos.

Ante la prosa de los antiguos romanos, Pero López siente un verdadero pánico, que comparte con muchos de sus contemporáneos —v. gr. el propio Bressuire— y bastantes de sus seguidores. Éste se manifiesta por lo que podría llamarse la obsesión lexical. [21] ¿Cómo dar cuenta de los

---

[20] Ottavio di Camillo añade otras dos causas posibles de la poca influencia en Pero López de las incipientes corrientes humanísticas: "su compromiso con los principios políticos y culturales de su clase, y ... la influencia que sobre él ejercieron los dominicos, a quienes favoreció con preferencia a las otras órdenes religiosas", en *El humanismo castellano del siglo XV* (Valencia: Fernando Torres, 1976), p. 30. Habría que matizar en lo que se dice de la influencia de los dominicos ya que Pero López, aun permaneciendo fiel a la devoción de su padre por los Predicadores, promovió la Orden de los Jerónimos, contribuyendo a la erección del monasterio de San Miguel del Monte.

[21] Comp. "los vocabulos ynotos e escuros" del prólogo de Bressuire en la traducción de Pero López. También "algunas palabras que no son mudables sin gran daño suyo" del corresponsal de Ruy López Dávalos. Pocas menciones, en cambio, relativas a la sintaxis que ofrecía sin embargo una dificultad sin duda mayor. Pero López introduce otra por iniciativa propia en su traducción del Prólogo de Bressuire: "ca las sentencias suyas son en alguna parte truncadas (que quiere dezir abreviadas e atajadas e suspensivas *que de una razon en que fabla non se partiendo della fablara en otra*". Las palabras en cursiva son un añadido de Pero López.

vocablos latinos sobre todo cuando corresponden a una realidad desconocida para los contemporáneos del traductor? Esta fijación en el léxico, que aparece en varios prólogos, denota un desconocimiento del mundo latino que, si bien autoriza los anacronismos, imposibilita todo verdadero acercamiento a su literatura y a su pensamiento. Pienso que Pero López tenía conciencia de esa enorme dificultad. Pero no veía cómo salvarla. Acudir a un idioma moderno que sirviera de intermediario podía ser una solución —es lo que intentó al traducir a Bressuire. Pero no pasaba de ser un subterfugio, aun si éste estaba avalado por una práctica corriente en aquella época. A las dificultades de interpretación del texto latino se añadían los errores y obscuridades del primer traductor, sin que fuera posible siquiera remediarlas.

Todo lo que antecede confirma, si aún fuera necesario, que la cuestión del humanismo de Pero López no debe plantearse. El canciller no era humanista ni podía serlo. Sin embargo abrió de modo decisivo la vía hacia el humanismo en Castilla, al restaurar el género de la traducción que había caído prácticamente en desuso desde Alfonso X. ¿A qué se debe que una actividad de tan fuertes antecedentes en Castilla —la escuela toledana del siglo XII o la del Rey Sabio— haya permanecido suspendida a lo largo de un siglo entero, hasta finales del XIV? No bastan razones históricas para explicar semejante bache. Las guerras civiles, la crisis social, un notable retroceso del interés por la cultura en las altas capas de la sociedad civil no han sido factores suficientes para impedir el desenvolvimiento de otros géneros. Baste el ejemplo de las crónicas reales que, a pesar de ser una producción muy necesitada de paz y de consenso social, siguieron componiéndose en la primera mitad del siglo XIV.

Los motivos verdaderos pertenecen a otro campo, sospecho que más ideológico que puramente cultural. En su cometido de dar a conocer textos pertenecientes a culturas extrañas, el traductor está expuesto a la competencia de las varias técnicas que se pueden colocar bajo el vocablo de *imitatio*. Éstas privilegian la referencia textual exterior, llámesele fuente o modelo. El texto referencial proporciona no sólo un tema o citas sino que se introduce substancialmente en el cuerpo de la obra sin ser sometido a un proceso de dislocación y asimilación. El autor se coloca bajo el amparo de la Autoridad. Muy distinto es el caso del traductor. Su actitud ante la obra es de respeto. Al procurar traducirla con la mayor fidelidad, proporciona a sus lectores una materia infinitamente más rica que la que pudiera resultar de un entresacamiento de citas o sentencias. Remite a la capacidad interpretativa del propio lector. Sería interesante observar si el desarrollo de la traducción como género a lo largo del siglo xv no ha desplazado el de los dichos, sentencias y demás obras de adaptación. Si éste fuera el caso, el papel de Pero López habría sido decisivo en ese cambio de rumbo de la mentalidad castellana.

En cuanto uno pretende estudiar el campo cultural e ideológico de los escritores medievales se encuentra enfrentado con una información gravemente lagunaria. De las traducciones del canciller, el mejor material para medir la cultura que había alcanzado, no existe más que una edición parcial de las *Décadas,* publicada tan sólo hace unos meses por Curt W. Wittlin. Mientras no se haya reunido un corpus amplio de esos textos, sólo se podrá emitir hipótesis más o menos aventuradas. La labor filológica que eso supone es enorme, más teniendo en cuenta la dificultad de identificar las versiones del texto que han servido de modelo. Sin embargo, éste es el único camino para que la crítica salga de los trillados que va recorriendo desde hace dos siglos. Ya es hora de penetrar en el detalle de los textos y dejar las generalidades a las que nos condena un conocimiento exterior, y forzosamente superficial, de las diversas traducciones.

Michel García

Sorbonne-Nouvelle, Paris

ON HENRY FIELDING'S RECEPTION OF *DON QUIJOTE*

C R I T I C S presently concerned with "Rezeptionstheorie", a discipline complementary to theories of composition or narration, have two responsibilities. The first is not new. They must analyze how the author — a reader of himself — attempts to guide the reading process by means of rhyme, rhythm, irony, significant emblems, repetitions, and all the rest. How is the unknown reader captured and brought into the text as a participant and friend? But the second is more challenging: that of understanding the text within readers, a realm at once subjective and historical where interpretation is regarded either as limited (correct or incorrect, plausible or implausible) or (according to at least one theorist) limitless. [1] In the case of the novel, however, the genre which transformed reading from scrutiny into what Ortega y Gasset described as a form of joyous submersion, [2] the two questions implicit in this logical division of effort (are we in the novel or is the novel in us?) are pointless. The addicted novel reader can only answer them with another question: "Who cares?" His habitual and yet marvellous symbiosis of consciousness with page is so seamless that the very notion of reception becomes dubious. Pierre Louÿs once mentioned tobacco as the only form of "volupté" unknown to the ancients, and Albert Thibaudet added a second, the silent "lecture des romans". [3] It is hardly coincidental that Parson Adams should have been equally fond of his Aeschylus (which he reads not philologically but as if he were Alonso Quijano reading *Amadís de Gaula*) and his pipe.

So conceived, it is clear that this particular way of reading, consecrated in the *Quijote* and reaching its apogee in the nineteenth century, is multiple in nature. Still, today, those of us who since childhood have so indulged ourselves read as many novels as we can of as many kinds (from trash to Tolstoy) as we can get our hands on and find time for. The

---

[1] Stanley Eugene Fish, *Is There a Text in This Class? The Authority of Interpretative Communities* (Cambridge, Mass., 1980).

[2] José Ortega y Gasset, "Ideas sobre la novela", *Obras completas* (Madrid, 1950-69), III, p. 410.

[3] Albert Thibaudet, *Réflexions sur le roman* (Paris, 1938), p. 239.

result is that we possess a treasure of shared fictional memories which novelists (all of them voracious readers) can use to communicate with us in what I have called elsewhere "novel-to-novel dialogue". [4] For example, the *Quijote* begins by communicating with the public in terms of a dialogue with the "common" reading of the time: romances of chivalry, the pastorals, and, above all, the first novel-length romance of roguery, the *Guzmán de Alfarache* which appeared in 1598. Its immediate and immense success was apparently what stimulated Cervantes (who found it gravely flawed) into undertaking his "answer". [5] This is well known, but what Hispanists have not meditated on in any systematic way (it is a cliché of our professional self-justification, but most of the detailed criticism is by outsiders!) [6] is the continuing dialogue of the *Quijote* with major novels of future centuries.

The list is both elastic and many-sided, ranging from direct influence to generic resemblance. A random sample might include Fielding (who wrote *Joseph Andrews* in the "manner" of Cervantes), Flaubert, Mark Twain, Dickens, and even such a non- or anti-Cervantine novelist as Hemingway. As we remember, *The Sun Also Rises* begins with poor Jake Cohen, an anti-anti-hero "incited" after reading one of the twentieth century's most "inciting" romances, *The Purple Land* by W. H. Hudson. [7]

The point is elementary. This is not just a question of learning by example or of genre, but rather of collective immersion in the same reading in such a way that the novelist can speak to his readers in a ready-made fictional "language". Or to say the same thing more directly, novels burgeon not only from observation and audition of known individuals and experienced society but also from enthusiastic or irritated absorption ("reception"?) of other novels. Henry Fielding adored the *Quijote* and detested *Pamela,* and his experience of reading both led to

---

[4] Stephen Gilman, *Galdós and the Art of the European Novel: 1867-1887* (Princeton, N.J., 1981), p. 93.

[5] Américo Castro, *Cervantes y los casticismos españoles* (Madrid, 1966), pp. 66-75.

[6] As far as I know, the best we have done is the theoretical discussion contained in Américo Castro's introduction to the Porrúa edition of the *Quijote* (México, 1960). An expanded version in English of that introduction is included in his *An Idea of History,* edited by Stephen Gilman and Edmund L. King (Columbus Ohio, 1977), pp. 77-142.

[7] The notion of the "incitación" (as opposed to "excitación") was originally coined by Castro to describe the active absorption of the romances of chivalry into the soul of Alonso Quijano, *Hacia Cervantes* (Madrid, 1960), p. 269. In the essay referred to in note 6, he extends it to such novels in the Cervantine tradition as *Le Rouge et le Noir* and *Madame Bovary.*

his creative dialogue with them on the pages of *Joseph Andrews* — and so too in the minds of the readers of all three. [8]

The case of *Pamela* is self-evident. In his first novel, the author of *Shamela* continues his debate with Richardson and with his hordes of titillated and lachrymose readers. The satirical theme is virginity and seduction, and to exploit it he invents Pamela's equally virtuous (but not hypocritical) brother, a protagonist as eminently anti-novelistic as Don Quixote was eminently novelistic. As an anodyne straight man within the raucous comedy, Joseph combines the chastity of his Old Testament namesake with the physique and face of a Greek god in livery. The rather perverse achievement of Fielding is to have created a genuine hero — brave, strong, handsome, virile, true-hearted, naturally "noble", and with perfect pitch — who in his unlikely virtue seems to be as "affected" as the stunted and distorted social types (parsons, squires, and innkeepers) whom he encounters. And far less interesting! [9] Within the novel the human antidote to Joseph is, of course, Parson Adams, and later the definitive correction was to be Tom Jones, equally good-natured and noble, but, as our grandparents still found, delightfully naughty, not fussy about "country matters".

It should be observed that Cervantes also made occasional fun of male chastity, as when Don Quixote, determinedly faithful to Dulcinea, at once provokes the possible ardour of Maritornes and Altisidora and resists what he believes to be their ravishing charms. However, in the Spanish novel such occasions are drawn in "caricatura" (as Fielding termed it), and the behaviour of both the tempted and the temptresses is "burlesque". Not so in *Joseph Andrews*. Both Lady Booby and Maritornes' role partner, Betty, the maid at the inn, although not described lasciviously, are attractive enough to be able to entice prospective lovers and choose among them, which is why Joseph had to be depicted as at once irresistible and ridiculously chaste in his male imitation of his sister. The assaults to which he is submitted are authentically passionate as contrasted to those which beset Don Quixote, and Joseph, in response to

---

[8] Homer Goldburg also considers Fielding's reading of Scarron, Marivaux and Lesage, *The Art of "Joseph Andrews"* (Chicago, 1969).

[9] Aurélien Digeon, *The Novels of Fielding* (London, 1925), p. 53. More recently critics have stressed the efforts of Fielding later on in the novel to portray his "hero" as less ridiculous (when we eventually learn of his true love, his initial comic chastity becomes more serious) and more interesting. Even so, without Parson Adams the "manner of Cervantes" would not have generated fresh novelistic delight.

Richardson, must be as innocent and adamant as his sister. One can imagine Fielding both preparing, and laughing at, what he knew would be the salacious "reception" of those particular scenes. In any case, what for Cervantes amounted to a single episodic strand of comedy (the disrobing of the knight by damsels, his seduction by daughters of nobility, and the rest) was at the beginning Fielding's central concern.

In view of this profound difference, a crucial question arises: how was it possible to engage in simultaneous dialogue with two such disparate novelists as Cervantes and Richardson? How could a satirical reply to *Pamela* be written "in imitation of the manner of Cervantes"? The answer, of course, is that it was not possible and that it was necessary to get Joseph out of domestic service, out of the clutches of Lady Booby, and on to the road. The change of tack results immediately in a series of narrative reminiscences of the *Quijote:* an adventurous journey punctuated by inns and unscrupulous keepers thereof; exposure (Lukacs' notion of novelistic "Obdachlosigkeit" [10] is carried to an extreme in Chapter XII of Book I), infliction of pain and humiliation, close attention to gestures and gait, and successive encounters with a gallery of eccentric individuals. These were the narrative means by which Cervantes (in creative dialogue with the picaresque tradition) had contrived to "turn fiction into reality". [11] In so saying, I do not defend the Romantic generalization that the theme of the *Quijote* is the conflict of the real with the ideal nor even present Cervantes and Fielding as precursors of nineteenth-century "realism". Theirs are stark and relatively vacant worlds if compared to the dense milieu and ambience of Balzac's Paris or Twain's Mississippi. [12] What we find both in the *Quijote* and in *Joseph Andrews* is what Max Scheler called "that primary experience of *resistance* which is the root of experiencing what is called 'reality' ". [13] The "root" (the beatings given and taken), as we now know, would eventually grow into the branches, leaves and flowers of future novelistic experience, but its own biological function is quite different.

---

[10] Georg Lukacs, *Die Theorie des Romans* (Darmstadt, 1965), p. 35.

[11] Henry Fielding, *The Journey of a Voyage to Lisbon* (Oxford, n.d.), p. 26.

[12] One can, of course, note in *Joseph Andrews* an increment of descriptive detail as compared to the *Quijote*. Weather, for example, is far more attended to. Nevertheless, the "world" created by Fielding with its stereotyped landscapes and its empty London is closer to that of Cervantes than to those which would be created in the century to follow.

[13] Max Scheler, *Man's Place in Nature*, translated by Hans Meyerhoff (New York, 1961), p. 14.

The above similarities have not escaped erudite attention. [14] However, less obvious is the fact that the voice of the narrator (Fielding himself as he wanted us to know him and not a persona) echoes and amplifies that of Cervantes. Seventeenth-century readers of the *Quijote* — to the disgust of Vladimir Nabokov, the author of that most cruel of novels, *Bend Sinister* — "relieved their melancholy and fretful spirits" [15] not with the mind-numbing suspense of the *Amadís,* but with gales of laughter. The more percipient among them did perceive, in addition to comic mishaps, an implicit critique of contemporary society, but at best they found in it a description of their neighbours and superiors [16] and at worst they attributed it to the author's grouchy old age and awareness of failure. [17] With well known exceptions, for example, the *comedias* of Alarcón and Quevedo's virulent "festivity", the Horatian notion of *castigat ridendo mores* was not typical of Golden Age Spain. Celebration more than castigation was the order of the day. In turbulently satirical eighteenth-century England on the contrary, silent readers (perhaps in part because emphatic translations made it more audible) began to hear and listen to the narrative voice of Cervantes which they received as ironically "grave". [18] Such was the "manner" of Cervantes which was Fielding's point of departure. By means of constant interruptions, interpolated sermons, at times jocose, at times serious, and always pretentious, mock professions of uncertainty, provocative chapter titles, and outrageous play with fractured English, he converted sly Cervantine understatement into deadpan over-statement. The reader of *Joseph Andrews* is asked explicitly to read between the lines.

Fielding had begun with the farcical skit entitled *Don Quixote in England* in which national "manners" were laughed *at* in theatrical space and time. But now in his "comic epic in prose" (the word "prose" means specifically the silent speech of the author on the printed page) the reader

---

[14] Martin Battestin, *The Moral Basis of Fielding's Art: A Study of "Joseph Andrews"* (Middletown, Connecticut, 1959), p. 170.

[15] Miguel de Cervantes Saavedra, *El viaje del Parnaso,* in *Obras completas* (Madrid, 1946), p. 85.

[16] "Y los que más se han dado son los pajes: no hay *antecámara* donde no se halle un *Don Quijote;* unos le toman si otros le dejan; estos le piden y aquellos le piden", *Don Quijote,* II, 4, *Obras completas,* p. 1390.

[17] Notably, Avellaneda, Cristóbal Suárez de Figueroa (*El pasajero,* Madrid, 1914, pp. 21 and 95), and — ruefully — by Cervantes himself in the *Viaje del Parnaso,* IV, where he is portrayed as "colérico y marchito" (*Obras completas,* p. 84).

[18] Norman Knox, *The Word Irony and its Context, 1500-1755* (Durham, N.C., 1961), pp. 168-171.

is enticed to explore hilarious national outwardness ("manners") *in* his own inwardness — his intimate consciousness of himself as a social creature. The novel, silently read, takes place in the mind and (as in the case of Alonso Quijano) captures the mind. Fielding, well aware of what he was about, states as an explicit intention "to hold the glass to thousands *in their closets,* that they may contemplate their deformity, and endeavour to reduce it". [19] What Cervantes had done gradually and unassertively in the course of the three sallies was now programmatic. *Joseph Andrews* was supposed to teach its readers how — in the words of Virginia Woolf — "to work themselves free". It may not be as deeply subversive as the *Quijote, Le Rouge et le Noir* and *Huckleberry Finn,* insofar as it only undermines social "affectation" while they lead us to question society itself as a form of value-perversion. But the ironical principle is the same.

Aside from learning from the *Quijote* how to feign a printed voice in order "gravely" to treat readers with therapeutic irony, Fielding also found therein invaluable lessons in narrative technique. To begin with, there is the interpolation of stories thematically related to the whole: for example, "The Unfortunate Jilt" and "The Rake's Progress" of Mr. Wilson who, when he finally divests himself of his "deformity", ends as a counterpart of Don Diego Miranda, the Knight of the Green Greatcoat. But what is most striking is that both Cervantes and Fielding, having been professional playwrights, are not only concerned critically with the sorry state of the art in their respective centuries and nations but also incorporate theatrical techniques within narration. Fielding himself praises *Don Quijote* for that very reason: it is superior — he maintains — to the female version by Charlotte Lennox insofar as the latter "partakes of the coldness of History or Narration", whereas the former "hath all the force of a Representation; it is in a manner subjected to the Eyes". [20] The point is convincingly illustrated in Jill Syverson's critical analysis of the reunion in the inn (I, XXXVI) with its immaculate timing, its entrances and exits, its positions on stage, as well as its use of disguises and recognitions. [21] As for *Joseph Andrews,* a typical example is the

---

[19] Henry Fielding, *Joseph Andrews,* III, I, edited by Martin C. Battestin (London, 1965), p. 159.

[20] Cited from the *Covent Garden Journal,* no. 24, by Glenn W. Hatfield, *Henry Fielding and the Language of Irony* (Chicago, 1968), p. 197.

[21] Jill Syverson, "Theatrical Aspects of the Novel: *Don Quixote, Joseph Andrews,* and the Example of Cervantes", *Revista de Estudios Hispánicos,* IX (1982), 241-248, at 243-245.

"*scene* of roasting" (my italics) which in many ways resembles the cruel charades staged for Don Quixote's benefit at the Duke's palace. [22] The rapprochement seems all the more likely in that the eloquence and dignity of Parson Adams' reply to the perverse squire and his company of curs reminds lovers of Cervantes of Don Quixote's splendid retort to the meddlesome "ecclesiastic". Pronounced before an amused audience in the dining halls of the palace and the manor, both elicit a very different dramatic response from the second "audience" of readers. Instead of laughing, we feel like standing up and cheering.

It is precisely in his creation of the Parson that Fielding reveals his genius as a reader of the *Quijote*. It is not that Joseph's travelling companion, like Wieland's Don Silvio de Rosalva, is in any sense a latter-day reincarnation of Cervantes' protagonist. As the title page specifies, what is imitated is the manner and not the man. And Fielding in his initial description goes on to stress the differences: "Mr. Abraham Adams was an excellent scholar" (meaning not an eccentric bookworm) who possessed "good sense, good parts, and good nature" (meaning although "ignorant of the ways of the world", not out of his mind). He is not mad, although on occasion he may dance with joy and snap his fingers "as if he had been mad". More crucially, he is not insecure in his vocation. Rather he professes his own variety of Christianity (in which he believes with the blind faith of his namesake) with unremitting zeal. Hence he is blessedly exempt from the cumulative doubt and disillusion as well as from the inner mutability which characterize the knight. Finally, although his nag is as unreliable as Rocinante, he is no mean opponent in physical combat. His arm is as strong as a leg, and his crabstick is far more deadly than the Manchegan's lance.

Nevertheless, although not Quixotesque, in one important respect Adams' characterization and his role are profoundly Cervantine. They correspond to Fielding's interpretation of both squire and knight as naïve. Martin Battestin explains his surname in precisely these terms:

In his tattered cassock or in his nakedness, he is one of the blessed perennial innocents of the world, a latter-day Adam who has not meddled with the tree of knowledge. Like the completely good natured man he is, when he is most himself, he acts generously on intuition and impulse, spontaneous in joy and sorrow — snapping his fingers, fetching a groan, dancing around the room in a rapture, brandishing his crabstick. [23]

---

[22] Goldburg, p. 211, and Battestin, p. 170.
[23] *Joseph Andrews,* XXXII.

In other words, this eighteenth-century Adam is surely the most appealing literary creature to have sprung from the special reverence for naïveté which was complementary to the use of grave irony. By which I mean that Fielding — as he believed Cervantes to have done before him — proposed to speak to the reader over the head of the candid protagonists [24] about the social distortions of human nature, while the latter in their spontaneous reactions to given situations would validate by example the worldly-wise commentary. It is curious to note here that, just as in the *Quijote,* there are varieties of naïveté which communicate with each other in dialogue. For example Joseph, who has had the experience of being in service, can at times explain to his friend the foibles and insincerity of those who are served.

If Parson Adams' function in the novel was to resemble that of Cervantes' pair (who were admired in the eighteenth century as forefathers of his particular form of revealing innocence), it is not surprising that Fielding should have been concerned (if not to imitate them as he did in the case of Partridge and Sancho) to incorporate traits of both in his new human creation. But what is remarkable is his brilliant success in so doing. How was it possible to blend characteristics taken from two such antithetical lives within a single life? Before attempting to answer, let us make sure that that is indeed the case. All three — each in his own way — possess a heart of "honest simplicity", but typically Sanchesque is the Parson's enjoyment of creature comforts. As little an ascetic as the Spanish squire, he adores good cheer: a fire, pleasant company and conversation, a mug of ale (the English counterpart of the wineskin), "a loaf and cheese". We can even imagine how readily Sancho would have shared a friendly pipe with him had he had the chance. The Quixotesque contribution is equally apparent. Both the Parson and the knight are incorrigible interrupters who, consumed with curiosity, interrogate all passers-by; both are quarrelsome and susceptible to sudden excesses of passion; both do not hesitate to rescue damsels in distress (although in the case of the Parson the distress and the rescue are genuine); both indulge themselves complacently in learned discourse; both ignore the impression made on others by their eccentric appearance; and both believe in the supernatural, whether in the form of enchanters or ghosts and witches.

---

24 Michael Erwin, *Henry Fielding: The Tentative Realist* (Oxford, 1967), p. 56.

Recognition of similar traits is neither a confirmation of the titular declaration of dependence nor a contradiction of the initial declaration of independence ("good sense"). In making both statements, Fielding, acclaimed by Stendhal as the founding father of the novel, [25] is as truthful as our own American founding father was supposed to be. Parson Adams is no more an imitation Don Quixote than he is an imitation Sancho. And yet, just as in the case of the creation of Huck Finn (not in *Tom Sawyer* but in his own novel), Fielding's immensely perceptive reading of Cervantes was crucial to his conception and gestation. What the English proto-novelist was the first to comprehend — to *live* in the intensity of his symbiosis with the Spanish text — was what Salvador de Madariaga two centuries later was to term the "quixotization" of Sancho and the "sanchification" of Don Quixote. For them it is the result of a slow process of shared experience, a growing together like that of a long-married couple, and what prevents its completion is an acute sense of personal identity founded chiefly on vivid memory, but also on private "domestic" grievances. However, for Fielding their gradual conjunction suggested the possibility of creating a completed, definitive portrait of naïveté. He would combine characteristics of the two as he knew them within the hermetic frontiers of an unquestioning religious vocation. And when they did not mesh, he would resolve all discrepancies by means of a central core of absent-mindedness. The extraordinary and often malicious capacity for recollection which preserves the individualities of knight and squire within what Hermann Cohen terms the "history" of their "love" [26] is precisely what is lacking in Parson Adams. Only so could fragments of their typification coexist so comfortably in his soul.

Book II, chapter XI, presents a striking example. Parson Adams' argumentative quixotism becomes sheer folly when, having been arrested

---

[25] Stendhal realized that, while Cervantes wrote the first novel, he conceived of his achievement as essentially a-generic or even anti-generic — a critique genre as such. Fielding, on the other hand, consciously and craftily converted that achievement into a viable new genre. Therefore, he and not Cervantes was the inventor of the novel: "Ce roman [*Tom Jones*] est aux autres ce que l'*Iliade* est aux poèmes épiques". *Mémoires d'un touriste, Œuvres* (Paris, 1929), I, p. 52.

[26] Hermann Cohen, like Lukacs, contradicts Goethe's notion of three *Naturformen* of literature (epic, lyric, and dramatic) by defining the novel as a separate narrative genre. However, his definition is at once opposite and complementary to Lukacs' metaphysical "rooflessness": "*Die Liebe erfordert ihre eigne Geschichte. So fordert die Lyrik die Liebesgeschichte heraus. So ruft sie über ihre eigenen Grenzen den Roman hervor*", *System der Philosophie*, Dritter Teil, *Ästetik des Reinen Gefühl* (Berlin, 1912), II, p. 122.

and almost "committed to gaol" by an intoxicated justice of the peace, he is unexpectedly identified as a "gentleman" by an acquaintance of the Boobys' and so discharged. The injustice of the proceedings — both the threatened committal without a hearing and the dismissal of charges because of status — is patent. Then after a long silence (during which the Parson "applied himself vigorously to smoking") when the justice "began to sing forth his own praises and to value himself exceedingly on his discernment in the case which had lately been laid before him", the erstwhile accused cannot hold his peace. Exactly as Don Quixote would have done, he "*quickly interrupted... his worship*", and a "dispute now arose, whether he ought not in strictness of law to have committed him, the said Adams; in which the latter maintained he ought to have been committed, and the justice as vehemently held he ought not". [27] The absurd quarrel is then itself interrupted by Fanny, and the following chapter finds the pair taking shelter from "a violent storm of rain in an inn or rather alehouse where Adams immediately procured himself with a good fire, a toast and ale, and a pipe and began to smoke with great content, *utterly forgetting everything that had happened*" (both italicized phrases are mine). The battle with the "ravisher", the chivalric rescue of the "damsel" (Fanny), the detention by the reward-greedy bird-catchers, and the threatening legal hearing all disappear from his mind as if he were — as indeed he is, literarily speaking — a split personality. Now a contented Sancho, he erases previous Quixotism from his mental *tabula*.

In conclusion, to those who understandably may cavil at the identification of Don Quixote's "madness" with naïveté and who find a much more convincing display of that quality in Sancho's governorship, I offer two favourite passages of mine, which, as we shall see, also appealed to Fielding. Prior to Don Quixote's single combat with the Knight of the Mirrors, Sancho describes his master to his colleague in squiredom, Tomé Cecial:

> ... no tiene nada de bellaco; antes tiene un alma como un cántaro; no sabe hacer mal a nadie, sino bien a todos, ni tiene malicia alguna; un niño le hará entender que es de noche en la mitad del día, y por esta sencillez le quiero como a las telas de mi corazón, y no me amaño a dejarle, por más disparates que haga. [28]

---

27 *Joseph Andrews*, II, xi, p. 127.
28 Cervantes, *Obras completas*, pp. 1423-24 (*Don Quijote*, II, xiii).

The person who knows Don Quixote best of all has just testified to the profundity of naïveté beneath the madness, that is, to his charter membership in the blessed fraternity of revealing innocence. It is typical of Cervantes that he should have presented Sancho as an authority on "simplicity".

The inherent nobility in Don Quixote's guilelessness becomes apparent in the following chapter after his victory when he raises the visor of his antagonist and discovers "el rostro mismo, la misma figura, el mismo aspecto, la misma fisonomía, la misma efigie, la perspectiva misma del bachiller Sansón Carrasco". [29] Face, physiognomy, image, picture (as well as the squire who, without his false nose, turns out to be Sancho's next-door neighbour back in Argamasilla) — everything indicates that Don Quixote's joy in having at long last defeated a knight errant in full armour with an escutcheon and a lady love is only illusory. His answer, of course, is that enemy enchanters have victimized him once again, but in the third sally images cannot be so easily discounted. Second thoughts are provoked, and those of Don Quixote confirm Sancho's view of him:

> Estemos a razón, Sancho —replicó Don Quijote—. Ven acá: ¿en qué consideración puede caber que el bachiller Sansón Carrasco viniese como caballero andante, armado de armas ofensivas y defensivas, y pelear conmigo? ¿He sido yo su enemigo, por ventura? ¿Hele dado yo jamás ocasión para tenerme ojeriza? ¿Soy yo su rival, o hace él profesión de las armas, para tener envidia a la fama que yo por ellas he ganado? [30]

In *Joseph Andrews* we hear a clear echo of this speech — an equally noble incomprehension of perversity — when Parson Adams discovers that the "gentleman" who enjoys the appearance of generosity does not intend to keep *any* of his lavish promises:

> But surely Joseph, your suspicions of this gentleman must be unjust; for what a silly fool must he be who would do the devil's work for nothing! and canst thou tell me any interest he could possibly propose to himself by deceiving us in his professions? [31]

The title of the chapter is explicit: "A very curious adventure in which Mr. Adams gave a much greater instance of the honest simplicity of his heart than of his experience in the ways of the world". Fielding has

---

29 Cervantes, *Don Quijote*, II 14, *Obras completas*, p. 1429.
30 Cervantes, *Don Quijote*, II, 16, *Obras completas*, p. 1432.
31 *Joseph Andrews*, II, XVI, p. 150.

understood Cervantes perfectly, just as Cervantes would have understood him.

An apparently minor question remains to be answered: why describe this sad and sordid episode as an "adventure"? All that *happens* is that the Parson is first "in an ecstacy" over the prospect of a three-hundred-pound living and all the rest, and afterwards expresses his perplexity, disappointment, and candid bewilderment. One answer might be that Fielding, like Lawrence Sterne, [32] is jousting ironically with the whole notion of adventure — whether comic or suspenseful or both — as the basic building block of novelistic structure. But if so, what about all the other genuine adventures to which Joseph and his "friend" are submitted? Another answer which I prefer is that Fielding is alluding to Don Quixote's similar ecstasy when in the darkness of the grove he hears the armour of another knight errant "clattering on the ground", an appropriately Homeric translation of Cervantes' "al caer le crujieron las armas". Then, "llegándose a Sancho, que dormía, le trabó del brazo, y con no pequeño trabajo le volvió en su acuerdo, y con voz baja le dijo: 'Hermano Sancho, aventura tenemos' ". [33] This is one of the most moving sentences in the entire novel and, if Henry Fielding heard it in the way my teacher, Augusto Centeno, taught me to hear it, his reception was of the highest fidelity.

STEPHEN GILMAN

---

[32] "Tis to rebuke a vicious taste which has crept into thousands... reading straightforward in quest of adventures..." Lawrence Sterne, *Tristram Shandy*, I, 20 (Oxford, 1926), p. 62.

[33] Cervantes, *Don Quijote*, II, 14, *Obras completas*, p. 1420.

"EXEUÇION PROVADA": ON LEGAL TERMINOLOGY IN THE *LIBRO DE BUEN AMOR*

334a	G	Por ende yo apongo contra el *exeuçion*
	S	E por ende yo propongo contra el *esençion*
349b	G	que puso la gulhara en sus *eseuçiones*
	S	que puso la gulharra en sus *exenpçiones*
353a	G	la *exuçion primera* es en si perentoria
	S	la *exençion* primera es en si perentoria
354a	G	la *exuçion* primera muy bien fue alegada
	S	la *exepçion* primera muy bien fue llegada
358c	G	por *exuçion* non pude condenar nin punir
	S	por *exepçion* non puedo yo condepnar nin punir
359b	G	sea *exuçion* provada non le faran otro castigo
	S	sea *exepçion* provada nonl faran otro castigo
360c	G	non por la *exeuçion* mas por que lo deve far
	S	non por la *exepçion* mas por que lo puede far
361a	G	Por *exeuçion* se puede la demanda desechar
	S	Por *exepçion* se puede la demanda desechar
361c	G	por *exeuçion* non puedo yo condenar nin matar
	S	por *exeçion* non puedo yo condepnar nin matar

A s medievalists know, the editing of a text requires the constant exercise of editorial judgement: choices have to be made between MS readings, and emendations made where the MSS do not make sense. [1] In effect, the editor presumes to know better than the copyists what the author intended. But in so doing he incurs the risk of unwittingly setting himself up as knowing better than the author what the latter meant. Every author makes unintentional errors, of course, and where these are obvious there is little harm in removing them. But if what is removed is neither an unintentional error by the author nor a later miscopying, but what was actually meant, the editorial "correction" becomes a misrepresentation. It may wish upon the author knowledge, carefulness or literary subtlety which he did not possess. Or it may reflect the modern reader's ignorance:

---

[1] For a useful discussion of copyists' errors, with special reference to the *Libro de buen amor,* see Alberto Blecua, *Manual de crítica textual,* Madrid: Castalia, 1983, 1.ª parte.

a MS reading universally condemned may turn out, in the light of further study, to be perfectly good. [2]

In editions of the *Libro de buen amor* one form of hypercorrection may be the imposition of strict classical orthography on the Latin quotations that occur. In some cases, the MSS have obviously garbled the Latin. One cannot, for example, seriously suppose that a medieval priest could write or intend such oddities as *cum is qui derun paçem* (374*b* in *G*) or *primo dieron vnium* (375*c* in *G*). But in many cases the MSS give what read like phonetic renderings of medieval pronunciation of Latin, as, for example, 374*d*, *in notibus estolite* (*S* and *T*), *in notebus estolite* (*G*). This may well have been not only how Juan Ruiz pronounced the words, but how he wrote them or expected them to be written. He was not drawing up a formal document for submission to ecclesiastical authorities, but quoting in the context of a Romance text probably intended for oral performance. And he may well have quoted from memory.

The case of legal terms is similar. The introduction of Roman Law into the Castilian courts must have meant the adoption of a number of Latin terms and their eventual Castilianization. Castilian lawyers' pronunciation of them would tend to be ahead of orthographic modifications in this process, especially while the normative effect of prescriptive texts such as the *Siete partidas* was still not widespread. The concentration of over fifty such terms in a single passage as early as 1330 is one more way in which the *Libro de buen amor* proves its exceptional qualities. What precedents for the written forms of these words would Juan Ruiz have had, apart, possibly, from the *Siete partidas*? [3]

The single passage I refer to is the story of the wolf accusing the vixen of theft before the monkey judge (sts. 320-371). This Aesopic fable, which

---

[2] I have tried to demonstrate this point recently in respect of st. 1506*b*: "¿'Ove nuevos cuidados'? ¿'Ove menos cuidados'?: Un problema textual y literario del *Libro de buen amor* (v. 1506*b*)", in *Homenaje a José Manuel Blecua*, ed. Félix Monge *et al.*, Madrid: Gredos, 1983, pp. 295-305.

[3] The following terms, all used in a legal sense and all direct from the Latin (some more evolved than others), occur in the story of Don Ximio: *abdiençia, abogado, acto, -a, acusar, acusaçión, aponer, apellar, asignar, asolver, conclusión, conde(p)nar, confesión, conplido, -a, conpusiçión, constituçión, criminal, defensión, demandar, derecho, dilatorio, exeuçión, furto, instrumente, judgar, juez, juizio, jurisdiçión, ladrón, legado* (as *llegado*), *legítimo, librar, litigar, mandar, notario, ofiçio, oponer, ordinario, partes, pena, perentorio, -a, petiçión, plazo, proçeso, pronunçiar, proponer, provar, rreconvençión, rreplicaçión, seer, sentençia, talión.* The following also occur in the story, but show other than purely phonological change: *abenençia* (ADVENIMENTUM), *atormentar* (TORMENTUM), *rresponsión* (RESPONSA), *testigo* (TESTIS), *vistas* (VISIS). The following occur elsewhere in the *Libro*: *abenir* (ADVENIRE), *approllaçones* (PROLATIONES), *decreto* (DECRETUM), *malefiçio* (MALEFICIUM).

is told with skeletal economy in the Latin versions which survive from the Middle Ages, is developed by Juan Ruiz into a brilliant demonstration of legal procedures based on Roman Law. [4] The wolf, himself an inveterate thief, accuses the vixen of stealing a cockerel (st. 323). His advocate delivers the accusation before the judge, Don Ximio, in correct legal form (sts. 324ff), ending with a demand for the death penalty (328c). The vixen exercises her right to ask for an advocate to defend her (st. 329). The judge duly allows her twenty days in which to find one, and adjourns the hearing (sts. 330-331). When the court reassembles (st. 332), the vixen's advocate, a powerful mastiff, enters two legal objections to the hearing of the wolf's accusation: firstly, the wolf is himself an habitual thief, with many convictions for the crime (sts. 333-336); secondly, he has been excommunicated for publicly maintaining a concubine, at the same time as having a lawful wife (sts. 337-338). These objections become the central issue in the case and form the basis for the judge's summing up (sts. 347-366). It is the word used for these objections (judicial exceptions in Roman Law) that I propose to discuss. As the variant forms of its nine occurrences show, it clearly gave the copyists some trouble, and they in turn have confused modern editors.

The Gayoso MS (G) gives what appear to be variations on the form *exeuçion*. The second letter is *x* eight times out of nine. The *e* that follows it is missing in four cases; the copyist writes *exuçion* each time, with a single *tilde* that is probably intended to serve as the abbreviation sign for both the *e* and the final *n*. The letter preceding the *ç* is clearly *u* each time, not *n*: both Ducamin and Criado/Naylor print *u*, and my own reading of the MS confirms it. [5] Either the copyist had *exeuçion* in his model, or else he heard what he thought was *exeuçion* when copying from dictation. The Salamanca MS (S) has *esençion* the first time (334a), but next produces what looks like a hypercorrection: *exenpçiones*. The

---

[4] For an indication of the surviving Latin versions of the fable, see Félix Lecoy, *Recherches sur le "Libro de buen amor"*, Paris, 1938, p. 130. For a discussion of the legal elements in Juan Ruiz's version, see José Luis Bermejo Cabrero, "El saber jurídico del Arcipreste", in *El Arcipreste de Hita, el autor, la tierra, la época. Actas del I Congreso Internacional sobre el Arcipreste de Hita*, Dirección: M. Criado de Val, Barcelona: S.E.R.E.S.A., 1973, pp. 409-415; Steven D. Kirby, "The Artistic Utilization of Law and Rhetoric in the Don Ximio Episode of Juan Ruiz's *Libro de buen amor*", Ph. D. Thesis, Univ. Kentucky, 1976; Henry Ansgar Kelly, *Canon Law and the Archpriest of Hita*, Binghamton, New York, 1984, cap. 4: "Procedure in the Court of Don Ximio".

[5] Juan Ruiz, *Libro de buen amor*, ed. Jean Ducamin, Toulouse, 1901; ed. M. Criado de Val and Eric. W. Naylor, Madrid: C.S.I.C., 1965.

third time the copyist drops the *p*: *exençion*. The fourth time (354*a*), he replaces the *n* by a *p*: *exepçion*. He retains this form for the next four occasions, but on the last occasion he writes *exeçion*, which suggests a careless omission of the *p*, but could represent an intended reversion to *exençion* (failing to add the *tilde* for the *n*).

The first editor of anything approaching a modern critical edition, Julio Cejador, appears to have followed *G* throughout, except for reading the copyist's *u* as *n*: he prints *esençiones* in 349*b*, but *exençión* in all other cases. [6] More recent editors — Chiarini, Corominas, Joset, Blecua — all of whom profess to apply neo-Lachmannian principles of textual criticism, fail to make any comment on the editorial decisions they make here. [7] Chiarini regularizes to *exepçión/exepçiones* throughout. Corominas and Joset regularize to *esençión/esençiones* (Corominas omits the cedilla). Blecua follows *S* the first three times, but from 354*a* on, where the copyist writes *exepçion*, he inserts an *n*: *exe[n]pçión*. Chiarini's choice of *exepçión* throughout clearly reflects his decision that it is the correct word in the context, regardless of what the MSS put. The others all appear to have inferred that the archetype reading was *esençion* or *exençion*, and to have seen *G*'s *exeuçion* as a nonsense reading (I assume they have not misread it as *exençion*). But if the archetype had *exençion*, how did *exeuçion* not only occur but persist in the branch to which *G* belongs, unless it was a form that made sense? Does not its rejection conflict with the cherished principle of *lectio difficilior*? And why should the copyist of *S*, after getting it right the first three times, change to *exepçion* and persist with that form? The impression is created that at the fourth occurrence he decided that he knew better than his model what was meant and made his own editorial emendation. If, however, we dissent from the editors and postulate that the archetype reading was *exeuçion*, there is less explaining to do. *G* has simply got it right, give or take a letter. In *S*, the initial *esençion* could have arisen from a misreading of the *u* and trivialization to a form the copyist knew. Or else he may have found *esençion* in his model (there for the same reason), and have begun by copying it uncritically. At the fourth occurrence, he decided that the word ought to be *exepçion*.

---

[6] Juan Ruiz, *Libro de buen amor*, ed. Julio Cejador y Frauca, Madrid; Clásicos Castellanos, 1913.

[7] Juan Ruiz, *Libro de buen amor*, ed. Giorgio Chiarini, Milan: Ricciardi, 1964; ed. Joan Corominas, Madrid, C.S.I.C., 1967; ed. Jacques Joset, Madrid: Clásicos Castellanos, 1974; ed. Alberto Blecua, Barcelona: Planeta, 1983.

A neo-Lachmannian *recensio* suggests that the archetype reading was more likely to have been *exeuçion* than *exençion* or *esençion*. But was it a correct reading or an error? The word is not, as far as I know, recorded in any dictionary or glossary. The *Tentative Dictionary of Old Spanish*, whose *Libro de buen amor* entries are by H. B. Richardson, only gives two forms, *exención* and *excepción*, and only refers to the *Libro;* both forms are stated to be derived from EXEMPTIONEM. This is manifest nonsense: the etymon of *excepción* can only be EXCEPTIO. The question is whether Juan Ruiz used a word derived from EXEMPTIO or one derived from EXCEPTIO. None of the studies referred to in note 4 above considers the question. Kirby attaches no significance to the variations in form in the MSS: what is meant is clearly a judicial exception. [8] His lack of concern presumably arises from his conviction that the judicial procedure described in the story is all derived from the *Siete partidas* of Alfonso X. The term for a judicial exception in the *Partidas* is *deffenssión,* [9] which Kirby considers to be derived from DEFENSIO as used in the *Decretals* of Gregory IX. *Defenssión* occurs in the story (349*a,* 352*a,* 364*d*), but in the sense of an argument in support of an exception, not of the exception itself. If Juan Ruiz was guided by the *Partidas* in respect of procedural law, it seems strange that when referring to the key procedural point in the case, he should use a term that does not occur in the *Partidas*.

Henry Kelly, in chapter 4 of his book, virtually ignores Kirby's thesis. He considers the source of the procedural niceties described in the case before Don Ximio to be Canon Law, essentially as described by the thirteenth-century jurist Gulielmus Durantus in the *Speculum Judiciale*. Kelly himself points out (p. 90) that both Canon and Civil Law derived their procedures from Roman Law, as codified by Justinian. But he fails to point out that the *Speculum* deals with Civil and Criminal Law as well as with Canon Law, as Gulielmus's prologue clearly states. [10] As the case before Don Ximio is a criminal case, it seems somewhat illogical to regard Canon Law as the source, rather than Roman Law. Further-

---

[8] Kirby, "Artistic Utilization...", p. 212.
[9] *Siete partidas,* III, tít. III, leyes viii, ix, x, xi. I have not been able to check the *Fuero Real* in its Castilian version, but the thirteenth-century Portuguese translation has *deffensõ*: Livro II, "Titulo de cõmo se sabya defender" (ed. A. Pimenta, Lisboa, 1946, p. 70).
[10] *Speculum Judiciale, lib.* I (1473 edn.), f. ii: "*In parte prima de personis in judicio intervenientibus disseretur. In secunda totus ordo iudiciarius in causis civilibus perstringetur. In tercia iudicia criminalia supponentur...*".

more, though Juan Ruiz apparently alludes to the *Speculum* in 1152*a*
("el Espéculo"), it is certainly not his only source of legal terminology,
as his use of at least a dozen terms from Castilian legal sources shows:
*alcalde, caloña, carta, costas, ençerrar rrazones, enfamado, enforcar, en-
plazar, fallar, malfetría, otorgar, pechar, quito*... Juan Ruiz may also use a
few Roman law terms not in the *Speculum*, where, for example, I have
so far failed to encounter AUDIENTIA, rendered as *abdiençia* (336*d*, 347*c*).
The term appears in the *Codex Justinianus*, and the *Encyclopedic Dictionary of Roman Law*, p. 370, states: "... unknown in the language of
classical jurists, the term is used in Later Imperial constitutions for legal
proceedings, the judgement included".[11] One might perhaps render Juan
Ruiz's use of it as "hearing of the case". His familiarity with legal matters
would seem to be quite broadly based, as well as of considerable depth,
certainly not confined to just one legal manual. It is difficult to believe,
therefore, that when introducing the key issue in this case he should use
any but the correct term.

Esençion/exençión can be ruled out immediately. EXEMPTIO is defined
by the *Encyclopedic Dictionary* (p. 462) as "Taking away a person summoned to court by force or fraud to frustrate the summons..."[12] DEFENSIO
is defined by the *Encyclopedic Dictionary* as the activity of defending
oneself in a trial; also as "procedural means by which one combats his
adversary's claim, an *exceptio*, for instance". This definition makes DE-
FENSIO a broader and less specific term than EXCEPTIO. The *Speculum
Judiciale* explains that DEFENSIONES are actions which bring a case to an
end by defending the accused (such as the agreed liquidation of a debt),
but not by preventing the hearing from going ahead. These latter devices
are EXCEPTIONES.[13] The *Encyclopedic Dictionary* defines EXCEPTIO as "A
defense opposed by the defendant to the plaintiff's claim to render it

---

[11] Adolf Berger, *Encyclopedic Dictionary of Roman Law*, Philadelphia (Trans.
Amer. Philosoph. Soc. vol. 43), 1953, *s.v.* AUDIENTIA. Robert Mayr (= Mayr-
Hartig), *Vocabularium Codicis Justiniani*, Pars I (Pars Latina), Prague, 1923, gives
a number of references to its occurrence.

[12] In Du Cange, EXEMPTIO is defined as follows: "Qua Monasteria ab episcopali
jurisdictione eximuntur. Vide. Monasteria exempta".

[13] *Speculum Judiciale, lib.* II, *partic.* I: *De Exceptionibus et Replicationibus.*
1. *núm.* 4: "*Defensiones illae proprie dicuntur, quae ipso iure tollunt et perimunt
omnem actionem. Hae enim et similes dicuntur proprie defensiones et non exceptiones ... quia licet defendant reum et per consequens repellant agentem, non tamen
excludunt actionem, cum nulla sit ibi actio; sed exceptio excludit actionem, ut dixi.
Largo tamen modo possunt dici exceptiones, eo quod repellunt, seu excludunt
agentis intentionem...*". D. G. DURANDI EPISC. MIMATENSIS, *Speculum Iuris...*, Franco-
furti, MDXCII.

ineffective...", that is, not an answer to the charge but a legal reason for not allowing the case to continue, if I understand it aright. The *Speculum Judiciale* has a whole section on exceptions (see note 13), and exceptions are discussed in both the *Decretals* of Gregory IX (*lib.* II, *tit.* xxv) and the "Clementinas", or *Constitutions of Pope Clement V* (*lib.* II, *tit.* x). Juan Ruiz alludes to the latter at the end of his prologue, and quotes its opening words: "Fidei catholice fundamento...", while the former is possibly referred to in 1148*d*, "los decretales". Professor Kelly's analysis of the case before Don Ximio (especially pp. 100-112) makes it clear that the law relating to exceptions was complex, and also that Juan Ruiz knew a good deal about it. The conclusion must surely be that the word he had in mind for the exceptions raised by the vixen's lawyer was, in its Latin form, EXCEPTIO. But in what form did he intend that it should appear in the text? Was Chiarini right as far as reflecting the author's intention is concerned, even if it meant throwing overboard the neo-Lachmannian rule book? Corominas's dictionary gives the first documented occurrence of *excepción* as the *Ordenamiento de Alcalá* of 1348. He presumably discounts the occurrence of *excepción* in the Salamanca MS of the *Libro* on the grounds that it is a scribal error of the early fifteenth century. There is, however, one occurrence of *excepción* in an earlier text to be noted, in an Aragonese document of 1331.[14] There may be others as yet unnoticed. In any case, we would still have to explain how *exçepçion* (or *exepçion*) got changed into *exeuçion* in the archetype.

All the legal terms derived from Latin which Juan Ruiz uses show some degree of Castilianization, even though some were clearly new and were presumably not yet to be found in the Castilian legal codes. The extent of the modification depended, no doubt, on how early they had been adopted and on how easily they were assimilable in their original form. Thus while *furto, notario* or *acusar* are scarcely altered, *judgar* has changed a good deal from JUDICARE, *juez* from JUDEX, *derecho* from DIRECTUS, *pleito* from PLACITUS. Those terms which had not yet received the formal recognition of being incorporated into legal codes such as the *Siete partidas* may well have been familiar to lawyers mainly by ear, as oral adaptations from the Latin forms. I suggested at the beginning that

---

[14] *Documento desconocido de Zaragoza del año 1331*, ed. Gunnar Tilander, Stockholm: Leges Hispaniae Medii Aevi VII, 1958, 36, 64: "Et renunciamos dia de acuerdo et diez dias pora cartas demandar et atodas otras et cadaunas excepciones et dilaciones de dreyto et de fuero contra la present carta jnpugnantes".

the concentration of so many terms taken from Roman Law in a Castilian text may have been exceptional, possibly without precedent, except for the *Partidas*. Part of Juan Ruiz's self-appointed task in telling the story (whether serious or merely playful) may have been to rub the nose of the *abogado de rromançe* (353*d*) in this new terminology. With a term such as EXCEPTIO, not used in the *Partidas* and not yet taken over to any extent, he may have had no written precedent for a Castilianized form, and he may have chosen to be guided by his ear — by what he heard from the lips of contemporary legists — than by the original Latin, with which, as an archpriest versed in Canon Law, he would be familiar. Latin -PT- was always subject to considerable modification in Castilian (SEPTEM > SETTE > *siete*, CAPTIVUS > *cabtivo* > *cautivo*, etc.). It was also not common, and derivations from -CEPTIO are hard to find in texts of the early fourteenth century, so that there would be few normative restraints on pronunciation or orthography. [15] It is easy to imagine that a real *trabalenguas* such as *excepción*, /ekstseptsjón/, would rapidly be modified by lawyers intent on showing off their familiarity with the term to /ekseβtsjón/ or /eksewtsjón/, or even /esewtsjón/. A nice orthographic representation of this would be *exeuçión*.

Even if we prefer to suppose that Juan Ruiz's own mental image of the written word was something like *exçepçion*, his pronunciation of it — when reciting the story aloud to friends, for example — may yet have responsible for the form *exeuçion* getting into the archetype. Either way, it seems prudent in this instance to heed the insistent message of the Gayoso MS, the more accident prone of the two certainly, but also the less given to linguistic updating or pedantic spellings. [16]

G. B. GYBBON-MONYPENNY

Hythe, Kent

---

[15] There are no other derivatives of -CEPTIO in the *Libro de buen amor*. In the *Obras completas* of Don Juan Manuel, ed. José Manuel Blecua, Madrid: Gredos, 1983, vol. II, "Glosario", one finds *conçebimiento* instead of *concepción* (in *Libro de los estados*, II, cap. 3; also *concibimiento*, *ibid.* II, cap. 8) referring to the conception of Christ; and *reçibimiento* instead of *recepción* (*Libro del cauallero et del escudero*, cap. XVIII); cf. D. G. Pattison, *Early Spanish Suffixes*, Oxford: Basil Blackwell, Publications of the Philological Society XXVII, 1975, cap. 5.

[16] It is, perhaps, relevant to recall that even in the fifteenth century a learned poet such as Juan de Mena, enriching his poetic vocabulary with deliberate Latinisms, frequently spelled words as he had learned to pronounce them in the Latin-speaking *milieu* of Salamanca University, producing such forms as *contrapuna*, *costançia*, *diçiones*, *eçede* (EXCEDIT), *inoto*, *reto* (RECTUS); see María Rosa Lida, *Juan de Mena, poeta del prerrenacimiento*, México, 1950, p. 261.

MÉS SOBRE LA INTENCIONALITAT DELS TEXTOS HISTORIOGRÀFICS CATALANS MEDIEVALS

N o fa gaire que Brigitte Schlieben-Lange, tot partint de premisses lingüístiques i del seu interès per la funció comunicativa de la historiografia medieval, formulava unes preguntes ben concretes sobre la intencionalitat de les quatre grans cròniques catalanes. [1] Malgrat la brevetat, el seu útil assaig arribava a unes conclusions força interessants que justifiquen la metodologia usada, consistent en interrogar unes obres determinades fent servir un qüestionari uniforme també determinat. Es tracta, si no vaig errat, de la tècnica emprada pels editors del GRLMA en impulsar la preparació d'una documentació sistemàtica que permeti després compulsar i contrastar tot un conjunt de textos des de la perspectiva desitjada.

Com que, pel que sembla, el volum del GRLMA destinat a la historiografia, malgrat la diligència dels benemèrits editors, ja fa anys que arreplega pols en els estatges d'uns impressors sense massa pressa, m'ha semblat oportú d'aprofitar l'avinentesa d'aquest homenatge a un dels catedràtics britànics més honrosament vinculats a la historiografia hispànica en general, i a la catalana en particular, per retornar al tema encetat per la investigadora alemanya, si bé ampliant el camp d'estudi a alguns dels textos més representatius documentats per mi mateix en el volum del GRLMA suara esmentat, i aprofitant no solament els pròlegs sinó també totes aquelles dades que considero més significatives a l'hora de tractar d'especificar la intenció de l'obra, la motivació que impel·lia la ploma de l'autor o compilador, i el públic a qui anava adreçada la literatura historiogràfica. D'aquesta manera, potser les notes que segueixen podran complementar la brillant síntesi de H. U. Gumbrecht, més aviat centrada en les literatures romàniques "més importants". [2]

---

[1] "Zu den Intentionserklärung der vier grossen Katalanischen Chroniken", dins *Miscel·lània Aramon i Serra. Estudis de llengua i literatura catalanes oferts a R. Aramon i Serra en el seu setantè aniversari*, vol. I, *EUC*, XXIII (1979), 533-41.
[2] Em refereixo de moment al seu llibre *Zwei Beiträge zum Historiographie-Band des Grundrisses der Romanischen Literaturen des Mittelalters* (edició en ciclostil, Witten/Bochum, 1981/2). Hi ha també previst tot un volum d'estudis basats en els resultats de la documentació recollida, segons el pla general de l'obra

1. La "Chrònica dels comtes de Barcelona e dels reys d'Aragó" o "Gesta Comitum" (s. xiv)

Aquesta crònica, considerada com una de les pedres angulars de la historiografia catalana, es conserva en llatí i en català i ofereix en la breu introducció —que, per cert, manca en dos dels millors còdexs— un bon resum de quins podrien ser els objectius de la historiografia oficial:

> Aquest llibre *mostra veritat, del primer comte de Barcelona* e *de tots los altres qui són venguts aprés d'ell,* e *de l'ordonament de tots los comtats qui són en Catalunya, e·ls noms e·ls temps* d'aquells qui ho han tengut los uns aprés dels altres; *e·l regisme d'Aragó com vench e com fo ajustat ab lo comtat de Barcelona; e dels fets* recaptoses e grans e nobles *qui són estats feyts per comtes e per reys* en lur temps. [3]

Si fixem l'atenció en els mots subratllats és prou evident la voluntat d'oferir: *1)* una versió veraç de la formació i organització dels primers comtats catalans, en especial del de Barcelona; *2)* de traçar la línia successòria; *3)* de referir-se a la dinastia aragonesa "ante unionem", a fi d'explicar com es va arribar a aquesta unió; *4)* de condensar la narració en uns protagonistes: els governants, i llurs gestes.

Val a dir que l'estructura del llibre s'adiu tan bé amb aquest programa que és possible de sospitar que el pròleg fou redactat "a posteriori" per un compilador prou conscient del fet que manejava materials molt diversos acumulats en diverses etapes a l'entorn d'un nucli original —els primers capítols— que crida de seguida l'atenció tant per l'estil com pel contingut. Així, la nostra crònica resumeix la durada del regnat ("tench lo comtat... X anys"), les qualitats morals, en especial les virtuts militars, la generositat i la cortesia ("fo molt bo d'armes; fo molt valerós e molt larch; ...bon d'armes, cortés e larch"), i qui fou el successor ("(E) aprés X/ d'ell..."). L'esquema i la intenció —que correspondrien als punts *1, 2, 4,* indicats més amunt— són, més o menys desenvolupats, els dels cronicons, genealogies i obituaris, on hom anotava de forma succinta el més essencial. No debades la crítica ha establert una relació entre aquesta

---

que hom pot veure al *Cahier de travail* preparat per Raymond Joly (Heidelberg, 1964) i al document mecanografiat *Diskussion zur Gesamtgestaltung des Historiographie-Bands des GRLMA* (sense lloc ni data). El mateix Gumbrecht m'ha comunicat per carta que no pensava tractar dels textos catalans.

[3] *Gesta Comitum Barcinonensium. Textos llatí i català,* edició de L. Barrau Dihigo i J. Massó Torrents, Cròniques Catalanes, 2 (Barcelona, 1925), p. 119, que hom pot comparar amb les pp. 21-2 de la versió llatina.

crònica i els cronicons de Ripoll, monestir fundat per Guifré i custodi de les despulles i de la memòria dels comtes cerdans que tant exaltaren i ennobliren aquell famós centre cultural. [4] Aquesta relació apunta naturalment a una possible motivació del compilador, un clergue relacionat amb Ripoll interessat en el manteniment i increment del patronatge reial (d'ací l'èmfasi en la generositat o llarguesa), i en recordar la importància històrica del monestir. Això explicaria també que la veritat mostrada en llatí i en romanç sigui una veritat oficial que disculpa i exonera i en alguns casos, com el de Ramon Berenguer IV, pel qual el cronista mostra especial predilecció, esdevé panegíric. Tanmateix, només en els tres darrers capítols el text pren una certa volada i s'organitza en una narració consistent.

2. "Libre dels Feyts" o "Crònica del rei Jaume I el Conqueridor" (s. xiv)

Si jutgem pel títol, la intenció d'aquesta crònica és la de resumir i transmetre a la posteritat una relació dels "fets ... que són estat feyts" per Jaume I. L'*incipit* del llibre ens recorda que aquests fets donen testimoni de la fe, que sense obres és morta, i hom ja ha remarcat que el monarca volia assenyalar com havia tractat sempre d'adequar els seus actes a les seves creences, transformant així la historiografia en un llegat o testament exemplar, tractant de transcendir la història —el bé i el mal— i referir-la al pla provident de Déu. [5] Pel que en sabem, el rei En Jaume era un home del tot identificat amb el "Déu lo quer" dels creuats, i de pregones conviccions religioses, capaces de convertir les flaqueses humanes en testimonis de la misericòrdia divina, la qual cosa ofereix una certa garantia d'objectivitat. No cal dubtar que el llibre té un to sincer de

---

[4] Les citacions precedents es poden veure a les pàgines 122, 125, 135, 138, i moltes d'altres. Vegeu la important introducció on hom afirma que l'autor de la traducció catalana "era ... un home d'església nascut a Ripoll" com ho provaria el seu interès pel monestir i el coneixement que en mostra (pp. LII-LIII). Sobre la tradició historiogràfica de Ripoll consulteu Miquel Coll i Alentorn, "La historiografia de Catalunya en el període primitiu", *ER, 3* (1951-2), 139-96 (pp. 187-94). Sobre la missió cultural d'aquell centre cal conèixer ara el magnífic estudi de Francisco Rico, *Signos e indicios en la portada de Ripoll* (Barcelona, 1976), p. 46.

[5] Schlieben-Lange, p. 536, cridà l'atenció sobre la forma verbal "lexam", típica dels testaments. Cito sempre per l'edició de J. M. Casacuberta, Col·lecció popular Barcino, 9 vols. (Barcelona, 1926-62). Resulta més fàcil de consultar l'edició de Ferran Soldevila de *Les quatre grans cròniques*, Biblioteca Perenne (Barcelona, 1971), 1-402. Hi ha versió anglesa de J. Forster i P. Gayangos, *The Chronicle of James I...*, 2 vols. (Londres, 1883).

confessió personal que l'ús constant del plural majestàtic fa més palès. Com és lògic tractant-se de la biografia d'un guerrer, les "gesta" són en general de caràcter bèl·lic, narrades sempre per un protagonista que s'adelita en remarcar, seguit seguit, quan i com havia sabut imposar el seu criteri personal, i de quina manera els esdeveniments acabaren donant-li la raó. El llibre és ple de verbs d'acció, i salta als ulls una considerable presència de "FAEM" ("Faem armar, cridar, demanar, llevar l'àncora, faem manament, fo nostre acord que feésem, etc."), prou reveladora de qui tenia tothora el control de la situació. Però és també cert que a mesura que hom va penetrant la psicologia no gaire complicada del monarca, hom resta convençut que, tal com ens assegura l'autor del pròleg, la grandesa dels fets exposats es fonamenta en una constant acceptació de part del rei d'un control superior, la qual cosa, almenys des de la perspectiva del seu temps, fa exemplars les seves accions. Sigui com sigui, el resultat pràctic, com podia anticipar molt bé el prologuista, no deixa de ser l'exaltació i enaltiment del monarca i la glorificació de la seva memòria entre els seus successors, que s'agradaven de llegir aquest llibre de lo "*bon* rei En Jacme..." [6] D'altra banda, convé recordar que, com en el cas precedent de la *Gesta*, un monestir, el de Poblet, "en lo qual monestir jau lo molt alt senyor en Jacme", tingué cura de copiar el millor manuscrit conservat i que hom va fer enllestir també la corresponent versió llatina, la de Fra Pere Marsili, on és molt més patent la intenció oficiosa de lloar el difunt i de conservar-ne la bona memòria. [7]

3. La crònica de Desclot (s. xiv)

Pel que fa a "lo libre qu.En Bernat Desclot dictà e escriví", o segona de les grans cròniques, tracta també "*dels grans feyts* e de les conquestes" dels "nobles reys que hac en Aragó qui foren del alt linyatge del comte de Barcelona" (Pròlech). En realitat aquests nobles monarques són Jau-

---

[6] El qualificatiu és de Ramon Muntaner, *Crònica*, edició de J. M. Casacuberta i M. Coll i Alentorn, Col·lecció popular Barcino, 9 vols. (Barcelona, 1927-52), I, c. 7: "Que aitant com lo món dur, se dirà 'lo bon rei En Jacme d'Aragon'". Pere El Cerimoniós dóna a entendre que s'agradava de llegir la crònica del seu predecessor: "Encara no érem gitats e legíem lo libre o crònica del senyor rei En Jacme, tresavi nostre" (edició d'A. Pagès, *Chronique catalane de Pierre IV d'Aragon, III de Catalogne, dit le Cérémonieux ou del Punyalet* (Toulouse-Paris, 1942), c. 3, 193, p. 228). N'hi ha ara versió anglesa de M. Hilgarth, 2 vols. (Toronto, 1980).
[7] El ms. 1 de la universitat de Barcelona, assequible en edició facsímil (Universidad de Barcelona, 1972), f. CCII. La versió llatina es conserva en el ms. 64 de la mateixa biblioteca.

me I i els dos Peres, i la desproporció entre els capítols dedicats a Pere el Gran i als seus antecessors justifica l'*explicit* del Ms. copiat per Coll i Alentorn i omès en l'edició Soldevila, on es parla ja de "lo llibre del rei En Pere, *dels bons feyts d'armes que ell féu* sobra sarrahins e altres gents, e com morí" (C 168). De manera que la història és una introducció a la de Pere el Gran (1276-85), "qui fo lo segon Alexandri per cavaleria e per conquesta" (Pròlech), a qui es dediquen els capítols 51-169.

De bell nou la historiografia es concebeix com una narració de les "gesta" reials, si bé Desclot, en calcar una famosa frase de l'evangelista Sant Joan (19,35) i dir: "E d'açò fa testimoni cel qui açò recompte en aquest libre, que vahé", (C 159), avala i potser sacralitza una mica el seu testimoniatge. Desclot tracta de definir el rei Pere a través de les seves accions, el que ell féu i el que féu fer als altres ("E lo rei féu endre- çar, preparar, fer, ajustar, repicar, etc."); accions que contrasten amb els mots buits del seu principal antagonista, Carles d'Anjou ("... *eyl dirà so que.s volrà e nós farem so qui.ns serà honor...*", C 100) i perfilen una fisonomia positiva del monarca. La sobrietat de l'estil i la proverbial discreció de l'autor, que mai no sol ficar cullerada, produeix un efecte d'objectivitat que, comptat i debatut, resulta una de les armes propagan- dístiques més eficients i subtils, puix que fins a un cert punt aconsegueix de dissimular la intenció de celebrar la glòria del sobirà regnant, dins del marc, sovint llegendari, de la tradició dinàstica. Que el llibre anava primordialment destinat al mateix rei i als "defensores" podria, potser, indicar-ho un dels velats consells que se li escapen gairebé sense voler al prudent secretari en parlar de les relacions amb Sancho de Castella i de la difícil situació d'Aragó, col·locat entre dues grans potències: "Per que *tot rey e tot seyor de terra* se dou gardar..." (C 76).

4. LA CRÒNICA DE MUNTANER (S. XIV)

Hom ha dit que el llibre de Muntaner, igualment destinat a magnificar el casal d'Aragó, té com a protagonista la "dinastia en tant que representa l'estat expansionista mediterrani". [8] Muntaner ens fa present del seu text com si fos una mena d'ex-vot en acció de gràcies pels favors rebuts de la Providència durant la seva llarga i accidentada vida d'aventures al

---

[8] Vegeu Josep Miquel Sobré, *L'Èpica de la realitat. L'escriptura de Ramon Muntaner i Bernat Desclot* (Barcelona, 1978), p. 76. Les citacions són preses de l'edició esmentada més amunt a la nota 6. N'hi ha també traducció anglesa de Lady Goodenough, *The Chronicle of Muntaner*, 2 vols. (London, 1920-1).

servei de la dinastia que vol exaltar ("... és raó que faça moltes gràcies a nostre senyor ver Déu e a la Verge madona santa Maria..., de la gràcia e de la mercè que m'ha feita". Pròleg). L'autor no vol tenir amagat el llum de la seva vasta experiència personal i es presenta com a predestinat pel mateix Déu per a recomptar la *Gesta Dei per Catalanos* ("... a Déu plau que tu recomptes aquestes aventures e meravelles com es altre no es viu qui ho pogués així ab veritat dir", C 1). Segons ell el seu text acompleix alhora una funció teòrica, transcendent, i una de pràctica o exemplar. Ambdues intencions es confonen i combinen, puix que es proposa de "comptar d'aco que en mon temps s'és fet", com a prova de l'ineluctable judici de Déu que fou qui va determinar la conquesta de Sicília pels catalans (C 60, 61-76), dant-los la victòria com a recompensa. Els futurs monarques faran bé d'aprendre i de recordar la lliçó de la història ("... per ço que qualque sia rei d'Aragon, que s'esforç de bé a fer e a dir e entenent les gràcies que Déus ha fetes en aquests afers que tu recomptaràs, a ell e a les sues gents, e que pens que de bé en mellor iran tots temps mentre ells vullen en veritat e en dretura metre e dependre son temps, *e que veja e conega que a la dretura ajuda tots temps Nostre Senyor. E qui ab veritat guerreja e va, Déus lo exalça e li dóna victòria...*" C 1). Tant és així, que per a ell resulten objectius identificables la glòria de Déu i la del casal d'Aragó, constant beneficiari passat i present de l'ajuda divina ("Aquest llibre senyaladament se fa a honor de Déu e de la sua beneita Mare e del casal d'Aragó", C 1; ... "basta que parle de la matèria per què aquest llibre se fa: ço és a saber, de la honor e de la gràcia que Déus ha feta ne fa al casal d'Aragó...", C 23). Serveix també el text per a fomentar la cohesió interna entre les distintes branques de la dinastia, sovint amenaçades per conflictes interns (llegiu el C 292 amb el famós exemple de la mata de jonc); objectiu al qual es sacrifiquen els fets històrics capaços d'enterbolir la visió idealitzada que hom proposa constantment al lector. No menys important és la tradicional funció d'encomiar al monarca. Es destaca que va saber sortir triomfant d'una pugna contra les dues grans potències del seu temps: "... contra l'Esgleia, qui és tot lo poder de crestians, e puis contra la casa de França, qui és pus antiga casa de reis qui sia en crestiandat..." (C 37). Muntaner vol fer arribar una discreta però molt clara amonestació al Papat, que ha comès l'error tàctic de combatre el successor del sanct rei Jaume (C 6, 32, 36, 52, 56, etc.). Resta encara el natural desig de l'autor de donar a conèixer els seus mèrits de guerra a fi d'obtenir no solament la glòria, sinó també el favor dels monarques als quals va dirigit el llibre i als quals no s'està de donar nombrosos consells: "E així, senyors d'Aragó e de Mallorques e de Sicília, qui eixits e sóts deixendents d'aquest senyor rei En Jacme... estats ab bon cor... (C 6); E plauria'm fort que el senyor rei d'Aragó posàs son cor en ço que io li diré... Per què, senyor fèts ço que faria bon aministrador" (C 36). En altres ocasions deixa entendre que també enclou entre els seus lectors una minoria selecta dels "defensores": "... e açò vull contar per tal que *reis e rics-hòmens* ne prenguen bon eiximpli" (C. 242 i 71); per què los almiralls e los capitans...; per què negun cavaller..." (C 134, etc.). Com a cavaller Muntaner perpetua la memòria dels fets heroics d'altres cavallers ("Per què io no us parle res d'afers que a mi esdevenguessen, si no fossen *fets qui es faessen per senyors...*" C 255), mots que no podien resumir millor el pregon sentit èpic d'aquesta crònica, i com ja hem vist, el de bona part de la historiografia catalana medieval.

5. La crònica de Pere el Cerimoniós (s. xiv)

De la propaganda més entusiasta i desbordada passem en la *Crònica de Pere el Cerimoniós* a la manipulació refinada i subtil, a la documentació minuciosa posada al servei de la raó d'estat i de l'ambició personal d'un rei de tremp absolutista i despòtic, que s'agrada de ser i de sentir-se el centre del poder i que lliga i subordina la cultura a aquesta ambició i al prestigi de la monarquia com institució.

Si ens atenem a la intenció del "Llibre en què.s contenen tots los grans fets qui són entreveguts en nostra Casa, dins lo temps de nostra vida", el pròleg és certament molt important. El sobirà presenta la seva història a manera d'un sermó, i desenvolupa "per conclusionem" el tema: "Non nobis, Domine, non nobis, sed nomini tuo da gloriam" (Ps. 115, 1), mitjançant tres proposicions rimades: *Domine*: "La *divinal*... creat"; *da*: "sia atribuit e *dat*"; *gloriam*: "pel bé reebut vol que Déu sia *loat*", fonamentades en les corresponents autoritats. D'aquestes proposicions la tercera sembla la més important. El rei Pere volia que el seu llibre, almenys a primera vista, fos una acció de gràcies a Déu *"per los dons diverses e gràcies multiplicades que havem reebudes en la nostra vida"* (Pròleg, 4), i les citacions bíbliques o autoritats emprades criden l'atenció sobre temes cabdals del llibre: les guerres i conflictes interns que plagaren el seu regnat (C 3-6), i dels quals fou alliberat (*eripuit me*) com altre David, mercès a la providència divina, "com llargament se conté en lo procés del present llibre". El rei ens vol fer creure que no féu escriure la crònica "a jactància nostra ne llaor", sinó a fi que els seus hereus "prenguen eximpli" admirant la bondat i misericòrdia divines, puix que la fe i la confiança en Déu converteixen les tribulacions i els perills en glorioses victòries. Com sabem això ja era un tòpic de la historiografia, però el lector atent guanya aviat la impressió que l'humil antítesi del tema: "No a mi Senyor, sinó a Vós", és, ben mirat, un miratge, o pura ficció, ja que en realitat la divina Providència no és altra cosa que un instrument del tot subordinat al *nós* autocràtic i cínic del sobirà. Resulta, doncs, que el llibre és un sermó, però un sermó d'auto-propaganda dedicat a ensenyar al poble els tradicionals "vitia et virtutes": els vicis dels enemics, en particular els de Jaume III de Mallorca, els dels membres de les Unions, i els de Pedro de Castella, degudament confrontats amb les virtuts del monarca, en especial la seva prudència i cautela o "bon consell". La *Crònica* ens presenta sovint al rei fent ajustar "los savis de nostre Consell" (C 3/182-3) i topem sovint amb els mots *Consell/ consellar* i *acordar* i *concordar*. Així, a més de repartir potser la responsabilitat de certes accions, es creava renom d'assenyat enfront d'un adversari imprudent i arrauxat, el malaurat monarca mallorquí, que el cronista ens presenta cridant com un boig: "Eu hai haüt *mal consell*. Eu hai perduda ma terra" (C 3/5). I precisament perquè Pere III està convençut que els *feyts* es subordinen a la raó d'estat i a una justícia trascendent que controla ell mateix i que atribueix a Déu, no amaga les seves crueltats i són tan contínues les referències a la Providència al llarg de l'obra. Es subratlla així més l'estructura lògica del text que no la religiositat del sobirà, el qual al final, a més a més, farà seva la més alta prerrogativa divina en afirmar, dut del seu caràcter meticulosament vengatiu: *Nullum malum impunitum, nullumque bonum irremuneratum* i *Mihi vindicta* (C 4/63).[9]

Segons el pròleg, el llibre va destinat als fills del rei i als seus "succeïdors", de manera que, com els textos precedents, seria una narració "de domo sua" ("dels grans fets... de nostra Casa", C 1/39), "pro domo sua". I tanmateix, atès que el rei Pere féu tot el possible a nivell diplomàtic i mitjançant campanyes de predicació intensiva en les esglésies dels

---

[9] Aquesta important sentència és presa de Sant Agustí, *Enarrationes in Psalmos, Enarratio in Ps. 118, Sermo 23,3* (*PL* 37, col. 1567). La trobo també a la *Glossa* de Pere Llombard al text de Rom. 2, 6 (*PL* 196, col. 1341). Es repeteix en *La fi del comte d'Urgell*, que estudiem més avall. (nr. 9). La segona citació és un text de Sant Pau, Rom. 1, 19. Els números dins parèntesi envien al capítol i paràgraf del text de la *Crònica*. Vegeu al·lusions a la Providència en els c. 2/37; 3/18, 22, 27, 46, 69, 99, 136, 147; c. 4/1, 63; 6/2, 12, 41, 60, 64, etc.

territoris usurpats per eliminar d'arrel les simpaties que inspirava la víc-
tima, no cal dubtar que el seu llibre, en particular el C 3, era una arma
més de propaganda política ("E, per tal que pus complidament sia vista
la raó...", C 3/1).

6. "LA CRÒNICA DELS REYS D'ARAGÓ E COMTES DE BARCELONA" DITA DE
"SANT JOAN DE LA PENYA"

En més d'un sentit aquest text complementa els de la *Gesta Comitum*
i d'altres fonts precedents, com la famosa *Historia Gothica,* que el rei
adapta i fa posar al dia d'acord amb els postulats de la seva política
oficial. Si és cert, com sembla, que la carta dirigida pel mateix Cerimoniós a l'abat de Ripoll al·ludeix a la tramesa d'aquesta crònica, tindríem
fins a un cert punt ben especificades de boca del mateix rei les raons que
l'impulsaven a fer custodiar el llibre, raons tanmateix que delaten la
intencionalitat del text. Són les següents, que copio per punts: *1.* "Per
tal com lo monestir de Ripoll és dels pus solemnes e antichs..."; *2. "Volem
que* en lo dit monastir *sia haüda memòria* dels reys d'Aragó e dels comtes
de Barchinona"; *3.* "E per ço com aquí no són ten complides ne ten ben
ordenades les cròniques dels dits reys e comtes com són en un libre que
nós havem fet e tret de diverses cròniques e istòries entigues, *las quals
contenen veritat*"; *4.* "Per ço a vós tremetem translat del dit libre, pre-
gant-vos que·l dit libre estigue en tal loch que *memòria sia haüda d'aquí
avant dels fets damunt dits...*" [10] Com que és també documentat que el
rei havia tramès exemplars de la versió llatina al monestir de Poblet i a
la catedral de València, resta confirmat el ja tradicional vincle entre la
historiografia catalana i els centres monàstics encarregats de custodiar
i difondre la veritat oficial registrada en les tres llengües oficials de la
Corona: el llatí, l'aragonés i el català. [11] En aquest sentit, aquí, com a les

---

[10] Segons E. González Hurtebisse, "La crónica general escrita por Pedro IV de
Aragón", *Revista de bibliografía catalana,* 4 (1904), 188-214 (pp. 190-1). Vegeu
l'edició a cura d'A. J. Soberanas, *Crònica general de Pere III el Cerimoniós dita
comunament Crònica de Sant Joan de la Penya* (Barcelona, 1961). El mateix Soberanas en preparà una edició crítica a la seva tesi doctoral, encara inèdita, *La
crònica de Sant Joan de la Penya. Materials per a la seva edició* (Barcelona, 1973).
La versió llatina la publicà A. Ubieto Arteta, *Crónica de San Juan de la Peña,*
Textos medievales 4 (Valencia, 1961). L'edició de Tomás Ximénez de Embún,
Historia de la Corona de Aragón (Zaragoza, 1876) conté els textos llatí i aragonés.
[11] Llegiu les introduccions de Soberanas i d'Ubieto, pp. 6 i 10, respectivament.
La tesi de Soberanas conté un stegma de la complicada transmissió d'aquest text
(p. 110), del què hi ha una versió extensa i una amb supressions que afecten alguns
capítols, com els 17, 18, 19, 20, 23, al·lusius a Castella, i que no degueren agradar
al rei.

Gesta comitum són força abundoses les al·lusions a la munificència règia, primer envers el monestir de Sant Joan de la Penya i després envers Ripoll, com és ara: "... li plagués enriquir lo dit monestir... E donà'ls e atorgà'ls un terme apellat Espelunca (C 11); ... e féu moltes gràcies a Sant Joan de la Penya (C 19); ... e deïcà lo monestir de Ripoll..., e aquell ennobleí de moltes heretats e bastí l'esgleia..." (C 28), etc. Queda clar, a més, que l'enaltiment del monestir és contemplat pels rei com un acte de glorificació de la mateixa corona i, en definitiva, de llurs pròpies persones, puix que no sol mancar la referència al caràcter de panteó reial: "... adugueren-lo al monestir de Sant Joan de la Penya, e soterraren-lo denant l'altar de Sant Joan... (C 17); E fou sebellit en lo dit monestir de Ripoll" (C 25). Res no té d'estrany, doncs, que un rei tan conscient del seu paper com desitjós de justificar-se davant la posteritat, volgués beneficiar-se del sistema.

7. LES "HISTÒRIES E CONQUESTES DELS REYS D'ARAGÓ E DELS COMTES DE BARCELONA" DE PERE TOMICH (S. XV)

El volum de Pere Tomich té un gran interès, per quant sembla reflectir un important canvi de perspectiva pel que respecta a la intenció. Tomich vol connectar les gestes dels reis i les glòries del país, és a dir la història oficial, a la història i tradicions de la noblesa catalana en general i a la dels seus protectors, els Pinós i Mataplana, en especial. [12] Tomich es presenta com a "petit servidor del noble e magnífic Baró e monsenyor mossèn Galçeran de Pinós..." (p. 10) i sembla voler captar la benevolència de Dalmau de Mur, a qui dedica l'obra, i de tota la seva poderosa nissaga. Per afalagar els seus senyors tracta de fer veure de quina manera llurs predecessors participaren sempre de forma activa en els fets de més trascendència i exalta així la funció i el sentit de la cava-

---

[12] L'única edició moderna és la de A. Bulbena, *Historias e conquestas dels Excellentissims e Catholics Reys de Arago e de lurs anteçessors, los comtes de Barcelona* (Barcelona, 1886), però hom pot emprar l'útil edició facsímil amb un índex de noms preparat per J. Saez Rico, Textos medievales 29 (Valencia, 1970). Un altre text on es fa l'apologia de la noblesa és el *Sumari de la població de Espanya i de les conquestes de Catalunya* d'un tal Berenguer de Puigpardines (S. XV o XVI?), on l'autor vol glorificar el seu cognom i es mostra preocupat pels canvis socials que afecten el seu estament: "Majorment perquè veu que en son temps van preterint los linatges de gent d'estat de la terra, per ço que molts gentils hòmens per no tenir eretatges se entren per habitar en les çiutats... e renuncien a gentilesa fent-se ciutadans, joristes hi escrivans e encara menestrals e altres vils oficis, fins a coltivadós de lurs pròpies mans". Vegeu Felipe Benicio Navarro, "La Crónica de Berenguer de Puigpardines", *Revista de ciencias históricas*, 2 (1881), 326-79 (p. 340).

lleria catalana fins al punt de posar gairebé la història del país al servei de la glòria i dels interessos d'una casta. Hi ha en el llibre una temptativa de justificació del feudalisme català i, entre altres coses, l'autor ens assabenta que les baronies de Montcada, Pinós i Mataplana són fundacions de Carlemany (C 23). A partir del C 24 no n'hi ha gairebé cap on no es faci esment d'algun Pinós acompanyant als comtes (C 35), rebent-ne mercès o castells (C 32, 34), participant en les conquestes de Mallorca, Almeria, València (C 35, 36, 39) o en les guerres d'Itàlia (C 42, 44). L'autor mai no deixa passar l'avinentesa d'allistar els noms dels cavallers que més es distingiren en cada regnat, i sol cloure cada capítol amb una relació dels nobles morts, i també de tot allò que ara encabiríem en les "notes de societat", com els matrimonis i les successions, que constituïen la clau dels poderosos lligams familiars i que permeten de fer-se una bona idea de l'estructura de poder de l'aristocràcia. Som informats, per exemple, que Jaume "El Just" va casar amb Elisenda de Montcada, filla de Berga de Pinós, i que un Galceran de Pinós s'uní en matrimoni amb una filla borda de Sanç de Mallorca (C 42). Guanyem també una idea de com era de densa la xarxa que unia entre si els Montcada, Cardona, Queralt, de Ballera, de Castre, Rocabertí, Melany, de Tramaset, etc. (C 45). Allò que més crida l'atenció en aquest text és que per primera vegada la historiografia no es subordina per complet als interessos de la dinastia, o personals d'un monarca, sinó que esdevé instrument de propaganda d'uns ideals i d'un estament ja bastant amenaçats (vegeu la referència als "remenses", C 24). Això permet d'establir una interessant comparació entre el llibre de Tomich i un altre text historiogràfic que n'és gairebé una còpia directa.

8. EL "RECORT" DE GABRIEL TURELL (S. XV)

Turell plagià sense manies l'obra de Tomich, que retallà ací i allà, bé eliminant-ne alguns capítols (C 1-2: 33), o integrant-ne molts d'altres en unitats més breus (C 3-4: 2; C 18-21: 34-5).[13] En general es pot dir que segueix de manera bastant servil l'estructura i el text del model sense que, a primera vista, sigui evident cap pla o intenció nova en els afegitons distribuïts al llarg de l'obra (C 14-6, 23, 30, 35, 40, 50, 62-3, 66, 71, 78, 82 117). Allò que més contrasta amb el model copiat és el

---

[13] Edició d'E. Bagué, ENC 67 (Barcelona, 1950). Indico entre parèntesi el capítol de l'original de Tomich i, seguit de dos punts, la corresponent adaptació de Turell.

desinterès de Turell per la informació sobre la noblesa, acumulada per Tomich al final de cada capítol. Turell sembla voler donar un nou sentit i una nova intenció al llibre que plagia. El seu propòsit és, en primer lloc, de deixar ben clara la vinculació de Catalunya i de les seves institucions a la França catòlica de Carlemany, que considera lliure de la nefasta influència d'alarbs, jueus, i fins i tot dels gots. Aquesta exaltació racista i religiosa ("Car la casa de França és la font clara que sutzura en si no monstra : catòlica té la creença, no comporta testimoni en la sua fe, jueus e moros de son regne té lançats... E aquesta nostra terra de Cathalunya se alegra de tu ésser poblada", C 43), és, si no vaig errat, un atac contra els castellans representats per la nova dinastia. Com que la llibertat i la grandesa de Catalunya es fonamenten en aquells nobilíssims orígens, es segueix que Ferran d'Antequera "rey ab pactes elegit..., és tengut servar les libertats..." (C 117). Ací rau, al meu entendre, la clau de la reelaboració que fa Turell del llibre de Tomich. Turell afirma les llibertats catalanes i el superior *pedigree* dels catalans davant un monarca estranger, indirectament titllat de moro o de jueu. Es més : Turell escriu com a *ciutadà honrat de Barcelona* que era, i s'identifica amb el *conseller en cap*, En Ramon Dezplà, el qual s'havia oposat al nou rei en defensa dels privilegis de la ciutat, és a dir, de les llibertats dels seus ciutadans i de tot un sistema polític de velles arrels històriques. Turell no s'està de comparar aquests ciutadans lliures amb el mateix monarca: *"D'aquestos ciutadans de Barcelona és lo stament tal, que algun rey no.l té... E són la conservació dels privilegis de Cathalunya. Car vist és, en les corts e altres parts, que tostemps la ciutat de Barçelona fa servar les coses. Aquestos no són solament ciutadans, mas cavallers en lo viure*, e representen los senats de Roma" (C 62). Vet ací, doncs, que un mateix text s'adapta, amb lleugeres variacions, a una intenció i a una mentalitat ben diverses i passa a ser instrument de propaganda dels poderosos burgesos de Barcelona que s'ufanaven de tenir "privilegi de poder portar or e fer tots actes com los vervessors" (C 63) competien amb la noblesa i no temien el rei. Curiosament aquests burgesos que s'havien oposat a Jaume d'Urgell pensant que un rei elegit *per pacte,* con Ferran, seria més fàcil de manipular d'acord amb llurs interessos, havien topat ara amb la decidida voluntat absolutista del castellà. La temàtica ens porta encara a un darrer text que convé de llegir conjuntament amb els de Tomich i de Turell.

9. "LA FI DEL COMTE D'URGELL" O "ESCRIPTURA PRIVADA" (S. XV)

Allò que confegeix especial importància a aquesta obra és que contesta, en nom de l'estament popular, les tesis de la noblesa i dels ciutadans representades pels dos llibres anteriors. [14] L'anònim autor de *La fi* acusa per activa i per passiva de traïdors a ciutadans i a cavallers. La seva intenció és tractar d'establir una relació de causa i efecte entre la terrible crisi de la guerra civil de 1458-79 i la injustícia comesa en el "Compromís de Casp", on Catalunya va trair-se en abandonar el Comte d'Urgell a la seva dissort:

> La causa qui·m ha mogut en scriure tan llarga e tan diffusament aquesta gesta, és estada perquè més fàcilment se puxe veure e verificar lo que damunt proposí, com diguí que lo peccat que la pàtria e lo rey no rebujaren cometre e perpetrar per la destructió e mort de aquest comte, és causa principal per la qual nostre senyor Déu nos ha donada e·ns done aquesta fort plaga de guerra qui és sobre nosaltres. Car, certament, ell fou venut... E la sua justítia..., fo axí mateix venuda... (pp. 97-8).

Tornem a la vella idea del judici de Déu i al vell *dictum* llatí de la *Crònica de Pere el Cerimoniós,* o sigui: "Cap mal sense punició, cap bé sense remuneració". [15] Un cop més la historiografia es posa al servei de la propaganda i un cop més hom tracta d'aprofitar el sentit providencial de la història. Les malaurances del present són conseqüència d'un passat també determinant d'un futur amenaçador. La tesi, repetida arreu, és que "aquest flagell de aquesta fortunal guerra... és estat donat per *vindicta* de la sanch e de la destructió del dit comte..., la qual, *a tracte dels ciutadans de Barcelona* qui llavors éram, ab tanta iniquitat e crueltat fou feta..." (p. 117). Hom assegura que els ciutadans de Barcelona i de Lleida causaren l'enderrocament de la nació catalana per defensar llurs mesquins interessos de classe. Traïren així llurs mateixes essències, puix que la missió de la Generalitat "era la deffensa de llur gran libertat e de tot lo Principat" (p. 99), i sense el suport material de la Generalitat, representat per la famosa bombarda "que tirava bé III quintàs" (p. 99), Ferran no hauria vençut la contesa. Una vegada coronat mostrà aviat que "volia ésser rey libero e franco" (p. 50-1) burlant així la confiança dels ciutadans, humiliats per l'arrogància dels castellans.

---

[14] Vegeu l'edició de X. De Salas Bosch, ENC 33 (Barcelona, 1931).
[15] Vegeu la pàgina 143. A la p. 142 insinua que el càstig era imminent, en forma de profecia: "... ja es llevave en Asia un porch senglar qui per ventura vindicaria les grans crueltats...".

La noblesa rep un tractament semblant. L'autor la fa responsable de la seva total decadència que contrasta amb la passada magnificència. En passar revista a les casades catalanes, enclosa "la casa del noble en Bernat de Pinós, qui llavors se parificave al stat de un comte" (p. 126), acumula en forma d'adjectius i superlatius les fortunes del passat i les misèries del present i vol que hom "no oblit de la grandíssima culpa, desídia e pusil·lanimitat del stament de la milícia e dels nobles altres senyós de aquest principat" (p. 123). Segons argumenta, com que el comte d'Urgell "fos lo cap, aprés la casa del rey, de la nobilitat de aquest principat" (p. 124), en fer-li traïció, l'aristocràcia es va trair a ella mateixa. Uns i altres —si bé la iniciativa es carrega a la Generalitat— "permeteren rompre e trencar aquella incorrupta e sancta línea masculina, introduynt en lo imperi sement strany e nació bàrbara..." (p. 138).

10. CONCLUSIÓ

En resum: la historiografia medieval catalana és hereva de la funció informativa, eminentment pragmàtica dels cronicons, genealogies i obituaris, que la lliguen a uns centres monàstics, Ripoll i Poblet, dipositaris de la memòria i de la tradició dinàstiques. La majoria de textos antics palesen la intenció de recordar els FETS "qui són estats feyts per comtes e reys". Bons fets, grans fets, fets "recaptoses... e nobles", o, en altres paraules que tradueixen el llatí Gesta (Comitum o Regum) i són un possible indici de la importància del text número 1: "fets qui es faessen per senyors". Allò que hom vol subratllar de les gestes és llur valor exemplar d'ensenyament moral i pràctic. La historiografia coincideix amb altres gèneres medievals com l'hagiografia, l'èpica, la predicació, els anomenats Specula Principum i la tradició clàssica i bíblica, en postular la necessitat d'aprendre d'uns models manllevats de l'antigor. Com que els textos historiogràfics són enllestits pels reis, o per encàrrec directe de reis, i van dedicats a reis presents o futurs i a llur entorn, la tria d'uns models pertanyents a la pròpia nissaga, a més de reforçar el sentiment de prepotència i l'esperit de casta d'un clan predestinat, explica el to familiar de testament d'algun dels llibres. Hom pretén, se'ns diu, "mostrar veritat", però el control directe i sovint personal del monarca regnant fa que aquesta veritat degeneri fàcilment en vivència carismàtica, apologia, legitimació o descarada propaganda. Aleshores la general acceptació del principi augustinià de la història com a manifestació de l'orde, del judici i de la providència divinals, forniran al poder establert un arma tan subtil com eficaç de justificació política. I, tanmateix, resulta engrescador de descobrir que el pas al segle xv marca una important línia divisòria entre els textos números 1-6 i els 7-9. Aquests darrers semblen evidenciar un canvi d'intencionalitat, possible indici d'un canvi de mentalitat i d'estructures. Un mateix text (7/8) adquireix connotacions ben diverses segons que sigui la noblesa o la burgesia la qui reivindiqui per a si la participació en les "gesta" de la reialesa. El darrer text (9), mescla de pamflet, de sermó i de novel·la gòtica "avant la lettre" (de la historiografia a la novel·la, com bé ho prova el *Tirant,* només hi ha una passa!), per allò mateix que es fa portaveu de l'estament popular sense rebutjar però el sentit providencial de la història, tracta de projectar el passat en un present i en un futur crítics, i acusa els estaments aleshores protagonistes de la historiografia: rei, nobles i en particular l'element nou, la poderosa burgesia, d'haver traït miserablement les essències històriques del país. [16]

ALBERT G. HAUF

Universitat de Galles, Cardiff

---

[16] Per raons òbvies d'espai no m'he proposat en el present treball de tractar tots els textos documentats ni d'oferir una bibliografia sistemàtica, d'altra banda assequible a les obres de consulta disponibles. Esmentaré, però, l'utilíssim *Repertorium Fontium Historiae Medii Aevi* publicat per l'Instituto Storico Italiano per il Medioevo, 4 vols. (Roma, 1967-1976), en curs de publicació, on hi figuren els textos historiogràfics catalans.

ON FIFTEENTH-CENTURY SPANISH VERNACULAR HUMANISM

IN the third book of the Catalan romance *Curial e Güelfa* there occurs
an odd and illuminating scene: Curial, the chivalric hero, who is sailing
about the Mediterranean in a galley, lands in Athens. From there he
journeys to Thebes — attracted by the literary associations of Statius's
Thebaid — and then to the temple of Apollo at Delphi, on the slopes
of Mount Parnassus, where he falls asleep and experiences a dream-vision.
Apollo and the nine Muses appear, and ask him to judge a case which,
according to Apollo, "és entre'ls vivents molt gran qüestió". It turns
out to be no more urgent than a debate between two accounts of the
Trojan War. [1]

All this seems out of place; Curial is supposed to be a knight errant,
not a bookworm. And the length and detail of the anonymous author's
treatment of Curial's Parnassian encounter make it difficult to explain
the episode simply as a piece of erudite tinsel. The problem disappears
if we forget *Curial e Güelfa*'s affinities with the *libros de caballerías* and
think more of its affinities with the fictional or fictionalized exemplary
"chivalric biographies" which were then so popular with noble readers
in Burgundy, France and Castile. The best known are Gutierre Díez de
Games' *Victorial* on Don Pero Niño, Count of Buelna; Boucicault and
Jacques de Lalaing's *Livres des faicts*; Antoine de la Sale's *Le Petit
Jehan de Saintré*, and Jean de Bueil's *Jouvencel*. These books were intended as mirrors of attitudes and behaviour for their own day. Curial's
name, which means "courtly", is a signpost of a similar aim in *Curial e
Güelfa*: Curial is not merely a romantic hero, but the model of a "verray,
parfit gentil knight". [2] This being so, a clue to the significance of the
episode of the Parnassian dream is the emphasis the author lays on the

---

[1] *Curial e Guelfa, text del XVᵉⁿ segle reproduhit novament del codex de la
Biblioteca Nacional de Madrid*, ed. R. Miquel y Planas and Anfòs Par (Barcelona,
1932), pp. 342-54.

[2] Miquel and Par connect the name with Alain Chartier's *Le Curial*, a translation of the Italian humanist Ambrosius de Milliis's letter to Gontier Col, *De vita
curiali* (*Curial e Güelfa*, p. 482, note to l. 38); a glance at Heuckenkamp's edition
shows that there is no connection. But Chartier's title shows how the name alone
must have invited an allegorical reading.

fact that his hero was an "home scientífich e qui nulls temps lexava l'estudi" (p. 342). The phrase picks up a concern with *sciència* that runs through many passages of Curial's story. As a boy he learnt grammar, logic, rhetoric and philosophy, and became a "poeta molt gran" (p. 7); and as a man he became an all-rounder:

> Es cavaller en parlar e en obrar, e en plaça e en cambra, e en liça e en tot loch. Daltra part, és molt abte e virtuós, savi e de gran e notable consell; pero no me'n maravell, car entre los grans philosofs, poetes e oradors, veig que es tengut en gran stima ... E, partit d'aquí, no lexà l'estudi, ans tractà tan reverencialment los libres, que tots quants lo conèxen ho han a gran maravella (p. 269). [3]

In other words, the episode is an allusion to the age-old topic about "arms and letters" *(sapientia et fortitudo)*, or the ideal conjunction of intellectual and physical prowess in the perfect warrior-knight, which Curtius has traced from Homer and Virgil right down to Castiglione and the Renaissance and beyond. [4]

But whereas in earlier times the warrior's *sapientia* broadly meant his prudence and cunning, Curial's *sapientia* is quite specifically portrayed in the Parnassian episode as a familiarity with classical literature. That makes this particular passage, in the fifteenth-century context, something more intriguing than a bookish *topos*. It is a reflection of social reality. We have only to think of Diego de Valera (c. 1412 - c. 1480), who fought on the Moorish frontier and travelled the courts of Europe as a knight errant, but also wrote poetry and copious learned treatises, among them one on the *Origen de Troya y Roma,* to find a real-life counterpart to Curial. [5] And there were many other contemporary examples of learned knights in the Peninsula: the historian and translator Pérez de Guzmán, the enthusiastic Livian Benavente, the "Latin Count" of Haro, the *érudits*

---

[3] The emphasis on "all-round" excellence prefigures Castiglione's ideal of the *cortegiano,* a point I return to below (see note 32); cf. the Italian's evocation of the model courtiers of Urbino: "nelle giostre, nei torniamenti, nel cavalcare, nel maneggiar tutte le sorti d'arme, medesimamente nelle feste, nei giochi, nelle musiche, in somma in tutti gli esercizi convenienti a nobili cavalieri, ognuno si sforzava di mostrarsi ... degno", Baldassare Castiglione, *Il libro del cortegiano,* edited by E. Bonora (Milan, 1972), p. 35.

[4] Ernst R. Curtius, *European Literature and the Latin Middle Ages,* translated by Willard R. Trask (London, 1953), pp. 174-79.

[5] See *Prosistas castellanos del siglo XV,* I, ed. M. Penna, BAE, CXVI (Madrid, 1959), pp. xcix-cxxxvi, for an excellent resumé of Valera's career and writings. The *Origen de Troya y Roma,* addressed to the noble lord Juan Hurtado de Mendoza, is there edited on pp. 155-59.

Duke Pedro of Coimbra and Prince Charles of Viana, the bibliophile Constables of Portugal and Castile, the soldier-poets of the Manrique, Guzmán and Stúñiga families, and above all that *uomo universale*, Santillana (1398-1458). Abundant evidence from fifteenth-century libraries, and from the pattern of thought reflected in fifteenth-century literature, shows that a growing class of noble lay readers in Iberia really were interested in precisely the kind of classical questions which appealed to Curial.

In fact, as we have long known, vernacular translations from classical authors were one of the forms of secular literature most enjoyed by the fifteenth-century lay reading public. The list available in one or more of the vernaculars — Castilian, Aragonese, Catalan, Valencian and Portuguese — included works or extracts of works by Livy (also Florus's *Epitome*), Caesar, Quintus Curtius, Josephus, "Trogus Pompeius" (Justin's epitome is meant), Valerius Maximus, Orosius, both Plinies, Plutarch, Procopius, Sallust, Vegetius, Frontinus, Polybius, Eutropius, Thucydides, Homer (and the *Ilias Latina*), Lucan, Virgil, Ovid, Cicero, Lucian, Eusebius, Palladius, Boethius, Seneca, Plato and Aristotle. [6] Dedications, provenance of surviving MSS and library inventories show that the patrons and sponsors and readers of these books (even, occasionally, their translators) were princes and noblemen. If the passage from *Curial e Güelfa* suggests that an involvement in classical book-learning was a desirable ideal in the *chevalier* of romance, the translations show that such an involvement, for some powerful and wealthy knights, and particularly in Castile, went beyond the merely ideal.

It is tempting to speculate why this interest in classical translation gained such a grip on Spanish readers at this particular time. What did they want from their tomes of ancient history and moral philosophy? Doubtless the chief thing was what any sane man seeks from literature, a relief from boredom and despair; that "singular reposo a las vexaciones e trabajos que el mundo continuamente trahe, mayormente en estos nuestros reinos" of which Santillana so eloquently spoke in a letter to his son

---

[6] Raw bibliographical evidence is amassed in M. Menéndez y Pelayo's *Bibliografía hispano-latina clásica*, ed. E. Sánchez Rayón, 10 vols. (Santander and Madrid, 1950-55); Th. S. Beardsley, "Hispano-Classical Translations printed between 1482 and 1699: A Study of the Prologues and a Critical Bibliography" (Ph. D. dissertation, University of Pennsylvania, 1961) makes a few additions. For a different type of evidence, see J. Lawrance, "Juan Alfonso de Baena's Versified Reading List: A Note on the aspirations and the reality of fifteenth-century Castilian culture", *JHPh*, 5 (1981), 101-22.

about a new translation of Homer's *Iliad* (c. 1446-1452). Fifteenth-century readers often added morally bracing *exempla* as a desideratum; and it sometimes seems as if they hoped to find this twofold "exemplo e consolación", as they called it, not so much in an aesthetic experience, as in the books' more pragmatic freight of "information". So Santillana remarks in the same letter, "si carescemos de las formas, seamos contentos de las materias". [7]

This heuristic approach links up with the omission from the list of translations of much of what we regard as most characteristic and precious in classical literature: lyric, satire and drama. So it is sometimes argued that the choice of classical texts preferred by Spanish readers implies not only a deficient aesthetic appreciation of classical literature, but also a lack of curiosity about the *quiddity*, the essential "otherness", of classical civilization and that this makes their interest in the classical world quite a different thing from the Italian Revival of Learning. But, it seems that the Florentine humanists of the early Quattrocento were no less concerned with didactic and moral readings of classical texts and showed no greater predilection for lyric, satirical or dramatic poetry than Spaniards. The exemplary purpose behind the study of ancient history and ethics which motivated a key figure like Leonardo Bruni (1369-1444) was supremely acceptable to his avid contemporary readership in Spain and often quoted as authority and protreptic: so, in the dedication to Prince Enrique of his immensely popular *Proverbios*, Santillana justified the use of "buenos exemplos" from Plato, Aristotle, Socrates, Virgil, Ovid, Terence and others by reference to

> Leonardo de Arecio, en una epístola suya al muy magnífico ya dicho señor rey [Juan II], en la qual le recuenta los muy altos e grandes fechos de los emperadores de Roma naturales de la vuestra España, diciéndole que los traía a la memoria porque ... por enxemplo de ellos a alteça de virtudes e a desseo de muy grandes cosas lo amonestassen. [8]

And this approach to the classics remained unquestioned among lay readers everywhere in Europe at least until the eighteenth century; so

---

[7] Marqués de Santillana, *Obras*, ed. A. Cortina (Madrid: Austral, 1946), p. 44. On *exemplo e consolación*, see further J. Lawrance, "The spread of lay literacy in Late Medieval Castile", *BHS*, 62 (1985), 79-94, at 82 and 88-90.

[8] *Obras*, p. 46. The letter of Bruni to which Santillana refers, a eulogy of Spain and the Spanish emperors of Rome, the first of several sent to Juan II, probably dates from 1434; see *Epistolae*, ed. L. Mehus (Florence, 1741), VII, p. 6. It achieved wide diffusion in the Castilian translation (for example, Biblioteca Nacional MSS 5732 and 8611; Santillana's copy, BN MS 10212).

that R. R. Bolgar defined the whole Revival of Learning as "the noblest elements in Roman morality organized to serve the Renaissance spirit". [9] In this respect at least the Quattrocento Italian humanists and the patrons of the vernacular translations of Spain were united.

Besides moral "exemplo e consolación", however, the prologues which Peninsular translators earnestly tacked on to their works often touted a more utilitarian idea: that the classical moralists, historians and epic poets offer important practical lessons to noble readers on the conduct of their profession and of the "republic's" affairs. This seems to mean in part that, for the new lay readership of the fifteenth century, classical literature provided almost the only available texts for a study of state-craft, warfare and secular ethics based on empirical examples. This point was made, for example, by the Portuguese translator of Cicero's *De officiis*, when he noted that though there were other "mui boos livros que trautam da philosophia moral ... os outros per a mayor parte screvem da theorica, e a tençom deste he de mostrar a pratica". [10] But the idea is also related to the so-called "revival" of chivalry. Roman *militia* was still believed, in all the courts of fifteenth-century Europe (Italy not excluded), to be a "source" in direct historical descent, and hence "mirror", of contemporary chivalry and knighthood. [11] The supposition that Roman *militia* had this direct historical relevance for the definition of a knight's duties and behaviour is a note that was sounded over and again in the prologues.

Both the practical bent behind the revival of classical history and its historical reflection on contemporary chivalry are illustrated at the outset

---

[9] *The Classical Heritage and its Beneficiaries* (Cambridge, 1954), p. 255. By way of a Renaissance example, one may quote the proem of Machiavelli (1469-1527) to his great commentary on Livy, the *Discorsi*: "ho giudicato necessario scrivere ... a ciò che coloro che leggeranno queste mia declarazioni possino più facilmente trarne quella utilità per la quale si debbe cercare la cognizione delle istorie", Niccolò Machiavelli, *Il principe e Discorsi sopra la prima deca di Tito Livio*, ed. S. Bertelli (Milan, 1960), pp. 124-25.

[10] *O livro dos oficios de Marco Tullio Ciceram, o qual tornou em linguagem o infante D. Pedro, duque de Coimbra*, edited by J. M. Piel (Coimbra, 1948), "Prologo".

[11] A classic example is Bruni's treatise *De militia*, twice translated into Castilian, once for Santillana and once for Rodrigo Manrique; see M. Schiff, *La Bibliothèque du marquis de Santillane* (Paris, 1905), pp. 113-16 and 361-63. It was much discussed by Castilian readers, e.g. the correspondence (1444) of Santillana and Cartagena in *Prosistas castellanos del siglo XV*, ed. Penna, pp. 235-45. Bruni defines the ideal knight by examining the pristine form of militia founded by Romulus, using Livy as chief source, and discusses how far knighthood in Bruni's own day lived up to the Roman ideal; see C. C. Bayley, *War and Society in Renaissance Florence: The "De militia" of Leonardo Bruni* (Toronto, 1961), pp. 316-36.

by one of the earliest and most influential of all the Spanish statements on the subject, the one set out by Pero López de Ayala in the prologue to his translation of three *Decades* of Livy, made from the French of Pierre de Bressuire at the behest of Juan I in 1386. Ayala recommended Livy's history to his fellow noblemen not as an example of antiquarianism, but as a lively document in the rules of chivalry and war. The King may, indeed, have intended the translation of Livy's extended hymn to patriotic self-sacrifice to act as a specific reprimand and *exemplum* to the Castilian knights whose selfish and uncooperative thirst for personal glory and lack of discipline had so recently led to disaster and ignominy at the battle of Aljubarrota. [12] Ayala writes:

> Plogo a la vuestra real magestat que este libro de Titus Livius, dó se ponen e cuentan las ordenanças que los príncipes e cavalleros [antiguos] guardaron en sus batallas, ... sea traído agora en público por que los príncipes e los cavalleros que lo oyeren tomen buen exenplo e buena esperencia e esfuerço en si, catando quánto provecho e quánta onra nace de la buena ordenança e de la buena obedencia en las batallas, e quánto estorvo e daño e peligro viene al contrario. [13]

In Ayala's conception, the chief lessons to be learnt from classical history were rules of war and strategy, though he also suggested, significantly, that the grandeur of Rome's legacy might inspire "esfuerço". The same narrowly military conception doubtless was in the mind of the many nobles who subsequently comissioned copies of San Cristóbal's version of Vegetius's *De re militari*, of its abbreviation *Libro de la guerra*, of a new version of Frontinus's *Strategemata*, or of the Castilian translations (based on Bruni's Latin and Pier Candido Decembrio's Italian versions) of Polybius's *De bello Punico*, Procopius's *De bello Gothico*, and Caesar's *De bello Gallico*. [14] Juan Alfonso de Baena, in the *Prologus Baenensis* to his

---

[12] P. E. Russell, *The English Intervention in Spain and Portugal in the Time of Edward III and Richard II* (Oxford, 1955), pp. 398-99. Russell also makes the point that Ayala, with his study of Livy and Vegetius, seems to have been the only man of his time capable of seeing that the defeat at Aljubarrota probably had something to do with faulty tactics and morale, not divine intervention.

[13] Pero López de Ayala, *Las Décadas de Tito Livio: edición crítica de los libros I-III*, ed. C. J. Wittlin, 2 vols. (Barcelona, 1984), I, pp. 215-17, at p. 217. The popularity of this translation is attested by numerous MSS, incunables, later editions, and mentions in library inventories. It was usually read in the abbreviated version prepared in the 1430s by the Count of Benavente.

[14] On Fray Alfonso de San Cristóbal's version of *Vegecio de re militari* (late 14th c.), see Schiff, *Bibliothèque du marquis de Santillane*, p. 75. The BN MS 6526 *Libro de la guerra* dubiously attributed to Villena (ed. L. de Torre in *RH* 38 (1914), 497-531) is simply an epitome; another, the *Dichos de Séneca* [sic] *en el fecho de*

famous *Cancionero* compiled for Juan II, thought it not simply instructive, but obligatory for nobles to study the "batallas, guerras e conquistas que en fecho de armas e cavallerías los muy esclarecidos *sus antecessores* antigos, enperadores e senadores e cónsules e dictadores de la muy famosa e redubtable cibdat de Roma fizieron e ordenaron e conpusieron e escrivieron". In his Frenchified and long-winded style, Baena spelled out the strategic benefits of such study:

> para que puedan e sepan ser cabdillos e governadores, capitanes de grandes gentes, e que sepan con pura discreción e con buen seso governar ... en ordenada justicia e buena dispusición e sabia ordenança todas sus gentes e huestes e batallas e conquistas e guerras. [15]

And the emphasis on soldiering continued to be of prime importance, to judge by the undiminished popularity of translations of military history, well beyond the turn of the century and into the Golden Age. [16]

---

la cavallería, and some *Dichos de Quinto Curcio,* are attributed equally apocryphally to Alonso de Cartagena (BN MSS 8830 and 17803). Of Frontinus there were an Aragonese, a Catalan, and two Castilian versions current during the century: see Schiff, pp. 34 and 141-42, and A. Rubió i Lluch, *Documents per l'història de la cultura catalana mig-eval,* 2 vols. (Barcelona, 1908, 1921), I, pp. 219 and 226; the second Castilian version, made by Diego Guillén de Ávila for the Count of Haro in 1487, was subsequently printed and reprinted several times (Beardsley, "Hispano-Classical Translations", pp. 25 and 127-28). Bruni's *De primo bello Punico* (1421), an unacknowledged crib of Polybius, was translated into Italian by Pier Candido Decembrio (Schiff, pp. 37-38) and then into Catalan by Francesc Alegre (Hispanic Society of America MS H.C. 387/4327); his Procopius, *De bello Gothico* (c. 1441), into Castilian for Santillana's cousin Fernán Álvarez de Toledo, Count of Alba (Schiff, pp. 357-59). Decembrio's Italian Caesar was translated into Castilian c. 1450 (A. Morel-Fatio, "La Traduction des *Commentaires* de César par Pedro Candido Decembrio", *Bibliothèque de l'École des Chartes,* 4 (1894), 345-48; Schiff, p. 65); on a second fifteenth-century translation, see note 16 below.

[15] *Cancionero de Juan Alfonso de Baena,* ed. J. M. Azáceta, 3 vols. (Madrid, 1966), I, pp. 7-15, at pp. 10-11.

[16] An example is *Los comentarios de Gayo Julio César* by Diego López de Toledo, son of Santillana's cousin, the Count of Alba, who became *comendador* of the Military Order of Alcántara. Done in the 1480s while Diego was still a page-boy at the court of Prince John, the version was subsequently published by Pedro Hagenbach in Toledo in 1498; Diego later revised the translation with the aid of better, printed texts, and rededicated it to His "Caesarean" Majesty Charles V. The book was reprinted time and again in the sixteenth century, the last edition being that of 1621 (Menéndez Pelayo, *Bibliografía hispano-latina clásica,* II, pp. 142-54; Beardsley, "Hispano-Classical Translations printed between 1482 and 1699", p. 23). A similar case is that of Appian's *Romaica,* a military history of the Empire: it was translated, via the Italian and Decembrio's Latin, by Captain Diego de Salazar for the Marquis of Berlanga as *Historia de todas las guerras civiles* (Rome, 1502 and many subsequent editions), and, as *Los triumphos de Apiano* (Valencia: Juan Jofre, 1522, etc.), by Juan de Molina for Rodrigo de

But this military and chivalric focus was not all there was to the classical movement in fifteenth-century Spain. A significant extension of Ayala's and Baena's view of the practical strategic lessons of classical history appeared when writers began to express the opinion that a knowledge of literature was an essential training not only for military prowess, but for more general lessons, and especially for fitting noblemen for their role in the governance of the polity. Such an opinion is clearly expounded, for example, in the interesting prologue which Alonso de Cartagena (1395-1456), Bishop of Burgos, prefixed to his compilation of the laws of chivalry, the *Doctrinal de cavalleros,* which he dedicated to the poet and Count of Castro, Diego Gómez de Sandoval, in 1446:

> Los famosos cavalleros, muy noble señor, que en los tiempos antiguos por diversas regiones del mundo florescieron, entre los grandes cuidados e ocupaciones arduas que tenían para governar la república e la defender e anparar de los sus adversarios, acostumbravan interponer algund trabajo de sciencia, *por que onestamente supiesen regir así aquellos cuyo regimiento les pertenescía, así en fechos de paz como de guerras,* entendiendo que las fuerças del cuerpo non pueden exercer auto loable de fortaleza si non son guiadas por coraçón sabidor. [17]

A classic formulation of the same theme occurs in the prologue to Santillana's *Proverbios.* Santillana kicks off with the customary exordial topic of "arms versus letters", fustigating the (perhaps imaginary) dolts who say that a prince need know only "how to administer his realms or conquer new ones"; he then leads in with Cartagena's argument:

> ¿Cómo puede regir a otro aquel que a sí mismo no rige? ¿Nin cómo se regirá nin se governará aquel que non sabe nin ha visto las governaciones e regimientos de los bien regidos e governados?

He winds up by citing the Catos and Scipios, Hannibal, Caesar, and more recent heroes in support of his peroration: that "la sciencia non embota el fierro de la lança, nin faze floxa el espada en la mano del cavallero". [18]

Mendoza, Santillana's (bastard) grandson, Marquis of Cenete (A. Bravo García, "Apiano en España: notas críticas", *Cuadernos bibliográficos,* 32 (1975), 29-39).

[17] I quote from Oxford, Bodleian Library MS Bod 597, fols. 115-116 (my italics). There are another 12 MSS and 3 early editions of this very popular work; see *Dissertation Abstracts,* LXIV, 12965, on G. L. Boarino's "Alonso de Cartagena's *Doctrinal de cavalleros*: Text, tradition and sources" (unpublished Ph. D. dissertation, University of California, Berkeley, 1964).

[18] *Obras,* pp. 46-48. For further examples of the rhetorical topic of "arms versus letters", see N. G. Round, "Renaissance culture and its opponents in 15th-Century Castile", *MLR,* 57 (1962), 204-15. Both Round and P. E. Russell, "Las armas

The heroes in Santillana's list, and particularly Caesar, were to become standard models of the spirit of the age. [19]

This development beyond a purely military focus reflected the fact that a greater range of classical works were available for the noble education. Enrique de Villena, in the monumental unfinished commentary on his translation of the *Aeneid* (c. 1427), chose to interpret that work as an "espejo doctrinal" of the type envisaged by Cartagena and Santillana; according to Villena's *Prohemio*, noble readers would find in Virgil's epic, among many other bizarre and esoteric scientific and moral lessons of his own peculiar devising, and the inevitable "esfuerço siquiere de osar cometer grandes fechos", lessons in politics: "las prácticas como libran ... en las cortes de los reyes, e saber regirse en las mobilidades dellas" (BN MS 17975, fol. 10^v). The lesson was plainly embodied in another of Villena's popular classical allegories, *Los doze trabajos de Hércules* (1417): in the prologue, where he once again performed the ritual of attacking the "boors" who affirm that learning is incompatible with arms by citing the standard counter-example of Julius Caesar, and by pointing out that the Romans, according to Valerius Maximus, "leían los buenos fechos de los pasados e virtuosos cavalleros por animar a tales e mayores cosas a los entonces vivientes ... afirmando que tal exercicio era pungitivo de virtud"; and then in the body of the work, where Hercules, "espejo actual a los gloriosos cavalleros en armada cavallería", was made not only a knight of unequalled prowess but also, rather like Curial, a considerable natural philosopher and scholar as well. [20] A more systematic exposition of the broadly political arguments for reading classical ethics and oratory as well as history was Cartagena's *Epistula ad co-*

---

contra las letras: para una definición del humanismo español del siglo xv", in his *Temas de "La Celestina" y otros estudios: Del "Cid" al "Quijote"* (Barcelona, 1978), pp. 207-39, argue on the basis of these *topoi* and other evidence, that there really was an overwhelming prejudice against letters; when the *topos* occurs, as it usually does, in contexts like the one quoted above, it is surely more reasonable to take it as meaning that such prejudice was being seriously challenged. In particular, I find it hard to believe, in view of the evidence I am discussing in this article (and see note 33 below), that there was any important current of opinion at the court of that eminently bookish King Juan II to warn Prince Henry of the fatty degeneration of the moral fibre inherent in the literary pursuits devised for him by his father.

[19] The *locus classicus* for Caesar as soldier-scholar is Decembrio's prologue to his translation of the *De bello Gallico* (fifteenth-century Castilian version in Menéndez y Pelayo, *Bibliografía hispano-latina clásica*, II, pp. 141-42).

[20] Enrique de Villena, *Los doze trabajos de Hércules*, ed. M. Morreale (Madrid, 1958), pp. 7-10. The popularity of the work is attested by seven MSS, two incunable editions, and a number of citations in library inventories.

mitem de Haro, a Latin letter on the proper criteria for building a noble-man's library addressed to a leading collector of the time; the edifying programme set out by the bishop here was backed up by his own cycle of translations from Cicero and Seneca, the latter apparently the most popular secular work written in Castilian in the fifteenth century. [21]

Eloquent statements of the civic duty of men engaged in the *vita activa* to busy themselves with letters began to appear with some frequency as time went on. This note is sounded, for example, in the stirring tribute to his kinsman, Fernán Pérez de Guzmán, included by Vasco Ramírez de Guzmán in the prologue to his translation of Sallust, where he states that as a "zelador de saber los grandes e antiguos fechos" Fernán Pérez may count himself amongst those who "con derecha voluntad estudian de acrescentar el bien público". [22] A fine later example is Gómez Manrique's dedication (1476) of a *Cancionero* to his friend and patron the Count of Benavente, where he takes yet another conventional swipe at any "slug-gards" who may still adhere to the "arms versus letters" topic:

> Comoquiera que algunos haraganes digan ser cosa sobrada el leer y saber a los cavalleros, como si la cavallería fuera a perpetua rudeza condepnada, yo soy de muy contraria opinión; porque a estos digo yo ser *conplidero* el leer e saber las leyes e fueros e regimientos e governaciones de los pasados ..., las quales doctrinas ¿en quién mejor nin tan bien pueden ni deven ser empleados que en aquellos que han de governar? [23]

An anonymous mid-fifteenth-century translator of Aristotle's *Politics* and *Economics* made a related point when he wrote in his prologue that he had been moved to translate the two works (then seen as part of a trilogy with the *Ethics*) because

> por la mayor parte vemos que todos los hombres que rigen ciudades y repú-blicas y cosas familiares no alcançan ser latinos, de donde muchas vezes les falta la manera de governar; a los quales pensé hazer beneficio, si con mi industria diesse camino para que sin necessidad de la lengua latina tuviessen preceptos con los quales supiessen bien regir y governar. [24]

---

[21] J. N. H. Lawrance, *Un tratado de Alonso de Cartagena sobre la educación y los estudios literarios* (Barcelona: Universidad Autónoma, 1979); K. A. Blüher, *Séneca en España: Investigaciones sobre la recepción de Séneca en España desde el siglo XII hasta el siglo XVII,* trans. J. Conde (Madrid, 1983), pp. 133-48.

[22] Schiff, *Bibliothèque du marquis de Santillane,* pp. 78-79.

[23] *Cancionero de Gómez Manrique,* ed. A. Paz y Melia, 2 vols. (Madrid, 1885), I, p. 2 (my italics).

[24] Printed, together with the Prince of Viana's translation of the *Ethics,* in Saragossa by Jorge Coci, 1509 (Beardsley, "Hispano-Classical Translations", pp. 24 and 118-19).

A similar topos, that translations of the classics themselves help to "benefit the republic" by educating its statesmen, also became entrenched: the Navarrese courtier and poet Hugo de Urríes, for example, in the prologue to his *Valerio Máximo*, written in 1467 and printed with a dedication to Ferdinand of Aragon in 1495, boasted that by bringing home this work from his travels as ambassador in England and Burgundy he was conferring a "singular beneficio" on his homeland. So too the soldier Diego López de Toledo, who translated Caesar before serving at the siege of Granada in 1492, claimed in his dedication to the ill-fated Prince John of Castile that his aims had been to "aprovechar mi tierra ... ca poco aprovechan las armas si no andan acompañados con consejo". Diego Guillén de Ávila, who dedicated his translation of Frontinus's *Strategemata* to the Count of Haro in 1487, repeated the claim to "aprovechar a nuestra castellana república", citing "aquella sentencia de Aristóteles donde dize que se deve más amar el bien público que no el propio". [25]

Another aspect of the fifteenth-century vogue for vernacular classics was the debate on "True Nobility". Fifteenth-century Spanish, Burgundian and French writers on this theme, as well as Italian ones, sought to establish, amongst other things, the classical topic that a nobleman's true virtue lies not in hereditary *prez*, but in his intrinsic public value to the body politic ("república" or "cosa pública"), a *virtù* which could consist as much in the knight's wise advice and knowledge as in his physical prowess. [26] An interesting contribution to this *De vera nobilitate* tradition was made by Diego de Valera, whose *Espejo de verdadera nobleza* — one of the three native Castilian works in the Count of Benavente's library in 1440, another being Villena's *Doze trabajos de Hércules* — was translated into French by a Burgundian courtier, Hugues de Salve. Valera was a tireless champion of a lettered and classically educated aristocracy; in one of his famous "open letters" to an unnamed friend, dated 1447, he

---

[25] The three quotations from Beardsley, "Hispano-Classical Translations", pp. 122-23, 126-27, and 127-28 (fuller version in Gallardo, *Ensayo*, III, pp. 151-52); see notes 16 and 14 above for details of the early editions.

[26] See C. C. Willard, "The Concept of True Nobility at the Burgundian Court", *Studies in the Renaissance*, 14 (1967), 33-48; M. Vale, "The Literature of Honour and Virtue", in his *War and Chivalry: Warfare and Aristocratic Culture in England, France and Burgundy at the End of the Middle Ages* (London, 1981), pp. 14-32; and S. Anglo, "The Courtier: the Renaissance and Changing Ideals", in *The Courts of Europe: Politics, Patronage and Royalty 1400-1800*, ed. A. G. Dickens (London, 1977), pp. 33-50, who describes the theme as "tilled by Dante, and trudged into mud by a host of writers throughout the fourteenth and fifteenth centuries" (p. 38).

affirmed: "sé esforçarme servir mi príncipe no solamente con las fuerzas corporales, mas aun con los mentales e intelectuales". [27] In another treatise, the *Tratado de las armas*, Valera supported his views with an appeal to Plato's concept of "philosopher-kings":

> Es verdadera aquella sentencia de Sócrates que dize "Entonces la tierra es bien aventurada, quando los príncipes della son sabios". [28]

Characteristically, the source for this quotation was not Plato's *Republic* (though the first six books of this were available in Spain in the Latin version sent to Juan II and dedicated in part to Alonso de Cartagena by Pier Candido Decembrio), but Vegetius's *De re militari*. The same authority, from the same source, was quoted by, for example, Pero Díaz de Toledo in the prologue to his gloss of Santillana's *Proverbios* and by Enrique de Villena in the "Vida de Vergilio" which precedes his *Eneida* (BN MS 17975, fol. 6). By the end of the century Plato's philosopher-kings had become a ubiquitous commonplace.

The eminently practical purpose of fitting themselves for their role in the governance of the commonweal, which Hexter and others have documented also in the reading tastes of the newly literate nobility of the fifteenth century north of the Pyrenees, [29] was thus the driving idea behind the rash of classical translations commissioned by Spanish noble readers in this period. But to see their aspirations in this light, as spurred and guided by new "civic" attitudes and aspirations, is already to bring them closely into contact with some — not all — of the attitudes and aspirations of Quattrocento Italian humanism. We may apply to the Spanish case Huizinga's memorable dictum: "between the ponderous spirit of the Burgundian and the classical instinct of the Italian ... there is only a difference of nuance". [30] Therefore the claim that Boscán's famous translation (1534) of Baldassare Castiglione's *Il libro del cortegiano* represented a "first wave" of Italian Renaissance ideas about the gentleman-courtier in the Spanish peninsula is slightly misleading, however important that publication may have been in other respects. [31] *Il cortegiano*'s portrait of

---

[27] *Prosistas castellanos del siglo XV*, ed. Penna, p. 7.
[28] *Prosistas castellanos del siglo XV*, ed. Penna, p. 173.
[29] J. H. Hexter, "The Education of the Aristocracy in the Renaissance", in his *Reappraisals in History* (London, 1961), pp. 45-70.
[30] J. Huizinga, *The Waning of the Middle Ages*, trans. F. Hopman (Harmondsworth: Penguin, 1972), pp. 68-69.
[31] Compare Russell's verdict in "Las armas contra las letras", pp. 209-10.

the perfect courtier, evoked from memories of the courts of the *condottiere* dukes of Urbino and Milan at the turn of the century no less than from such impeccably Renaissance sources as Cicero's ideal of the orator-statesman, had been forestalled in many details by medieval writers on chivalry and Burgundian writers on True Nobility, so that the ideal is hardly "Italian". [32] And I have been arguing that Castiglione's concept of the well-born and cultivated professional soldier, with his easy but deep acquaintance with classical literature ("full-time dilettante" as Anglo wittily puts it), had been taken for granted in Spain for a considerable time before. After all, as Curtius observes apropos of the "arms and letters" topic, the combination was "nowhere ... so brilliantly realized as in Spain's period of florescence in the sixteenth and seventeenth centuries"; would this not point to a remarkable *volte-face*, if it were really the case that Castilian noblemen in the fifteenth century had been extraordinarily hostile to letters? [33] On the basis of the evidence presented here, Garcilaso, far from pioneering the idea of the well-read soldier, simply put into practice the established ideals of two generations of kinsmen such as Santillana and Manrique.

To return, finally, to Curial's Parnassian dream: in the interview with Apollo and the Muses, Curial was called upon to judge a curious dispute over the relative merits as *cavallers* of Achilles and Hector. If it is right to see this in the context of the new-found desire of the nobility to find out about and model itself on the exemplars of ancient virtue, then it becomes easier to comprehend the interest of original readers of *Curial e Güelfa* in the question of whether Homer or Dares was to be given the greater credit, or of whether Achilles or Hector was the better *cavaller*.

---

[32] Anglo, "The Courtier: the Renaissance and Changing Ideals", *passim*. On p. 40 he notes that accounts of court festivities in *El Victorial*, for example, "antedate Castiglione's Urbino by a century, and represent a tradition of courtliness extending back at least to the thirteenth century". See also note 3 above.

[33] Curtius, p. 178. That there were nobles who did not care for letters is of course not in question; letters are always a minority concern, and it is the size of that minority and the climate of opinion which matter. Whatever the force of the other evidence adduced to prove the existence of an abnormal climate of hostility to letters among the Castilian nobility, the suggestion that the "arms versus letters" *topos* (see note 18) was to a degree peculiar to Castile seems questionable. Hexter's article (note 29) gives abundant examples of "arms versus letters" commonplaces from France and England (where there was no *converso* problem, no *Reconquista*) and in texts which reach well into the seventeenth century. As Russell points out ("Las armas contra las letras", p. 210), Castiglione's own important discussion of the "arms and letters" theme opens by attributing the contrary topic not to the Spaniards, but to the French (*Il libro del cortegiano*, p. 84).

Echoes of that interest sound elsewhere too. Gómez Manrique, for example, in a gloss on the eleventh *copla* of his long consolatory poem to his sister Juana, Countess of Castro, commenting the lines:

> aquella cibdad muy fuerte troyana
> de cuyos triunfos, onores e glorias
> están llenos libros e grandes estorias,

remarks that although his sister, as a woman, may not personally have read the histories of Troy, she will most certainly have heard of the *porfía* between Homer, Dictys and Dares: "no creo que en la sala de vuestro palacio algunas vezes no se aya debatido". [34] And comparisons between the heroes of antiquity were a popular pastime, started by the craze for Plutarch's *Parallel Lives*. [35]

Curial's quandary hinges on a traditional issue, the historical veracity of the rival accounts. Homer, the supporter of Achilles, is accused of having been too poetic: "fa creure moltes coses que no les hach Achilles, ne passaren axí com ell escriu". So Curial has, reluctantly, to find for Dictys and Dares, supposed eye-witnesses from opposite sides who wrote the unadorned "truth". The terms of this discussion, though lifted from countless medieval predecessors, are also connected to a common topic in fifteenth-century discussions about classical literature: namely, the authenticity of "history" and its superiority to the idle fables of romance. [36] The debate on the authenticity of Homer was one of the most

---

[34] *Cancionero de Gómez Manrique*, I, pp. 209-41, at pp. 219-20. Santillana represents the Queen Mother of Aragon, Leonor de Albuquerque, in an *arboleda*, enjoying a reading by her ladies-in-waiting of "novellas e plazientes cuentos"; these were punctuated by "antigas gestas ... de Troya y de Tebas" (*Comedieta de Ponça*, coplas XLV-XLVIII). Such vignettes, which could be multiplied, suggest a milieu in which the *matière de Rome* was completely familiar to polite society, including ladies. For the popularity of the *Historia Trojana* (c. 1280) in Catalonia, see *Les Històries troyanes de Guiu de Columnes traduïdes al català en el XIVèn segle per en Jacme Conesa*, ed. R. Miquel y Planas (Barcelona, 1916), pp. xv-xviii; on the medieval Homer-Dares debate, see H. Buchthal, *Historia Troiana. Studies in the History of Mediaeval Secular Illustration*, Studies of the Warburg Institute, 32 (London-Leiden, 1971), pp. 1-8.

[35] Examples are Pier Candido Decembrio's *Comparazione di Gayo Julio Cesare ed Alessandro Magno*, trans. Martín de Ávila for Santillana (BN MSS 8549 and 10140, and an incunable version of 1496); the pseudo-Lucianic *Dialogue of Alexander, Hannibal and Scipio on the glory of arms*, anonymously translated (BN MS 9522, fols. 113ᵛ-122ᵛ); and, of course, the opening pages of Díez de Games' *El Victorial*.

[36] Brian Tate himself has noted that López de Ayala's attack on chivalric romances was linked to his translation of Livy by this "sustitución de los libros de caballerías por los historiadores clásicos" (*Ensayos sobre la historiografía peninsular del siglo XV*, Madrid, 1970, p. 46). Pérez de Guzmán argues that histories

interesting test-cases. Early in the 1440s a number of attempts were made by Juan II, through the offices of Cartagena, to gain access to Homer's account of the Trojan War, doubtless for comparison with the splendid Alfonsine translation of Benoît de Sainte-Maure's *Roman de Troie* (that is, an unwieldy 30,000-line verse romance version of "Dares and Dictys" made about 1165) in his royal library. An order was accordingly des-patched to Pier Candido Decembrio at Milan to send a Latin translation. Decembrio, after much delay, sent only five books and a "Life" of Homer. Meanwhile, the King's chronicler and secretary of Latin letters, Juan de Mena, was commanded to produce, in Cordova, a version of the *Ilias Latina*. [37] Mena's *prohemio* to his version, the *Ilíada en romance* (as it is entitled in MSS and early editions), naturally alludes to the debate about Homer's veracity; here, the Cordoban author's enthusiasm for the "seráphica obra" of the "vaticinante poeta ... monarcha de la universal poesía", expressed with an eloquence which had scarcely ever before been achieved in Castilian prose, allows him to come to an evaluation of the relative worth of Homer and his rivals different from the time-honoured one still favoured, half-heartedly, by the author of *Curial e Güelfa*; this, despite the fact, which Mena himself bemoans in extrava-gant terms, that the *Ilias Latina* is no more than a miserable botch of the grand original. Mena derides with scorn the medieval versions of the Trojan saga, and especially the *Historia Troiana* of the parvenu Guido delle Colonne, whose insults to Homer were flatulent boasts, "atrevi-miento sin freno", in view of the fact that Homer "fue en tal tiempo que bien pudo ser informado por vista de ... la troyana captividad" while he, Guido, lived in the time of good King Alfonso XI:

> ¿Y qué supiera Guido ni aun todos los otros de quien él rebuscó para escrevir si ovo seído Troya, si por la seráphica y quasi divinal obra de Homero como de original no lo ovi[e]sse avido? [38]

---

and chronicles which are full of "cosas estrañas e maravillosas" — he cites the "trufa o mentira paladina" of Pedro del Corral's *Crónica sarrazina* as an exam-ple — should be censored "for the good of the republic" (*Generaciones y semblan-zas*, ed. Tate, p. 1). The idea comes from his mentor Alonso de Cartagena's stric-tures on the lack of verisimilitude of "Tristani ac Lanceloti Amadisiive ingentia volumina, quae absque aliqua aedificationis spe animum legentium oblectant, illiusque "torneamenti" narratio, quod apud Toletum Roderici regis temporibus factum fuisse depromitur, quam audivi nudius tertius compositam esse" (*Un tra-tado de Alonso de Cartagena*, ed. Lawrance, p. 54).

[37] A. Morel-Fatio, "Les Deux *Omero* castillans", *Romania*, XXV (1896), 111-29; C. Fabiano, "Pier Candido Decembrio traduttore d'Omero", *Aevum*, 23 (1940), 36-51.

[38] Juan de Mena, "*La Ylíada en romançe*" *según la impresión de Arnao Guillén de Brocar (Valladolid, 1519)*, ed. M. de Riquer (Barcelona, 1949), p. 39. See also

In the wake of all this, not many years later, Santillana commissioned a Castilian translation of Decembrio's Latin version of the five books of the *Iliad* from his son, the future Cardinal Pedro González de Mendoza. [39]

Of course, this desire to recapture from the ancient texts a more authentic portrait of antique heroes was never incompatible with a continuing taste for medieval texts; the *Crónica troyana,* in particular, in the translation attributed to Pero López de Ayala, which to judge by library inventories and extant MSS was tremendously popular in the fifteenth century, remained in print, in at least fifteen editions, until 1587. [40] Nevertheless, the *concurrent* popularity of the classical texts implies, in my view, just the sort of developing critical faculty which, on other grounds, is sometimes denied to the patrons and translators of Juan II's court. The purpose of my paper has been, in fact, to propose that these translations represent something we could call "vernacular humanism". [41] It has always seemed to me that the least relevant argument one could bring to bear against seeing some sort of renewal of the classical spirit in the fifteenth century in Spain would be that the Spanish humanism of this time was not carried out in the Latin of Valla and Poggio. Of course, the use of Latin made a great difference: though one eminent scholar has recently confirmed Wilamowitz's old dictum that, with the exception of Valla and Politian, the humanists were not philologists, [42] the Italian brand of humanism was more professional, more scholarly, perhaps more profound. But scholarship was not necessarily more important than translation for the eventual achievement of the Renaissance in literature: the splendid fusion of classical forms with the life and thew and muscle of the living languages. Besides, Latin humanism was not, contrary to common belief, the only form of humanism practised in Italy, or even in Florence; the works of Leonardo Bruni and Pier Candido Decembrio, for instance, the chief representatives of Italian humanism for the court

---

the interesting dedication to Don Hernando Enríquez by the printer's hack, Alonso Tudela, *ibid.,* pp. 29-31, which refers to the "philosopher-kings" *topos.*

[39] Schiff, *Bibliothèque du marquis de Santillane,* pp. 1-7.

[40] Beardsley, "Hispano-Classical Translations", p. 20.

[41] I adapt the term from J. Monfrin, "La Connaissance de l'Antiquité et le problème de l'humanisme en langue vulgaire dans la France du XVᵉ siècle", in *The Late Middle Ages and the Dawn of Humanism outside Italy,* ed. G. Verbeke and J. IJsewijn (Louvain-The Hague, 1972), pp. 131-70; see also his "Humanisme et traductions au Moyen Age", in *L'Humanisme médiéval dans les littératures romanes du XIIᵉ au XIVᵉ siècle,* ed. A. Fourrier (Paris, 1964), pp. 217-62.

[42] E. J. Kenney, *The Classical Text: Aspects of Editing in the Age of the Printed Book* (Berkeley-Los Angeles-London, 1974), p. 18.

of Juan II, circulated freely in Italian translations, frequently indeed in translations by their own hand. [43] There was in fact a growing lobby in Florence (Rinuccini, Alberti, Politian, Landino) in favour of the *volgare* for many types of writing; this reflects the fact that professional Italian humanists were servants, not masters — their patrons, the nobility and *condottieri*, often required a type of culture much more akin to the vernacular humanism of their Spanish and Northern European counterparts than to that of the Florentine *érudits* and *antiquaires*. [44] And lastly, when Latin humanism did arrive in Spain, under the aegis of Nebrija, it brought about changes certainly less wide-ranging, and arguably less significant to the Renaissance in its Spanish avatar, than the nowadays despised vernacular humanism of the previous generation. Pompous Italian visitors to Spain at the end of the century, as Russell and Round have shown, were fond of scoffing at Spaniards' lack of Latin; they fell into the trap of supposing that a Renaissance which was different from theirs was not a Renaissance. History suggests that the truth was more complex.

J. N. H. Lawrance

University of Oxford

---

[43] L. Bertalot, "Zur Bibliographie der Übersetzungen des Leonardus Brunus Aretinus", *Quellen und Forschungen aus italienischen Archiven und Bibliotheken,* 37 (1936-1937), 178-95, and 38 (1937-1938), 268-85; V. Zaccaria, "Sulle opere di Pier Candido Decembrio", *Rinascimento,* 7 (1956), 13-74.

[44] R. Sabbadini, *Storia del ciceronianismo e di altri questioni litterarie nell'età della Rinascenza* (Turin, 1885), pp. 122-36; P. O. Kristeller, "The Origins and Development of the Language of Italian Prose", in his *Renaissance Thought and the Arts. Collected Essays* (Princeton, 1980), pp. 119-41; C. Grayson, *A Renaissance Controversy: Latin or Italian?*, Inaugural Lecture, Taylor Institution, 1959 (Oxford, 1960); and J. E. Seigel, *Rhetoric and Philosophy in Renaissance Humanism: The Union of Eloquence and Wisdom, Petrarch to Valla* (Princeton, 1968), pp. 226-54.

A TYPICAL EXAMPLE OF LATE MEDIEVAL CASTILIAN ANARCHY? THE AFFRAY OF 1458 IN ALCARAZ

T H E sources for fifteenth-century Castilian history contain eloquent testimony about the apparently endless riots, disorders and uprisings which characterised urban life, particularly during the reign of Henry IV. Yet although the horrors and bloodshed of the anti-semitic pogroms are in some cases particularly well documented, [1] very little is actually known about the other episodes of urban anarchy. How many people participated in these disorders? What actually happened? How many were killed or injured? What bonds of political and social cohesion operated at the level of street anarchy? By good fortune a detailed enquiry into an affray in the town of Alcaraz in 1458 survives. It takes the form of an *información, pesquisa* or *inquisición* which was carried out by Pedro de Silva, *corregidor* of Alcaraz, and Gonzalo Carrillo, one of Henry IV's military commanders and member of the royal council. Eighty-four pages record the testimony of some twenty witnesses, all of them *vecinos* of Alcaraz. All of them, in varying degrees, had been eye-witnesses of part or all of the events. Many of them had actually participated in the affray and tried to explain what they and others were up to. Moreover since both the affray and the witnesses were "local", there was no difficulty in identifying individuals, streets, and even houses. Names were named with extraordinary profusion. The enquiry even records snatches of direct speech overheard by the witnesses. We can almost, as it were, discern what individuals were actually thinking. And of course the evidence of any individual witness can be cross-checked with that of others. In short, as far as I know, this extraordinary document is the only example so far found which enables the historian to attempt an "anatomy" of an affray. [2]

Alcaraz, in the present-day province of Albacete, was of considerable strategic importance during the later medieval period, and its involvement

---

[1] See, for example, the account of the horrors perpetrated during the Toledan *alboroto* of 1467 against the *conversos* in E. Benito Ruano, *Toledo en el siglo XV* (Madrid, 1961), pp. 93-102.

[2] The document is in the Archivo de los Duques de Medinaceli, *sección* "Medinaceli (Las Navas)", *legajo* 309-33. Numbers in brackets refer to the folios of this document.

in a whole series of political struggles with the Manrique *comendadores* of Santiago, the Marquis of Villena, the Fajardos, and even the Moors of Granada has been ably documented by Aurelio Pretel Marín.[3] The same author has also recorded internal *alborotos* and uprisings for 1444, 1456, 1460, 1463 and 1474-5.[4] Obviously we are here faced with a succession of disorders of which the affray of 1458 is but one example. Such disorders took place within a town which was built on steeply rising ground and dominated, at the top, by the *alcázar*. As might be expected, the "centre" of the town was made up of the *calle mayor*, which terminated in the *plaza mayor* where there were two churches with large towers — the Torre de la Trinidad and the Torre del Reloj. It was in and around these areas that the epicentre of the affray of 1458 was located.

What, then, happened on the 10 January 1458? The story is complicated and perhaps the easiest way into it is through the testimony of one of the witnesses. García González de Vizcaya did not himself participate in the disorders, but he was sufficiently inquisitive to try and find out what was going on. He had heard that a certain Fernando de Bustamante had arrived at Alcaraz to discuss matters with the *corregidor*, Pedro de Silva, at the *tenerías*, which were located on the outskirts of the town (36ʳ). As will be seen, Fernando de Bustamante had been exiled from the town because of his activities as a *malhechor*, and this fact alone was sufficient to raise García's curiosity. And in effect our witness was in the *calle mayor*, asking questions, when the *corregidor* returned from his interview at the *tenerías*. García watched him pass and then scurried up to the *plaza mayor*, where once again he watched the *corregidor*, accompanied by knights and footsoldiers, heading for the *alcázar* (36ʳ). At this point, presumably because nothing momentous seemed to be happening, García went about his business. But shortly after, as he was standing at the door of the church of the Trinidad, he heard *cierto rumor* coming up the *calle mayor*. Turning to look, he saw Juan de Fontanar, Juan de Bustamante and the Ballesteros brothers, accompanied by knights and soldiers, galloping up the *calle mayor*, armed to the teeth and shouting "¡Armar, armar, señores!" (36ᵛ). Some of these men then chased after one or two of the *corregidor*'s men who fled through the cemetery of the Trinidad and took refuge within the church itself. At this point García

---

   3 Aurelio Pretel Marín, *Una ciudad castellana en los siglos XIV y XV (Alcaraz, 1300-1475)* (Albacete, 1978).
   4 *Ibid.*, pp. 91-94, 113-15, 121-27 and 160-65.

prudently left the scene and went to his *posada*. But later curiosity once again got the better of him and he returned to the *plaza mayor*. By this time the rebel soldiers had taken the *Torre del Reloj* and were busy making palisades and other defences (36ᵛ). García recognised Juan de Bustamante and Bartolomé del Horno, who appeared on the tower, and he went on to name others whom he had seen in the initial invasion up the *calle mayor* (36ᵛ-37ʳ).

García's testimony was limited, but it is clear from the evidence of other witnesses that the "invasion" or "uprising" had been well planned and that the meeting at the *tenerías* was a ruse. In fact two witnesses, a father and son, had been in Fernando de Bustamante's company during the days prior to the affray when Bustamante had been nearby in Viveros and La Canaleja (8ʳ-9ᵛ, 21ᵛ-23ᵛ). The son, indeed, had acted as a go-between between Bustamante and the *corregidor*, and he had observed them at the *tenerías*, talking apart and secretly for about an hour (21ᵛ). What exactly was discussed by the two men is not revealed by the *pesquisa*. Witnesses said in general terms that Bustamante went to the *tenerías* "sobre ygualar estos fechos", and to "ygualar a los fuera echados e desterrados" (6ʳ, 10ʳ). At the same time, however, his purpose was to "engañar" the *corregidor* (12ʳ). One witness claimed that "oyo desir al dicho Fernando de Bustamante que entendia de fablar con el dicho corregidor que lançasen fuera desta dicha cibdad a los Guerreros, sy non que darian tras los unos e tras los otros" (22ʳ). It may be, then, that Bustamante had cherished some vague hope of a successful outcome to the discussions, although all the evidence points to a deliberate trap. While the interview was actually taking place the rebels were already prepared in a "çelada so los çerrillos de Cabeça Gorda" (31ᵛ) and although Bustamante failed to trick the *corregidor* into letting him into the town for a meal (16ʳ-16ᵛ), the rebels easily gained entry into the town via the Puerta de Montiel and the Puerta Nueva (16ᵛ).

Who were these men, the *desterrados*, and what were their aims? Henry IV, referring to them as "delinquents" and *malhechores* who had been exiled from the town because of "ciertos insultos e muy feos fechos", named them as Fernando de Bustamante and his brother Juan, Juan de Claramonte, and the brothers Juan and García de Ballesteros (1ᵛ). [5] For their part Pedro de Silva and Gonzalo Carrillo, who pronounced a

---

[5] Henry IV's letter ordering the *pesquisa* is dated Madrid, 16 January 1458, and is transcribed on folios 1ᵛ-3ᵛ of the *pesquisa*.

sentencia after the *pesquisa,* have left us their version of the story. [6] According to them there had been a considerable history of trouble in the town prior to the affray. Fernando and Juan de Bustamante had aided and protected "omes malos e de mal ley e ladrones" and "malhechores". These men had constituted themselves into a kind of nocturnal alternative government. For example Sancho de Brotes, Fernando's *criado,* had made himself *alcalde,* and Fernando de Alarcón, Juan's *criado,* had appointed himself *alguasil.* These "alternative" officials carried *varas,* disarmed those "que de noche andaban por esta çibdad" and generally allowed robberies and other misdeeds to take place. The Bustamante brothers had done nothing to prevent all this. Indeed they themselves had gone around "armados de noche", "alborotando" the town against the *corregidor* and the last time that the *corregidor* had visited the town, in December, they had armed themselves against him and in favour of Juan de Ballesteros. For all these reasons these men had been expelled from the town. As for the affray itself, the objective of the *desterrados* was all too evident. The ringleaders had come "con entençion e proposyto de echar desta dicha çibdad a mi el dicho Pedro de Sylva e sy quisiera resistir ... de me ferir o matar o me ynjuriar".

The evidence of the witnesses more or less backs up this version of the events, but affords further clues. Among the many persons named, for example, Sancho de Brotes and Fernando de Alarcón, the nocturnal *alcalde* and *alguasil,* are identified as armed rebels (8ᵛ, 10ᵛ, 14ᵛ, 17ʳ, 22ᵛ, 27ʳ). And in answer to a rather leading question, witnesses naturally said that the aim of the affray was to expel the *corregidor* from the town. Juan de Fontanar, for example, had urged everybody in the *calle mayor* to go up to the *plaza* and throw out the *corregidor* (16ᵛ-17ʳ), and Juan de Ballesteros had been heard shouting that "no era su justiçia salvo robador e non corregidor" (9ʳ). But there was more to the affray than this. The leaders were regarded as being hostile not just to the *corregidor* but to "king's men". One witness, for example, stated that he went home to put his house into a state of defence because he had heard that the rebels wanted to sack it "por [ser él] servidor del rey" (17ʳ). Moreover the rebels themselves talked rather vaguely about their *contrarios.* In his testimony Mendo de Ballesteros, brother of the ringleaders Juan and García, revealed that they planned to fight in the *plaza* against their

---

[6] For the *sentencia* and for what follows, see document 32 of the same *legajo* 309 in the same archive in which the *pesquisa* is located.

contrarios and indeed that this was their *voz* or rallying-cry (40^r-40^v). But who were these *contrarios*? As has been seen, Juan Sánchez de Morales, who had been in Fernando de Bustamante's company and was well informed, testified that Bustamante wanted to expel the family of the Guerreros (22^r). And in effect we shall see that the affray was also about tensions between the oligarchical families and *bandos* of Alcaraz. For this very reason, perhaps, the rebels did not see themselves as *malhechores*. When one witness said to three of them that "en ora mala aqui entraron", they had replied that "asy se ganaban las honras" (28^v).

Initially the invasion or uprising was a complete success and the rebels were soon in control of most of the key points of the town apart from the *alcázar*. They had relied on speed and surprise and had moved quickly to invest "casas fuertes e torres e yglesias de la dicha çibdad" (4^r). Juan de Fontanar had been detailed to take the Torre de la Trinidad (11^r-11^v), Juan de Bustamante and García de Ballesteros took the Torre del Reloj (22^r, 28^v, 39^v), and the Torre de San Miguel was also invested (33^r). Of course the men in the towers had to be provisioned: wine, bread, firewood, clothes, and even weapons duly poured in from the house of the mother of the Ballesteros brothers, from Juan de Fontanar's home and from the houses belonging to Pedro García del Poso, and Ruy González de Llerena (6^v, 8^v, 11^r-11^v, 28^v, 40^r-40^v). Meanwhile the houses of Fernando de Bustamante, Juan de Ballesteros, Juan de Fontanar and Pedro Ruiz Zapatero became the rallying points and strongholds of armed men. Numerous people inside the town, named in ordinate detail, armed themselves and went to help the rebels. Bartolomé del Horno and Juan Carrasco, for example, were seen in the Torre del Reloj, and witnesses admitted that they had been in the rebels' houses from the start and had taken up arms "en su favor" (15^r, 22^v, 27^r). Most, too, seem to have been well armed. The men in the Torre del Reloj had lances and large shields (27^r) and most of the leading participants, apart from Fernando de Bustamante who was on foot, were on horseback and armed (23^v, 27^r, 36^r-17^v).

However, it was one thing to secure military control of *torres* and *casas fuertes,* but what was to be the next move? The rebels, in fact, were caught in a position not too dissimilar to that of Colonel Tejero after his initial success in the attempted *coup* of 23 February 1981. The *corregidor* was safely entrenched inside the *alcázar* and the only way forward was to secure further and powerful support. In fact the leaders had counted on such support from within Alcaraz, but as negotiations dragged on throughout the night it became clear, so to speak, that the Brunete division and General Armada were not going to materialise.

There were some twelve to fifteen leading oligarchical families in fifteenth-century Alcaraz. The leading rebels certainly belonged to some of these. As early as 1292, for example, a Bustamante was *alcalde del rey*, and during the fifteenth century members of the family held offices in the urban oligarchy.[7] We know, too, that both Fernando and Juan de Bustamante were *hidalgos*, because it was on the technical point of breaking the *hidalgo's pleito homenaje* and *juramento* that Pedro de Silva proceeded against them.[8] Both the Ballesteros and Claramontes were also oligarchical families and provided rebel leaders.[9] Less prominent in the affray, but actively participating, were individuals from other leading families such as the Fontanar, the Córdoba, the Llerena, and the Tellado.[10] Nevertheless the commitment was not wholehearted in all cases and many families would be too hostile even for the rebels to consider asking for their support. It is hardly surprising, for example, that not one member of the important family of the Guerreros was involved and nobody from the equally important families of the Noguerol or Bustos is mentioned in the *pesquisa* or even alluded to by the witnesses. It was imperative, therefore, that allies and potential allies should be canvassed and brought into line by both sides and it was to this task that the night hours were devoted. But from the very start things started to go wrong for the rebels.

Their first step was to demand support from "pledged" allies like Gonzalo Pinero and Pedro de Henarejos. Fernando de Bustamante, for example, went in person to Pinero's house and told him to arm himself and his men and join the rebels. This Pinero promptly did and turned up with his armed *amigos* and *parientes*. But having done so, he asked the rebels why he had been summoned and then, astonishingly, he not only proceeded to make a statement but he demanded that an *escribano* should give him a written testimony of its contents. The statement was punctilious. The rebels had demanded Pinero's support and he had accordingly turned up with his armed men in order to demonstrate that he was prepared to help them against their enemies. However, Pinero added, it was clear that the rebels had entered the town without the approval

---

[7] A. Pretel Marín, *op. cit.*, pp. 62, 73 and 80.
[8] This is stated in the *sentencia:* see above, footnote 6.
[9] A. Pretel Marín, *op. cit.*, pp. 73, 111, 168 and 176.
[10] *Ibid.*, pp. 73, 111, 120, 143, 168, 170, 176.

of the *corregidor* and he, Pinero, in no way intended to help them against the *corregidor* (18ᵛ-19ᵛ).

Having got the *testimonio* of his statement, Pinero wanted to return home, but he was persuaded by Fernando de Bustamante to accompany him and mediate in another possible source of support. This time the objective was the house of Bustamante's aunt and her sons, and Pinero's presence was probably calculated to soften the strained relations between these two branches of the family. But Bustamante failed to get the *favor* and *ayuda* of his cousins and the old lady turned him down flat by saying that "nunca dios quisiese que ella nin sus fijos fuesen contra la justiçia" (19ᵛ).

Once again Bustamante and his companions set off, but this time they planned to use a third party in order to obtain the support of two nobles, Rodrigo and Vasco Frutoso (15ᵛ, 20ʳ). The man chosen for this mission was Juan de Claramonte the Elder whose son, Juan de Claramonte the Younger, was one of the leading participants in the affray. The Elder Claramonte was clearly worried about his son and seems to have spent most of the night on horseback, armed with a sword and shield and accompanied by two foot-soldiers, visiting interested parties (14ʳ, 27ᵛ, 35ᵛ). The evidence of the witnesses suggests an ambivalent attitude. On the one hand he was heard to say in the *plaza* that it grieved him that he was old but that he had sons and enough grain and wine to help (the rebels) (32ʳ-32ᵛ); but, on the other hand, he was seen drawing up at Fernando de Bustamante's house and shouting "Aqui mal fecho. Aqui mal fecho" (35ᵛ). This, then, was the man who was sent off to secure the help of the Frutosos. The evidence of Rodrigo Frutoso, however, suggests that Claramonte the Elder was mainly concerned about his son. In effect he asked the Frutosos

... que les ploguiese poner en estos fechos algund remedio por que non se perdiese su fijo. E que ellos le dixeron que non le podian poner remedio ninguno en este fecho. E que deque esta respuesta le dieron que les dixo que les ploguiese de ser todos en vna opinion para echar al corregidor de esta çibdad por que non fisiesen justiçia de su fijo sy la meresçia. E que ellos le respondieron que eran fidalgos e que avian fecho juramento e pleito omenaje al corregidor de ser con la justiçia del rey e con el dicho corregidor e que ante morrian que non ser contra la justiçia del rey e con el dicho corregidor. E que entonçes les dixo el dicho Juan de Claramonte que pues non querian ser con el que les rogaua que non fuesen en ayuda del corregidor e que se estouiesen en su casa quedos e que ellos se convernian con el corregidor e lo echarian fuera desta çibdad (13ᵛ).

Once again, therefore, the rebels failed to secure additional support.

Meanwhile, in another part of the town, important developments were taking place in the house of the *bachiller* Diego González de Montiel, a personage of substance who was to become an *oidor* of the royal *audiencia* and a member of the royal council.[11] Some fifty armed men had gathered in the *bachiller*'s house (17ʳ) and it is a tribute to his deviousness that some witnesses at the *pesquisa* thought that he was supporting the rebels whereas others were equally convinced that he was on the *corregidor*'s side. In fact he seems to have employed a form of psychological warfare in order to manipulate the rebels into a losing position, pretending first to be on their side and then leaving them stranded. Early on the *bachiller* visited the house of the rebel leader, Juan de Ballesteros, and said: "Juan de Ballesteros, demostradme la gente que theneys aqui". He was shown some forty armed men and he then said to Ballesteros: "Sabed que vos quiere el corregidor venir a prender. Por eso defendeos bien, que para los que salieren para la otra parte en su favor yo thengo en mi casa reparo para dar en ellos" (17ʳ). In the light of subsequent events, this was a masterly move by the *bachiller*. He had discovered the number of armed men at Ballesteros' disposal without revealing the extent of his own support. More important, Ballesteros was made to feel that the rebels were already on the defensive, that the *corregidor* was poised to attack and that the balance of power lay with the *bachiller* and his men.

The *corregidor*, for his part, clearly felt that he could count on the *bachiller*'s party and he had confirmed this by messenger (25ʳ). The next step, therefore, was to let the news filter through to the rebels that they had failed to gain the support of another powerful man — the *bachiller* himself. The opportunity to do this came when Claramonte the Elder turned up. "Bachiller", he said, "¿que mandays?". "Esto aqui", came the reply, "para seruiçio del rey con estos mis parientes para quando el sennor corregidor me enbiare a llamar" (26r). Not surprisingly this reply provoked a later visit by two representatives from the rebels who must have been anxious by now to establish what exactly the *bachiller*'s position was. "Sennor. Juan de Ballesteros e Fernando de Bustamante e Juan de Bustamante nos enbian aca a vos, que ellos e sus parientes quieren poner vna sospecha al corregidor, que sy vos sy quereys ponerla" (26ʳ). The *bachiller*, of course, refused to do this, but it is a tribute to his skill

---

[11] The *bachiller* was also an *oidor* and royal councillor during the reigns of John II and Henry IV according to Pretel Marín, *op. cit.*, pp. 169 and 304-05.

that he also seems to have persuaded the two rebel representatives to find out for him what the rebels were up to (32ᵛ).

By early morning it was apparent that the rebels' position was untenable and that their potential support had crumbled badly — they had failed to recruit Gonzalo Pinero and his party, the Bustamante cousins, the Frutosos and above all the wily *bachiller*. In fact in the morning Pinero brought his men to the *alcázar* to serve the *corregidor* and they remained in his service until the rebels surrendered the towers (21ʳ). As for the *bachiller*, the words of one witness put the matter succinctly: "... por causa del dicho bachiller se fueron los que asy heran entrados contra el dicho corregidor, e avn que despues oyo desir que el dicho sennor corregidor auia seydo muy gososo por lo que el dicho bachiller auia fecho, por que era seruiçio del sennor rey" (25ʳ).

There can be little doubt that this affray in Alcaraz was regarded by the authorities as being one of the utmost gravity. It provoked a stern letter from Henry IV demanding action and it was followed by an extensive enquiry headed not just by the *corregidor* but by an important military official brought in for the purpose, along with his men, from Murcia. It appears to be a classic case of urban anarchy, involving political and social violence, the complete disregard of royal justice and royal officials by *malhechores,* and armed conflict and bloodshed. Yet it is worth looking at this "anarchy" more closely.

The most obvious starting point is to total up the numbers who were killed and wounded during the fighting. In fact the total number of the killed and wounded, on all sides, was precisely nil. Moreover the only episode of "fighting" which took place bears the hallmark of farce. At the very start of the affray one of the *corregidor*'s men, taken unawares, took refuge inside the church of the Trinidad. Quickly found and disarmed, he was then apparently allowed to flee and was described by one witness as being *desgreñado* (24ᵛ). Presumably this might just count as an injury, but it is worth reflecting that almost any contemporary football match produces more injuries among the players (let alone the spectators). The analogy may sound far-fetched, but it is certainly worth pondering whether fifteenth-century Castilian *alborotos* and disorders of this type were also governed by "rules" which limited the extent of the violence.

Much of what happened in Alcaraz depended upon the bonds of cohesion, or the lack of cohesion, among the various groups involved. Chief among these were the bonds of kinship. Gonzalo Pinero testified "que el se armo e otros amigos e parientes suyos" (19ʳ). The *corregidor* counted on the support of the *bachiller* "e sus parientes" (25ʳ), and the *bachiller* for his part told Claramonte the Elder: "Esto aqui para seruiçio del rey con estos mis parientes para quando el sennor corregidor me enbiare a llamar" (26ʳ). Similarly it was the rebels "e sus parientes" who wanted the *bachiller* to level a *sospecha* against the *corregidor* (26ʳ). The witnesses give enough evidence to support these vague references to *parientes*. [12] In the *bachiller*'s house on the night in question, for example, there were his own brother, Alfonso González de Montiel, three brothers with the surname Alcalá, three men bearing the name Algasi and two bearing the name Siles. Among the invaders there were two Bustamante brothers, three Ballesteros brothers (who were later helped by their mother), a Tellado father and son, two Platero brothers and two Cabrejano brothers (and possibly one of their sons and another relation). Then, of course, there were those who joined in once the affray had started: Juan de Claramonte the Elder trying to help his son, the two sons of Juan Sánchez de Albacete and the two sons of Alfonso López Zapatero.

But in addition to these kinship links, there were other bonds of cohesion. The participation of some is to be explained by the fact that they were already in the service of others. For example Sancho de Brotes and Fernando de Alarcón, as has been seen, were *criados* of the Bustamante brothers and three men are all described as "mozos de Diego el Sastre" (11ʳ). Of greater interest are the links of *fe*, implying an oath of faithfulness or a definite pledge of support. Thus Pedro de Henarejos explained his actions in terms of the *fe* which he had given to the rebels: "... dixo ... que se armo, pero que no se armo para contra la justiçia saluo por la fe que este testigo les auia dado ..." (35ʳ). Likewise Bustamante had summoned Pinero and his men "guardando aquella fe que le tenia dada", and when they did turn up, the rebels once again asked Pinero "que les guardase la fe que les avia prometido para les ayudar e fauoresçer" (18ᵛ-19ʳ). Significantly, at no point in their evidence did either Henarejos or Pinero deny that they had pledged their *fe*. Lastly, of course, many individuals talked in terms of loyalty to the Crown, interpreting this as being support for the king's officials and the royal justice which they administered. The Frutoso brothers stood by their oath as *hidalgos* to be on the king's side, Fernando de Bustamante's aunt

---

[12] Folio numbers are not given for what follows because, being scattered throughout the *pesquisa*, the evidence would require extensive references.

refused to bring her sons out "contra la justiçia", Pinero argued that his
fe did not extend to supporting the rebels against the *corregidor* and the
bachiller had brought his men out in support of Pedro de Silva.

The abiding impression from the evidence is that all these bonds
— of kinship, service, *fe,* and loyalty to the Crown — were very real
and yet very unstable and that they were also potentially contradictory.
Presumably before embarking on such an affray, the leaders would have
made their calculations about the potential support which they could
expect from *parientes,* friends and allies who had pledged their *fe.* But
only practice would reveal whether their calculations were correct and
each type of potentially cohesive bond might be defective. The Ballesteros
brothers, for example, must surely have thought that another brother,
Mendo, would support them. Yet Mendo himself appeared as a witness
in the *pesquisa* (39^r-40^v). Worse still their uncle, Juan Jordán, declared
in his evidence "que cree que quantos males ay en esta çibdad que lo
a causado Juan de Ballesteros" and it would even seem that the uncle
had attached himself to the *bachiller's* party during the crisis (31^r-32^v).
Similarly Fernando de Bustamante obviously hoped that his cousins
would be persuaded by family loyalty, but he was wrong. Men counted
on kinship links, but they did not invariably work. The same was true
of the pledges of *fe,* as the actions of Pinero demonstrated. And, as far
as loyalty to the Crown was concerned, despite the impressive statements
of a few individuals, there was obviously a substantial number of people
willing to attempt an attack on the royal *corregidor.*

The instability of these bonds of loyalty, therefore, would seem to
provide the grounds for anarchy, violence and bloodshed. Yet, presented
with the breaking of bonds, the men in Alcaraz did not resort to violence
but seem, instead, to have obeyed certain dignified "rules" of behaviour.
Absurdly, it may seem, Gonzalo Pinero, in the middle of the rebels'
headquarters, dictated his views to a royal *escribano* and demanded a
written testimony of how he had kept to his *fe,* while at the same time
refusing to fight because his *fe* did not cover an attack on the *corregidor.*
Why did the rebels not kill him on the spot, or at least insult and abuse
him? Instead, off he went with Fernando de Bustamante to visit the
latter's aunt! And when the aunt refused her family's help, why did Bustamante not threaten revenge? Why did Claramonte the Elder not revile
the Frutosos for refusing to save his son? It would almost seem as if
a voting procedure took place that night and, after all the votes of the
relevant parties had been cast, the outcome of the affray was decided.

Negotiations and "votes", not fighting, decided the issue. If all Castilian affrays were like this, then fifteenth-century violence would seem to be a remarkably sophisticated, even peaceful, phenomenon.

Why, then, did Henry IV and his officials take such an interest in this particular incident in Alcaraz? After all, resistance to royal justice and attacks on *corregidores* were almost commonplace. Pretel calculates that in Alcaraz itself *corregidores* were expelled in 1451, 1460 and 1463. [13] Moreover, if the rebels had succeeded, this would not have been the first time that Pedro de Silva suffered such an indignity, for in 1440, in a similar incident, the *corregidor* had been expelled from Segovia. [14]

The answer may be that all such incidents gave rise to a *pesquisa* and that it is only by accident that this particular *pesquisa* has survived. But it is far more likely that the royal anxiety arose from the fact that the affray of 1458 was only one element in a much larger and complicated picture.

In his evidence Juan Jordán had blamed his nephew, Juan de Ballesteros, for all the troubles plaguing Alcaraz. He did not give reasons for this statement, but another witness, none other than the *hidalgo* Rodrigo Frutoso, gives us the essential information. In his evidence Frutoso stated that:

> ... sabe que quando fase Juan de Ballesteros que lo fase con fauor que tiene de Alfonso Fajardo. Preguntado como lo sabe, dixo que por que el dicho Juan de Ballesteros le dixo que el dicho Fajardo le escrive cartas, e que tiene un hermano con el dicho Alfonso Fajardo que biue con el, e que se alaba publicamente que tyene fauor con el, e que agora que esta con el dicho Fajardo en Lorca. E que sabe el testigo que el dicho Juan de Ballesteros se desafio con Diego de Aguayo, criado del rey, por que el dicho Diego de Aguayo tenia la bos del rey contra Alfonso Fajardo, e el dicho Juan de Ballesteros tenia la bos en ayuda e fauor de Fajardo. Preguntado como lo sabe, dixo que por que ge lo dixeron en aquesta çibdad algunos vesinos della, e es asy verdad (13^r).

According to this crucial evidence, therefore, we learn that yet another Ballesteros brother "lived with" Alonso Fajardo, and that Juan de Ballesteros acted with the *favor* of Fajardo and had challenged Diego de Aguayo, a royal supporter who was also, incidentally, the nephew of Gonzalo Carrillo, one of the two officials entrusted with carrying out the *pesquisa*.

---

[13] Pretel Marín, *op. cit.*, p. 171.
[14] See Pedro Carrillo de Huete, *Crónica del Halconero de Juan II*, ed. Juan de Mata Carriazo (Madrid, 1946), p. 304.

Much more important, however, were the activities of Alonso Fajardo. During 1455 and 1456 Alcaraz had been caught up in frontier warfare, its lands had been ravaged, its finances exhausted and it was alleged that Alonso Fajardo had aided and abetted the Muslim attacks. [15] Then, early in 1457, Henry IV intervened decisively in the political struggle for domination in the south-east of the kingdom. He confirmed Pedro Fajardo in the *adelantamiento* of Murcia and entrusted him with the task of crushing his cousin, the "traitor" Alonso Fajardo. [16] It was to the latter, a friend of the king of Granada and his Muslim commanders, that the leaders of the affray were allied. During 1457 Alonso Fajardo's Christian and Moorish troops attacked the lands of Murcia, the *maestrazgo* of Santiago and the *arcedianazgo* of Alcaraz. It was at this stage that Henry IV sent in Gonzalo Carrillo with two hundred knights and in fact Carrillo almost immediately trapped one of Fajardo's expeditions in the Alcaraz region, while the men of Alcaraz themselves managed to neutralise the Fajardo stronghold of Letur. [17] By mid-October Alonso Fajardo was in serious trouble: his *alcaide* of Alhama had betrayed him and surrendered the fortress to Carrillo, and the royalists under Pedro Fajardo and Carrillo had defeated him and his Moorish allies at Molina. [18]

It was at this stage that Alonso Fajardo retreated into his stronghold of Lorca and, as Frutoso's evidence shows, one of the Ballesteros brothers was there with him. Later the royal forces would close in on him, including Gonzalo Carrillo and a contingent from Alcaraz under Pedro de Silva. [19] Meanwhile, however, Fajardo tightened his links with his Moorish friends and gave his "favour" to the attempted preemptive strike against Alcaraz in January 1458. Small wonder that the royal authorities were so interested in the affray and that its leaders found it difficult to secure additional support during that long January night of negotiations.

ANGUS MACKAY

University of Edinburgh

---

[15] Pretel Marín, *op. cit.*, pp. 111-13.
[16] *Ibid.*, p. 115.
[17] *Ibid.*, p. 117.
[18] *Ibid.*, p. 118; J. Torres Fontes, *Don Pedro Fajardo, adelantado mayor de Murcia* (Madrid, 1953), pp. 76-77.
[19] Pretel Marín, *op. cit.*, p. 118.

THE ADMIRAL OF CASTILE AND ANTONIO DE VELASCO: *CANCIONERO* COUSINS

Don Antonio de Velasco al Almirante, pintándole:

De gatilla tiene el tono
quanto más alto se entona;
de la cinta arriba es mono,
de la cinta abajo es mona.
Patillas de macho toma,
y las piernas de vençejo.
Algo tiene de conejo,
mucho tiene de paloma.

MP2, fol. 231ᵛ

HERNANDO del Castillo's *Cancionero general* (11CG), first printed by Cristóbal Kofman in 1511 and an enormous commercial success in expanded editions throughout the sixteenth century, features compositions attributed to "El Almirante" and "Antonio de Velasco".[1] In common with the great majority of *Cancionero general* poets, the two men have since remained little more than names and rubrics. This is a situation which can be only partially accounted for by the relative scarcity of documentary evidence among the surviving prime sources for the late fifteenth and early sixteenth centuries; there has also been a marked lack of critical interest, until comparatively recently, in the aspirations and aims of a group of poets who frequently practised genres which can be seen to be "difficult". The verses of these poets frequently contain elliptical or obscure allusions to the events and personalities of the time; a high proportion of these allusions will remain impenetrable, however, until more is known about the personalities, places and relationships in-

---

[1] Hernando del Castillo, *Cancionero general* (Valencia: Cristóbal Kofman, 1511); reproduced in facsimile, with introduction, índices, and appendices, by Antonio Rodríguez-Moñino (Madrid: Real Academia Española, 1958). For the most recent and most detailed description of its contents, see Brian Dutton, *Catálogo-Índice de la poesía cancioneril del siglo XV*, 2 vols. in one (Madison: Hispanic Seminary of Medieval Studies, 1982), I, pp. 163-87. Dutton's work analyses 190 manuscripts, and 221 editions compiled between 1474 and 1520; in this article I adopt Dutton's classification system throughout.

volved. [2] My aim in this article is to identify and throw a little more light on the characters of the Admiral of Castile and Antonio de Velasco.

In the first edition of 11CG Hernando del Castillo included only two compositions of "El Almirante". These were the twelve-line *canción* "Quando de vós me partía" (fol. 127ᵛ) and the two-line *invención* "La mejor vida es aquella" (fol. 141ʳ). Rodríguez-Moñino (pp. 152 and 169) attributes to the Admiral a third composition, "Es pena grave el tormento" (fol. 127ᵛ). The attribution, however, is due to an oversight by the editor, who failed to notice that the *canción,* with its rubric "otra suya", is immediately prefaced by a *canción* attributed to "un galán". [3] In 1511 Castillo appears not to have considered the Admiral a major poet, and it would seem reasonable to deduce that unless the compiler included his verses simply because they were among those which he had to hand, the Admiral was then accorded a place in the collection principally out of deference to his family pedigree.

The Enríquez family, directly descended from Alfonso XI of Castile, was one of the richest and most influential in Spain. The title of *Almirante de Castilla* was bestowed in 1405 on Alonso Enríquez, one of the bastard sons of Fadrique Enríquez of Castile, who in turn was a bastard son

---

2 The work of Juan Bautista Avalle-Arce, who has rescued Pedro de Cartagena, the Vizconde de Altamira and Perálvarez de Ayllón from oblivion, is an admirable example of what can be achieved in terms of biographical research. See, for example, *Temas hispánicos medievales* (Madrid: Gredos, 1974), pp. 280-367; "Cartagena, poeta del *Cancionero general*", *BRAE*, XLVII (1967), 287-310; "Más sobre Pedro de Cartagena, converso y poeta del *Cancionero general*", *Modern Language Studies*, XI (1981), 70-82; "Algo más sobre el poeta Vizconde de Altamira", *Crítica Hispánica*, II (1980), 3-12. Avalle-Arce has recently drawn attention to what may prove to be one of the most valuable single sources of information on this period, in the form of Gonzalo Fernández de Oviedo's *Batallas y quinquagenas*, the massive second part of which is preserved, in an autograph copy of 1026 fols., in the Biblioteca Universitaria at Salamanca (MS 359). He describes his find in "Fernández de Oviedo, biógrafo inédito. Muestras de una edición", *Anuario de Letras*, XVIII (1980), 117-63, along with an announcement that the text is shortly to be published by the University of Salamanca in its collection "Tesoro Bibliográfico". Professor Avalle-Arce has generously allowed me to see, in advance of publication, the *Diálogo* from *Batallas* (fols. 271ʳ-80ᵛ) which is relevant to the Admiral of Castile (the part devoted to Antonio de Velasco is missing from the Salamanca MS), and I should like to express my appreciation here for the practical help which he has afforded me in the preparation of this article.

3 Jacqueline Steunou and Lothar Knapp, *Bibliografía de los cancioneros castellanos del siglo XV y repertorio de sus géneros poéticos*, 2 vols. (Paris: Centre National de la Recherche Scientifique, 1975-78), correctly list this poem as anonymous (I, p. 409 and II, p. 145), as does Dutton, *Catálogo-Índice*, I, p. 172). Unfortunately, the Admiral is omitted from the Author Index of Dutton's *Catálogo-Índice*, so that there is no quick way of determining how many of his compositions are included in the 411 collections analysed therein.

of Alfonso XI, and it remained hereditary in the family for precisely three hundred years from that date. The fact that Alonso Enríquez's mother was commonly reputed to have been "una judía hermosa", known as Doña Paloma, led to a constant series of gibes and accusations about the *pureza de sangre* of the Enríquez family throughout the fifteenth and sixteenth centuries. In Francesillo de Zúñiga's *Crónica burlesca del emperador Carlos V,* for example, Charles V's jester, himself an open *converso,* refers jocularly, in a letter to the fourth Admiral, to the unshakeability of their friendship. The text of the most reliable manuscript, MS 6193 of the Biblioteca Nacional, Madrid, reads simply: "Vuestra Señoría sea cierto que la liga y amistad que hicimos, por mí nunca se quebrará; y por Vuestra Señoría menos, porque nunca grillo quebró lanza ni otra cosa". [4] The text printed by Pascual de Gayangos, however, which is characterized by a number of later and evidently corrupt insertions, amplifies the sentence with a clear allusion to the fourth Admiral's rumoured Jewish origins: "y también porque la sangre sin fuego hierve, según el deudo que yo é vuestra señoría tenemos". [5] Rumours about the Enríquez's Jewish blood are to be found in the proceedings of the Inquisition, but Fernández de Oviedo vehemently denounces these as malicious gossip, names Alonso Enríquez's mother as the wife of a steward in his father's household, and insists that Alonso was brought up by the Jewess in order to "encobrir a la madre verdadera e disimular el parto". [6] The prime candidate for the authorship of the two 11CG compositions must be this "amigo" of Francesillo de Zúñiga, Fadrique Enríquez, the fourth admiral in the line, as suggested by the rubric to a ten-line *copla* of Tapia, "Gran dolor es veros yr" (11CG, fol. 16ᵛ), which is addressed to "don Fadrique Enríquez, Almirante de Castilla".

On the death of his father Alonso, Fadrique inherited the family holdings in the Palencia area, along with the stronghold of Medina de Rioseco, and was appointed to the *almirantazgo* and the *veintecuatría* of Seville by the Catholic Monarchs, Ferdinand and Isabella, on 14

---

[4] Ed. Diane Pamp de Avalle-Arce (Barcelona: Crítica, 1981), p. 160.
[5] BAE, XXXVI, 49b.
[6] See Nicolás López Martínez, *Los judaizantes castellanos y la Inquisición en tiempo de Isabel la Católica* (Burgos: Seminario Metropolitano, 1954). More details of the Enríquez family can be found in Florentino Pérez Embid, *El almirantazgo de Castilla hasta las capitulaciones de Santa Fe* (Sevilla: Escuela de Estudios Hispano-Americanos, 1944), and Enrique Martínez López, "El rival de Garcilaso: *Esse que de mi s'está reyendo*", BRAE, LXI (1981), 191-281, at 211, n. 34.

February 1490. [7] Ferdinand was the Admiral's first cousin, the son of Juan II of Aragon and Fadrique's aunt Juana Enríquez de Córdoba; the family connections with the recently created County of Haro were also close, since Fadrique's mother was María de Velasco, the sister of Pedro Fernández de Velasco, the first Constable of Castile, and daughter of Pedro Fernández de Velasco, first Count of Haro. [8] The relevant genealogy is as follows:

TABLE I

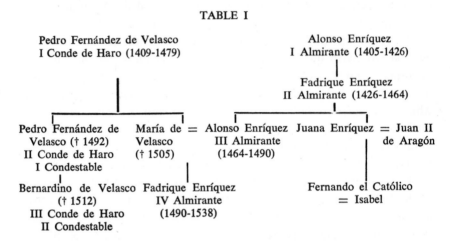

Birthdates are notoriously difficult to unearth, but a passing reference by Fernando del Pulgar in his *Crónica de los reyes católicos* reveals that in 1481 Fadrique Enríquez had not attained his twentieth birthday: Pulgar's text makes it clear that he was then old enough to become involved in a squabble with the Leonese Ramiro Núñez de Guzmán over

---

[7] Alonso López de Haro, *Nobiliario genealógico de los reyes y títulos de España*, 2 vols. Madrid: Luis Sánchez, 1622), I, p. 399, gives the date of Alonso Enríquez's death as May 1485, but appears to be in error. Fadrique's official appointment to the *almirantazgo*, succeeding "dicho almirante vuestro padre, por quanto es finado", is confirmed by a document signed by Ferdinand and Isabella on 14 February 1490 (Archivo Municipal Sevillano, Tumbo de los Reyes Católicos, III, fol. 326ᵛ, quoted by Pérez Embid, *El almirantazgo*, p. 159).

[8] Pedro Fernández de Velasco could be the *Condestable* who contributes an *invención* to 11CG (fol. 141ᵛ), based on the term "penas" with its dual sense "feathers", "suffering". Francisco Rico, "*Un penacho de penas*. Sobre tres invenciones del *Cancionero general*", *Romanistisches Jahrbuch*, XVII (1966), 274-84, analyses the word-play convincingly, but does not concern himself with identifying the author. Pedro Fernández died in 1492, and was succeeded by his son Bernardino, who became the second *Condestable* of Castile. Either could be responsible for this *invención*.

seating arrangements next to the ladies of the court in Valladolid, and thus we can reasonably assume an age of eighteen or nineteen, and a birthdate of 1462/63. [9] Pulgar devotes a whole chapter to the events in Valladolid, from which the young Fadrique emerges as a headstrong and difficult young man, who offended Isabella sufficiently to be consigned after the episode to a period of exile in Sicily. Later chronicle entries, however, show that by 1489 he had sufficiently reinstated himself in the favour of the Queen to play a full part in the Granada campaign; he was involved, along with such noblemen as the Duke of Alba, Juan Téllez-Girón and Juan Pacheco, in the siege of Baza. [10] Fernández de Oviedo comments that "por su mucho valor y edad y generosidad [fue] muy acatado e estimado, e por su prudencia e persona muy bien quisto e amado"; López de Haro, who describes him as "muy excelente señor, de grande esfuerço y valor", records his presence at the capitulation of Granada in 1492. [11]

The evidence of the *cancioneros,* however, along with that of Charles V's jester, Francesillo de Zúñiga, and the *chistes* recorded in the sixteenth century by Luis de Pinedo, suggest that the courage in battle alluded to by the chroniclers must have been achieved in the face of a daunting lack of inches, and that Fadrique's achievements as a poet were handicapped by a less than perfect musical tone. Antonio de Velasco refers in a *canción* (MP2, fol. 231v, reproduced at the head of this article) to the Admiral's "tono de gatilla", his "piernas de vençejo", and to rabbit-like and dove-like qualities not entirely appropriate to the man of action. Dr. Melgar advises (MP2, fol. 231v), that:

> Al Almirante no miren,
> que no le pueden mirar,
> y aunque de cerca le tiren,
> no le podrán açertar.
> Es jota de saber,
> y mínimo de natura...

---

[9] Edition and study by Juan de Mata Carriazo, 2 vols., CCE, V-VI (Madrid: Espasa-Calpe, 1943). Fadrique's uncle, Pedro Fernández de Velasco, is reported as interceding on Fadrique's behalf with this plea to the queen: "Señora, yo traigo aquí a don Fadrique, mi sobrino, e lo entrego a Vuestra Señoría, para que mande hazer dél lo que por bien toviere: pero vmillemente le suplico que considere que no á veynte años, y que esta hedad no es avn bien capaz para saber el acatamiento e obidiençia que se deve a los mandamientos reales" (I, cap. 121, p. 443).

[10] *Crónica de los Reyes Católicos,* II, caps. 242, 247 and 250.

[11] *Batallas,* fol. 271r; *Nobiliario,* I, p. 399.

The musician and poet Gabriel is no less unkind, in a poem addressed to the Admiral and preserved on the same folio:

> Con pulgas y con dolor
> es inpossible, señor,
> poder dormir la persona;
> y más una mona
> que le cantava al albor.

Fadrique Enríquez was, by all accounts, an unexceptional singer and a dramatically small man. [12]

The honorific title of *Almirante* was hereditary, and seafaring skills were not a prerequisite for succession. Not surprisingly, therefore, the only reference to Fadrique's prowess as a sailor which I have been able to trace (his name is conspicuously absent from accounts of sea-battles fought in the wars of Granada) involves a diplomatic mission to Flanders. In 1496, by command of Ferdinand and Isabella, the fourth Admiral of Castile conducted the *infanta* Juana ("la Loca") to Flanders, to join her husband, the Archduke Philip the Fair; he returned with Philip's sister Margaret, the bride-to-be of the *infante* Juan. [13] Fadrique reached the height of his political power during the revolt of the *comuneros*: in 1520, along with his cousin Íñigo Fernández de Velasco, third Constable of Castile, and Cardinal Adrian of Utrecht, Charles V's former tutor, he became joint governor of Spain during Charles's absence in

---

[12] Francesillo de Zúñiga likens him to a "ratón con gualdrapa" (*Crónica burlesca*, XXIX, p. 167). Luis de Pinedo, *Sales españolas o agudezas del ingenio nacional*, BAE, CLXXVI, pp. 97-118, includes four jokes concerning Fadrique Enríquez (pp. 99a, 103a, 112b and 113a), all of which concern his diminutive stature. I reproduce two of these:

El Conde de Urueña y el Almirante Don Fadrique, estando reñidos sobre cierta cosa que el conde había dicho del Almirante, el Almirante le escribió una carta de desafío, y el Conde, después de haber detenido muchos días al mensagero, le respondió por otra carta que decía:

> Muy ilustre Señor:
> vuestra carta rescebí,
> que ni quiero matar mono,
> ni que mono mate a mí.

Porque el Almirante era muy pequeño.   (p. 99a)

El Almirante D. Fadrique servía de maestresala un día a la Reina Doña Isabel, y Don Juan de Mendoza hacía aire con un ventalle, porque era verano, y una vez descuidóse, y díjole la Reina: —Por qué no echas aire? Respondió: —Señora, por no levar la maestresala de la mesa.
(El Almirante era muy pequeño)   (pp. 112b-13a)

[13] *Nobiliario*, I, p. 399. López de Haro gives the impossible date of "mil quatrocientos y sesenta y nueue" (Juana was born in 1479).

Flanders, and played a vigorous and dedicated part in imposing peace on the country. The Emperor subsequently honoured him with the Burgundian Order of the Toison d'Or. [14] Fadrique's concerned exchange of letters in 1524 with Gonzalo Fernández de Oviedo on "los males de Spaña y la causa dellos" is preserved in MS 7075 of the Biblioteca Nacional, Madrid, and has recently been edited and studied by Juan Bautista Avalle-Arce. [15] Four letters survive from Antonio de Guevara, Bishop of Mondoñedo, dated between 1528 and 1534 and addressed to the Admiral; these suggest that Fray Antonio found himself somewhat harassed by the prolixity of the ageing Admiral's correspondence. [16]

During his period of exile in Sicily Fadrique married the wealthy Ana de Cabrera, Condesa de Módica and Vizcondesa de Cabrera y Bas, and contemporaries and chroniclers of the period frequently use one or other of these ancient Catalonian titles, referring to him loosely as Fadrique de Cabrera or Conde de Módica. Dr. Melgar is thus able to combine a pun on the Admiral's title with a slighting reference to the Admiral's wit and stature in the conclusion to "Al Almirante no le miren", quoted above:

> Es jota de saber
> y mínimo de natura;
> y porque módico fue
> módica fue su natura.

He had no official claim to either title but he was, in his own right, third Count of Melgar, Lord of Medina de Rioseco, Mansilla, Rueda, Aguilar and Villabrajima, and one of the richest men in Spain, with an annual income estimated by Fernández de Oviedo at fifty thousand ducats. [17] Ana de Cabrera's death in 1523 appears to have profoundly affected Fadrique; Francesillo de Zúñiga observes in a letter of 1527 that "las nuevas que acá hay, son que dicen que Vuestra Señoría se quiere meter fraile", and

---

[14] Fray Prudencio de Sandoval, *Historia del Emperador Carlos V* (BAE, LXXX, p. 319); Fernández de Oviedo, *Batallas*, fol. 280ᵛ. For the leading part played by Fadrique Enríquez in settling the troubles of 1520-21, see Sandoval, Libros VII-IX, *passim*.

[15] In "Dos preocupados del Siglo de Oro", *Anuario de Letras*, XIII (1975), 113-63.

[16] *Epístolas familiares de Fray Antonio de Guevara*, ed. José M. de Cossío (Madrid, 1950), I, pp. 199-203, 204-08, 213-18 and 459-69.

[17] Cf. Luis de Salazar y Castro, *Historia genealógica de la casa de Lara*, 4 vols. (Madrid, 1694-97), II, p. 47, and Fernández de Oviedo, *Batallas*, fol. 280ᵛ.

cannot resist the almost obligatory joke about the Admiral's size. [18]
Although in practice Fadrique did not take holy orders, he did establish
a Franciscan house in Medina de Rioseco, and there is one literary
survival from this period of late religious activity. This is *Las quatrocientas respuestas a otras tantas preguntas,* a collection of uninspired verse
by the Riosecan friar Luis de Escobar, who twelve years after Fadrique's
death dedicated his book to the sixth Admiral "don Luys Enrriquez
Almirante de Castilla y doña Ana de Cabrera duquesa de Medina su
muger". [19] Fadrique Enríquez died childless in 1538, and was buried
alongside his wife in the monastery of San Francisco de Rioseco; his
younger brother Fernando succeeded him as Admiral of Castile. [20]

José María Azáceta and Alfred Morel-Fatio are among the very few
critics to identify Fadrique Enríquez and draw attention to his involvement with the world of letters. Azáceta describes the Admiral as "una
figura literaria de alguna calidad", and Morel-Fatio observes that "don
Fadrique, quatrième *almirante* de la famille des Henriquez ... fut l'ami
ou le protecteur de tous les poètes de son temps". [21] Although Morel-
Fatio offers no evidence for his claim, the *Cancionero del Ateneo Barce-
lonés* (BA1) supplies a little support in the form of two *coplas* composed
by "un gentil hombre de casa del senyor Almirante" and addressed to
the daughter of Miçer Halcón. [22] It also seems probable that Gabriel [de
Mena], *el músico,* who figures prominently in the *Cancionero musical de
Palacio* (MP4), and is described as "cantor de la capilla del Rey" in
11CG, fol. 149[v], passed from the service of Ferdinand to that of the

---

[18] Francesillo advises his friend not to take the step, on the grounds that his
tiny body would be incompatible with the friar's habit: "porque con el hábito
parecería Vuestra Señoría duende-casa" (*Crónica burlesca*, XXVIII, pp. 160-61).

[19] Fray Luis de Escobar, *Las quatrocientas respuestas a otras tantas preguntas,*
2 vols. (Valladolid: Francisco Fernández de Córdoba, 1550-52). In practice there
are four hundred questions and answers in each of the two volumes, making eight
hundred in all. Although the title-page describes the author as "no nombrado, mas
de que era frayle menor", the Franciscan took great care to record his name for
posterity in an acrostic, and a note on the fly-leaf of the copy preserved in the
Biblioteca Nacional of Madrid (R. 2090-91) correctly identifies him as "Fr. Luys
de Escobar religioso observante de conv[to] de Rio Seco como de Jaca".

[20] *Nobiliario,* I, p. 400; Diego Gutiérrez Coronel, *Historia genealógica de la
casa de Mendoza,* ed. Ángel González Palencia, 2 vols. (Madrid: Sucesores de
Ocaña, 1945), I, p. 126.

[21] José María de Azáceta, *Cancionero de Juan Fernández de Ixar,* 2 vols.
(Madrid: CSIC, 1956), I, p. lxxxiv; A. Morel-Fatio, *L'Espagne au XVIe et au XVIIe
siècles* (Heilbronn: Henniger Frères, 1878), p. 499.

[22] These begin "Ante vuestra senyoría" (fol. 226[r]). See Pedro-Manuel Cátedra,
Poemas castellanos de cancioneros bilingües y otros manuscritos barceloneses (Exeter: EHT XXXIV, 1983), pp. 57-58.

fourth Admiral, most probably on Ferdinand's death in 1516. The rubric
to Gabriel's letter in verse "Muy magnífico señor" (MP2, fol. 231^r),
contains a reference to the "Almirante, su señor", and is addressed to "el
adelantado, hermano del Almirante", [23] while a reply of Juan de Mendoza to the Admiral in MP2, fol. 230^v, in addition to providing yet another
slighting reference to the latter's lack of inches, accuses the Admiral of
using his servants as ghost-writers, and begins:

> De la copla que a mí toca
> no es vuestro más del papel;
> siento las manos de Coca,
> oyo la voz de Gabriel;
> y pues qu'esto anssiés
> no tengo ningún remedio,
> pues que son contra mí tres,
> o a lo menos dos y medio... [24]

There is also evidence in the *Cancionero general* of 1554 of close
contact between the fourth Admiral and Juan de Boscán. Boscán ad-
dresses five compositions to the Admiral (Morel-Fatio, 27, 30, 31, 46,
48), and one to a friar (Luis de Escobar?) in the name of the Admiral
(Morel-Fatio, 29); there are two compositions addressed by the Admiral to
Boscán (Morel-Fatio, 26 and 45) [25] and one by "un frayle" (Escobar
again?) "respondiendo a Boscán en nombre del Almirante" (Morel-Fatio,
28). These exchanges rule out the remotest possibility that the *Almirante*
in question could have been Fadrique's father, Alonso, since the latter
died in 1490 when Boscán, by the most generous of estimates, could have
been no more than three years old. Boscán turned away from the writing
of poetry in traditional Castilian metres after his encounter with Andrea
Navagiero in 1526; this group of poems can thus be dated with security
within the first quarter of the sixteenth century, and we can be certain
that the Admiral in question was Fadrique Enríquez, the fourth of the line.

---

[23] Gabriel's *carta* also occurs in the *Cancionero general de obras nuevas* (Zaragoza, 1554), ed. Morel-Fatio in his *L'Espagne*, pp. 489-592.

[24] The reply, with some textual variants, also appears as no. CXX of the
Cancionero de Juan Fernández de Ixar, ed. Azáceta. I have not been able to
identify the mysterious "Coca" of line 3. He may simply have been the amanuensis.

[25] Four of these compositions (Morel-Fatio, 26-29) feature in the *Cancionero
de Ixar.* The Admiral's *coplas* "Pidos por merçed, Boscán" (cxv) produce the reply
"Otro mundo es el que ando" (cxvi) from Boscán; these are followed by further
respuestas, one by "vn frayle" to Boscán in the name of the Admiral (cxvii), and
one by Boscán to the friar in the name of the Admiral (cxviii).

Like the Admiral of Castile, Antonio de Velasco has just two compositions attributed to him in 11CG. Both are *canciones:* "Témesse mi triste suerte" (fol. 125^v) and "Si'l mal que vós m'aveys hecho" (fol. 127^v). Antonio's *mote* "Espiritus promptus est / caro autem es infirma" is also cited in Garci Sánchez de Badajoz's *Infierno de amores,* fol. 121^r. Unlike the Admiral, however, and much to the puzzlement of Marcelino Menéndez y Pelayo, he was in the course of the sixteenth century to become one of the admired poets of his generation, and *cancionero* collections, both manuscript and printed, increasingly feature his compositions. Dutton lists twenty-three compositions by Antonio de Velasco recorded before 1520.[26] Dutton's author index also includes a phantom "Antonio Velasco", to whom are attributed the *mote* "Yo que me pierdo por fe", 16RE, fol. 123^r (for which Resende's rubric reads "Dom antonio de valasco"), and the poem "Eu vi loba de Solia", 16RE, fol. 162^v (where Resende's rubric is "Outra a lobacurta de solia que fez don antonyo" and which clearly refers back to the "dom antoneo de valasco" mentioned in the heading to the preceding poem. This gives a real total of twenty-five compositions attributed to Antonio de Velasco; they are spread over a total of seven *cancioneros*: LB1, MP2, TP2, MN14, 11CG, 14CG, 16RE.

Antonio de Velasco is one of the thirty-eight characters chosen by Garci Sánchez to people the Erotic Hell of his *Infierno de amores,* but Garci Sánchez's editor, Patrick Gallagher, after drawing attention to the difficulties involved in collecting and arranging available scraps of information on the characters cited by Garci Sánchez, is able to devote rather less than a page of his "Critical Analysis" to Antonio. Biographical comment is confined to a misleading description of him as "the Conde de Nieva and the brother of Sancho de Velasco", and the more accurate observation that he was "the Commander and Deputy-governor of Burgos in 1521".[27] Menéndez y Pelayo considered Antonio worthy of a page of commentary (largely devoted to an anecdote told by Juan de Valdés), but made no attempt to identify him.[28] Neither Menéndez y Pelayo nor

---

[26] *Catálogo-Índice,* II, p. 196.

[27] *Infierno de amores* appears in 11CG, fols. 120-22, ed. Patrick Gallagher, *The Life and Works of Garci Sánchez de Badajoz* (London: Tamesis, 1968), pp. 97-112. For Gallagher's notes on Antonio and his spurious brother Sancho see pp. 221-23. Julia Castillo, *Cancionero de Garci Sánchez de Badajoz* (Madrid: Editora Nacional, 1980), p. 325, has no comment to make on either stanza 29 or Antonio de Velasco.

[28] *Antología de poetas líricos castellanos;* I quote from the Edición Nacional, vols. XVII-XXVI (Madrid: CSIC, 1944-45), of Menéndez y Pelayo's *Obras com-*

Gallagher enthuses about Antonio's literary ability: "Lo que hay de él en los *Cancioneros* nos le muestra más bien como hombre de mundo que como literato" (Menéndez y Pelayo); "he took no more than a dilettante interest in letters" (Gallagher).

Fortunately, the famous surname Velasco, along with the loose but helpful allusion to him as "Conde de Nieva", provide sufficient clues for an identification to be made. [29] Velasco is the family name of the Condes de Haro. Pedro Fernández de Velasco was created first Count of Haro by Juan II in 1430 as a reward for services rendered in the struggle against the Infantes de Aragón. The third son of his marriage to Beatriz Manrique was Sancho de Velasco, Lord of Arnedo and las Arenzanas (and thus uncle of Fadrique Enríquez, the son of Sancho's sister María). Sancho's wife, María Enríquez de la Carra, bore him two children, Antonio and Francisca. The elder of these, described incorrectly by López de Haro (*Nobiliario,* I, p. 183) as "segundo Conde de Nieua", is our poet.

López de Haro turns to the Condes de Nieva later in *Nobiliario* (I, pp. 565-66), and the complexity of the situation becomes evident. The second Count of Nieva was not Antonio de Velasco, but Pedro de Zúñiga. Pedro's eldest son Diego López de Zúñiga married Francisca de Velasco, and succeeded his father as third Count of Nieva: Pedro's daughter Francisca married the courtier and poet Antonio de Velasco, and subsequently succeeded her brother to the *condado* of Nieva. Velasco brother and sister married Zúñiga brother and sister: both women were called Francisca: Antonio de Velasco, after his wife became Condesa de Nieva, was frequently referred to as Conde de Nieva, although the only titles to which he could legitimately lay claim were those to the *señorío* of Arnedo and las Arenzanas inherited from his father.

---

pletas. Antonio de Velasco is discussed in vol. III of *Antología, Obras completas,* vol. XIX, pp. 156-57.

[29] He is referred to thus by Fray Prudencio de Sandoval, *Historia del Emperador Carlos V* (BAE, LXXX, p. 424).

TABLE II

Pedro Fernández de Velasco
I Conde de Haro

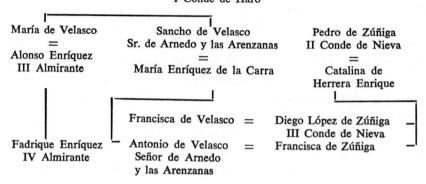

Antonio de Velasco was thus the first cousin and contemporary of Fadrique Enríquez, the *Almirante* of the *cancioneros*.

Antonio had no brother called Sancho, and the apocryphal character created by Gallagher arises from a failure to notice that stanzas 29 and 30 of the version of *Infierno de amores* preserved in 11CG have been copied out of order. Stanza 29 of the poem is dedicated to Antonio de Velasco, and reads as follows:

> Passaua mal sin medida
> don Antonio de Velasco,
> y ell esperança perdida,
> dezía con muy gran vasco:
> "Perdónesseme la vida,
> cruel amor" diziendo: "pues
> de matarme gana aués,
> y en ello mi mal se afirma,
> mi voluntad lo confirma:
> y *espiritus promptus es*
> *caro autem es infirma.*"

The following stanza in 11CG (30 in Gallagher's edition) begins with the line "Vi a don Sancho, su hermano", and gives rise to the confusion: this stems from an unawareness that the verse which mentions "don Sancho, su hermano" should precede, rather than follow, stanza 29. The first line points back to stanza 28, dedicated to Diego de Castilla, and the reference is to Sancho de Castilla, *maestresala* of Queen Isabella, and younger brother of Diego de Castilla, documented by López de Haro as Señor de Gor y el Boloduy. [30]

López de Haro records the date of death for Antonio's father Sancho as 1493, but gives no dates for Antonio. Resende's *Cancioneiro geral* (16RE) is of some help, however, since Antonio's *invención* "Que se pierda la memoria" (fol. 161^r) and his five-stanza gloss on it "Si son çeruelas de veras" (fol. 161^r) are prefaced by the rubric "De don Antoneo de Valhasco, esta[n]do en rrey nosso señor em Çaragoça, a hunas çeroylas de chamalote que fez Manuel de Noronha...". The reference can only be to the festivities held in Saragossa when Manuel I of Portugal, with his wife Isabella, went there to be sworn in as heirs to the Spanish throne by the Aragonese *cortes*. [31] This took place in 1498, and so we can be sure that Antonio was old enough to be composing in that year. He was still alive, and governing the city of Burgos at one point during the revolt of the *comuneros* in 1521; [32] I have so far been unable to trace a reference to the date of his death.

Although the surviving poetry of the two cousins is variable in quality, the best of their writing has literary merit, and was to attract the attention and admiration of scholars as eclectic as Juan de Valdés and Baltasar Gracián. Elsewhere, I have attempted a critical evaluation of some of their *cancionero* verse in the light of the observations of both Valdés and Gracián. [33] Here, my principal aim has been to identify the two noblemen and to trace their family and historical circumstances. I hope thus to have given some flesh to Fadrique Enríquez and Antonio de Velasco and to have situated them, as young courtiers in the late fifteenth-century court of the Catholic Monarchs, in the historical context of their most productive period of literary activity.

IAN MACPHERSON

University of Durham

---

[30] *Nobiliario*, I, pp. 156-57.

[31] García de Resende, *Cancioneiro geral* (Lisbon: Hermam de Campos, 1515; facsimile ed., New York: Hispanic Society of America, 1904; repr. New York: Kraus, 1967). The poem also appears in LB1, fol. 37^v, which can be dated around 1500.

[32] Sandoval, BAE, LXXX, p. 424.

[33] See my "Conceptos e indirectas en la poesía cancioneril: el Almirante de Castilla y Antonio de Velasco", in *Estudios dedicados a James Leslie Brooks*, ed. J. M. Ruiz Veintemilla (Durham: University Press, 1984), pp. 91-105.

THE *ALEXANDRE* "ENIGMA": A SOLUTION

T H E problem presented by the discrepancy between stanza 1548 and
the final stanza (2675) of the *Libro de Alexandre* was apparent to commentators on the work well before Alfred Morel-Fatio discovered the
Paris MS (*P*) in 1888. [1] The older Osuna-Madrid MS, which dates from
the end of the thirteenth century or the beginning of the fourteenth and
has Leonese linguistic features, mentions *Gonçalo* in st. 1548*d* and yet
claims in its explicit that the work was written down by Juan Lorenzo
de Astorga, whom some critics took to be the author (these included
Tomás Antonio Sánchez, Ramón Menéndez Pidal and María Rosa Lida
de Malkiel): [2]

st. 1548 (MS *O*):

> Bien semeio en esso que fue de Dios amado
> quando fue a su guisa el Rey soiornado
> mando mouer las sennas exir fuera al prado
> e dixo a Gonçalo ue dormir que assaz as uelado

st. 2675 (MS *O*):

> Se quisierdes saber quien escreuio este ditado
> Johan Lorenço bon clerigo ⁊ ondrado
> [natural] de Astorga de mannas bien temprado
> el dia del iuyzio Dios sea mio pagado Amen
> Finito libro // reddatur [s]ena magistro. [3]

---

[1] Alfred Morel-Fatio, *"El libro de Alexandre", manuscrit espagnol 488 de la
Bibliothèque Nationale de Paris,* Dresden: Gesellschaft für romanische Literatur,
vol. X, 1906.

[2] D. Tomás Antonio Sánchez, *Colección de poesías castellanas anteriores al
siglo XV,* 4 vols., Madrid: Antonio de Sancha, 1779-90, vol. III (1782), republ. by
Florencio Janer, *Poetas castellanos anteriores al siglo XV,* Madrid: BAE, vol. LVII,
Rivadeneyra, 1864; Ramón Menéndez Pidal, *El dialecto leonés,* Oviedo, 1962 (republ.
from *RABM*, XIV (1906), pp. 128 and 294-311); María Rosa Lida de Malkiel,
La idea de la fama en la edad media castellana, Mexico and Buenos Aires: Fondo
de Cultura Económica, 1952, *passim.*

[3] The quotations are taken from the palaeographic edn. of Raymond S. Willis,
Jr., *El libro de Alexandre: Texts of the Paris and the Madrid Manuscripts,* Princeton and Paris: Elliott Monographs, vol. 32, 1934; repr. New York: Kraus, 1965.

If, however, we survey the comments made about the poem up to 1888 when the second extant MS was found, we shall see that other attributions had been made. These early comments have been neglected in recent criticism, yet we should examine them closely if only because the persons who made them, in some cases, saw manuscripts of the poem which were different from the extant ones. The earliest mention of the *Libro de Alexandre*, apart from the *cuaderna vía* poems that quote from it, was made by the Marqués de Santillana, in his *Prohemio y carta;* he appears to have regarded the *Alexandre* as one of the earliest, if not the earliest, narrative poem in the Spanish vernacular, since he cites it first.[4] He does not, however, refer to the author by name, appearing to regard the work as anonymous, or simply not attaching any importance to the question, in typical medieval manner. Yet we can be fairly sure that he happened to have access to one of our extant MSS, the Osuna-Madrid, which was in his library at Guadalajara and later formed part of the library of the Duques del Infantado. In 1841, when the house of the Infantado merged with that of Osuna, our MS passed to the famous Osuna Library, having earlier survived a fire at Guadalajara, and in 1884, when that important library was acquired by the Spanish Government, it entered the MSS collection of the Biblioteca Nacional.[5] Santillana had read the poem, most probably in MS *O,* but he did not attribute it to Juan Lorenzo de Astorga (whom he may well have taken to be the copyist only), and there is no sign that he took the reference to *Gonçalo* in stanza 1548 as a reference to authorship. To Santillana, it seems, we owe the present-day title of the work.

Also in the fifteenth century, eighteen stanzas of the *Alexandre* were quoted by Gutierre Díez de Games in his *Vitorial,* or *Crónica de don Pero Niño,* in a passage where he is discussing the four greatest princes in history.[6] He took the quotation from a MS of the poem that is unknown to us, this fragment being known as *G'.* Games does not attribute the poem to any author, possibly because the MS he saw did not do so.

---

[4] *El proemio e carta,* ed. Manuel Durán in Marqués de Santillana, *Poesías completas,* II, Madrid: Clásicos Castalia 94, 1980, pp. 209-223, at p. 218.

[5] The first guard-folio gives the present signature: Vit. 5-10 "Poema de Alexandro", and the earlier sigs.: Ant. Ii-167; V-4-4; ii-5-10; Segura. Plut. III. Lit. M. No. 8, with 188 on the spine.

[6] Ed. Juan de Mata Carriazo, Colección de Crónicas Españolas, 9 vols., Madrid: Espasa Calpe, 1940-46, pp. 13-15; see Willis edn. of the *Alexandre,* introduction, pp. xxii-xxiii.

The next commentator, in chronological order, was Francisco de Bivar, who died in 1635. In his posthumously published *Marci Maximi Caesaraugustani, viri doctissimi...*, in which he defends the antiquity of the Spanish language, he cites various Latin works and then, under the heading *Vetustissimi Hispani metri exemplum*, he gives us nine and a half stanzas of the *Alexandre*. He himself tells us that he copied them from a very old parchment MS in his possession which had come from the monastery of Bugedo near Burgos. He clearly states that its author is unknown: *Autor igitur Annonymus* [*sic*].[7] This would seem to suggest that the lost Bugedo MS did not have an authorial attribution of any sort in its explicit, since Bivar got quite far into the text of the work (he quotes sts. 787-93, 851 and 1167-68*b*) and it would be surprising if such a bibliophile did not examine the last folio, especially since he would be keen to find a date there (he actually supposes it to date from the early years of the twelfth century). What reinforces the likelihood that the Bugedo MS was no more helpful as to authorship than the extant Osuna-Madrid, is that Bivar goes on to say that the *Alexandre* appears to be from a similar period as the battle of Simancas and the life of St Aemilianus written by El Maestro Don Gonzalo, the MSS of which are in the monastery of San Millán. He says he does not dare to guess if the same author also wrote the history of Alexander. This statement would lead one to suppose that, if there was the slightest suggestion in the lost Bugedo MS that Gonzalo de Berceo had written the *Alexandre*, Bivar would have pounced on it with some satisfaction. To Bivar goes the doubtful glory of first connecting Berceo with the *Alexandre*, at least until the reappearance of the Paris MS.

A few years later, in 1663, José de Pellicer Salas Ossau y Tovar, *cronista del rey*, in his *Información por la casa de Sarmiento y Villamay* (fol. 35ʳ), also discusses the *Alexandre*, but we cannot be sure what MS was available to him. He attributes the work to Alfonso el Sabio, but adduces no evidence for such a bold attribution. He was wrong about so many other things that perhaps we should not pay it too much attention; T. A. Sánchez later declared that Pellicer made the attribution "sin más prueba de su afirmación que su palabra y autoridad" (*op. cit.* III, p. xiv). Nevertheless, the comment may be significant in that it gives

---

[7] Francisco de Bivar, *Marci Maximi Caesaraugustani, viri doctissimi continuatio Chronici omnimodae Historiae ab Anno Christi 430 (ubi Flav. L. Dexter desiit) usque ad 612 quo maximus pervenit...*, Madrid: Diego Díaz de la Carrera, 1651, pp. 335-37.

grounds for believing that the MS which Pellicer saw did not state who the author was. Pellicer's royal attribution was later repeated without discussion by Nicolás Antonio. [8]

The next important commentator was Tomás Antonio Sánchez himself, when he was preparing his *Colección de poesías castellanas anteriores al siglo XV*, the third tome of which appeared in 1782. He tells us how the then Duque del Infantado had a copy of the poem made for him, which the duke allowed him to collate with the original MS (*O*). Sánchez reviews most of the earlier commentators: he discards Pellicer's attribution to Alfonso X, keeps in mind Bivar's suggestion about Gonzalo de Berceo, on which he comments that if it has to be one of these two, Berceo is the more likely; but he then goes on to reveal his "feliz descubrimiento de este códice" (*O*), which permits him to find out [*averiguar*] that "Juan Lorenzo Segura de Astorga fue su verdadero autor". Sánchez admits that the verb *escreuir* in the last stanza of MS *O* could mean that Juan Lorenzo was only a copyist; he also speculates that the final stanza might be a spurious addition; he is worried that Juan Lorenzo should call himself a *bon clerigo e ondrado*, which Sánchez thinks is somewhat improper; on the whole, however, he is convinced in Juan Lorenzo's favour as author.

And there things stood for almost a century, until Alfred Morel-Fatio published his *Recherches* in 1875, [9] still some years before his discovery of the fifteenth-century Paris MS. Here he rejected the attribution to Juan Lorenzo, regarding him as copyist only, and also the attribution to Gonzalo de Berceo, on grounds of language, sources, style, etc. Up to this point, the discrepancy between stanza 1548 (connected to Berceo by Baist) and the explicit in the Osuna-Madrid MS had been a problem, especially for those who rejected Berceo as author. When Morel-Fatio was consulted by the Bibliothèque Nationale in 1888 about an entry in a bookseller's catalogue describing an "Historia de Alejandro Magno, en coplas y lenguaje muy antiguo por Gonçalo de Berceo, natural de Madrid, manuscrit du quinzième siècle sur papier", he urged them to buy it and then identified it as the MS earlier listed in a seventeenth-century printed catalogue of the MSS for sale at the Convent of the Discalced Augustinians of Lyon in the Faubourg de Croix-Rousse, which he had earlier

---

8 *Bibliotheca vetus*, III, p. 458.
9 Alfred Morel-Fatio, "Recherches sur le texte et les sources du *Libro de Alexandre*", *Romania*, IV (1875), 7-90.

noted in his *Recherches*. The Paris MS turned what had been a problem into an enigma, an apparent chiasmus, since not only did it attribute the work to Berceo in its explicit but it also mentioned a *Lorente* at the very point where the Osuna-Madrid MS mentioned a *Gonçalo:*

st. 1548 (MS *P*):

> Bien semeio en esto que era de Dios amado
> Lorente ve dormir casaras velado
> quando fue a su guisa el rrey sojornado
> mando mouer las señas e sallyr fuera al prado

st. 2675 (MS *P*):

> Sy queredes saber quien fizo esti ditado
> Gonçalo de Berçeo es por nonbre clamado
> natural de Madrid en sant Mylian criado
> del abat Johan Sanchez notario por nonbrado. [10]

The discovery of this second MS led to a long controversy which is still with us. Gottfried Baist in 1891 considered it proof of Berceo's authorship [11] and he was followed in Germany by Emil Müller in 1910, who thought the work was written by Berceo in his youth. [12] But Morel-Fatio was not convinced and in his edition of the Paris MS published in 1906 he regarded the final stanza of MS *P* as a false attribution to Berceo made in the fifteenth century. [13] Nor were the contemporary Spanish scholars persuaded; Menéndez y Pelayo asked in 1892: "¿no había en Castilla más Gonzalos que Gonzalo de Berceo? Precisamente, el ser tan vulgar en España ese nombre entonces y ahora, mueve a creer que está tomado aquí equivalente de Fulano". [14] Menéndez Pidal in 1906 turned Baist's argument against him: if *Gonzalo* in MS *O* was proof that the attribution to Berceo in the explicit of MS *P* was correct, then equally the mention of *Lorente* in MS *P* was proof that Juan Lorenzo mentioned in the explicit of MS *O* was correct; in addition there was the

---

[10] The Paris MS is Ms. esp. 488 of the Bibliothèque Nationale (see note 1 above).

[11] "Eine neue Handschrift des spanischen *Alexandre*", *Romanische Forschungen,* VI (1891), 292.

[12] *Sprachliche und textkritische Untersuchungen zum altspanischen "Libro de Alexandre"*, Strasbourg: Heitz, 1910, p. 50.

[13] *Edn. cit.,* p. xxi.

[14] Marcelino Menéndez y Pelayo, *Antología de poetas líricos castellanos desde la formación del idioma hasta nuestros días,* Madrid: Hernando, 1890-1908, II (1892), pp. lxi-lxxviii.

matter of the Leonese form of the rhyming words in the text.[15] In 1938 Ruth-Ingeborg Moll rejected the attribution to Berceo on source grounds: Berceo always employed in each of his works one source text only, whereas the *Alexandre* had employed many.[16]

The battle continued unresolved until Emilio Alarcos Llorach's *Investigaciones* were published in 1948: he rejected both attributions on grounds of dialect and the places mentioned in the text.[17] At this point it is interesting to note that all the critics save two regarded the reference in st. 1548 as a reference to the author's tiredness during the act of composition. The two exceptions were Menéndez y Pelayo, who apparently regarded the comment as a reference to *Fulano*, perhaps to any member of the public listening to a recitation of the poem, and Alarcos, who thinks it a joke:

> Yo creo que la broma no va dirigida al autor mismo —o al copista— sino a cualquier "ombre bueno" del público —llamárase Lorente o Gonçalo, ambos nombres muy comunes—, que se adormeciera escuchando el poema (*op. cit.*, p. 55).

Only two further suggestions have been made. The late Niall Ware suggested in 1967 that the resemblance between *Lorente* in st. 1548 in

---

[15] "El libro de Alixandre" (rev. of Morel-Fatio's edn.), *Cultura Española*, VI (1907), 545-52.

[16] *Beiträge zu einer kritischen Ausgabe des altspanischen "Libro de Alexandre"*, Würzburg: Mayr, 1938, pp. 2-3. In his lengthy defence of Nelson's long-propounded thesis that Berceo composed the *Alexandre* before his "spiritual conversion" to hagiographical literature, Gilberto Triviños fails to dispose of Moll's argument about the *Alexandre* poet's use of multiple sources against Berceo's normal practice: "Berceo también combina dos o más fuentes de diferente naturaleza (oral y escrita)", see his *"Vagar doma las cosas:* sobre la edición crítica del *Libro de Alexandre"*, *Thesaurus*, XXXVIII (1983), 564-92, at 584. Berceo could be shown handling two written sources only in his late addition of the miracle of "La iglesia robada" to his *Milagros de Nuestra Señora* and possibly his use of an as yet undiscovered source for the prologue of the same work (unless that was already present in the MS of the *Miracula* available to him at San Millán). Neither Nelson nor Triviños appear to have considered the likelihood that the many linguistic and stylistic similarities between the *Alexandre* and Berceo's works could be explained by the Riojan poet's having closely studied the earlier and probably first poem written in *cuaderna vía*, the *Alexandre*, and drawn techniques from it just as most of the other later poets in this metre did. (See also Harriet Goldberg, "The Voice of the Author in the Works of Gonzalo de Berceo and in the *Libro de Alexandre* and the *Poema de Fernán González"*, *La Corónica*, 8 (1979-80), 100-12, where serious objections to Nelson's hypothesis are raised). One might well re-phrase Menéndez y Pelayo's words and ask: "¿No había en España más poetas que Gonzalo de Berceo?"

[17] Emilio Alarcos Llorach, *Investigaciones sobre el "Libro de Alexandre"*, Madrid: *RFE* anejo núm. XLV, 1948, pp. 50-55.

MS *P* and *Juan Lorenzo* in the explicit of MS *O* is probably no more than coincidental. [18] He considered that the *Gonçalo* mentioned in st. 1548 in MS *O* and the attribution to Berceo in the explicit of MS *P* were the readings in a MS which was a common ancestor of *P* and *O*. He even speculated that the scribe of *P* altered st. 1548 from *Gonçalo* to *Lorente,* which was probably his own name. Although this explanation may seem to strain coincidence too much, the importance of Ware's article lies in his separation of *Lorente* from *Juan Lorenzo,* and his discussion of possible scribal confusions in st. 1548. He also speculated that either two copyists far removed from each other in time tried to deny Berceo the honour of authorship, or alternatively that there was a deliberate attempt on the part of some early copyist to pass off the work as Berceo's by introducing two spurious stanzas.

The only other proposed solution has been put forward by Brian Dutton in 1971: he had earlier accepted the veracity of the information given in the final stanza of MS *P* about Berceo's biography, [19] and he now put forward a striking solution: an accident in a thirteenth-century scriptorium, in which two copies of the *Alexandre,* each in two tomes, stood side by side on a shelf. [20] The accident would have consisted of someone taking vol. 1 of one set and vol. 2 of the other, and *vice versa.* Thus one MS originally had *Gonçalo* in st. 1548 and in the explicit, while the other had *Lorente* in st. 1548 and *Juan Lorenzo* in the explicit. But there are serious problems with this explanation: the *mester de clerecía* poems were commonly copied either in quarto or in folio; not one has ever been found in two tomes. [21] Both the extant MSS of the *Alexandre* are quartos, but the folios of *P,* the paper MS, are somewhat larger

---

[18] N. J. Ware, "Gonçalo, Lorenço, Lorente: an *Alexandre* enigma", *BHS,* XLIV (1967), 41-43.

[19] "The Profession of Gonzalo de Berceo and the Paris Manuscript of the *Libro de Alexandre*", *BHS,* XXXVII (1960), 137-45; see also his "Gonzalo de Berceo: unos datos biográficos", in *Actas del Primer Congreso Internacional de Hispanistas,* Oxford: Dolphin Book Co. Ltd., 1964, pp. 249-54.

[20] "A Further Note on the *Alexandre* Enigma", *BHS,* XLVIII (1971), 298-300.

[21] Most of the MS copies of Berceo's poems are contained within compendia of his works which were bound up in single tomes; see Claudio García Turza, *La tradición manuscrita de Berceo, con un estudio filológico particular del ms. 1533 de la Biblioteca Nacional de Madrid,* Colección Centro de Estudios Gonzalo de Berceo, 4, Logroño: Instituto de Estudios Riojanos, 1979, and Isabel Uría Maqua, "Sobre la transmisión manuscrita de las obras de Berceo", *Incipit,* I (1981), 13-23. Most other medieval Spanish narrative poems are contained in MS tomes consisting of three or more works bound together; the *Poema de Mio Cid,* the *Libro de Alexandre* and the *Libro de buen amor* are almost exceptional in surviving in separately bound tomes, partly, no doubt, because of their length.

(190 × 263 mm) than those of *O* (163 × 258 mm). The copyists preferred where possible to have an exact number of stanzas on each page: *P* has seven per side and *O* eight, thus *P* consists of 193 fols. and *O* 153. Both the extant MSS have lacunae in different places, but there are more in *O* than in *P*. So what a chance it would be to find two *MSS* of the same work ending at the same point at the bottom of a verso folio at the exact end of a gathering, especially since the gatherings nearly always vary in their number of folios within any given MS, and then for them to be bound up in separate tomes! This is to leave aside the problem that the extant MSS have divergent dialectal forms, yet one can see no trace of any change in linguistic forms before and after st. 1548 in either MS. A brilliant theory, then, but totally unconvincing. One must also observe that both Ware and Dutton have no doubt that st. 1548 refers to the author.

I have studied the two most recent editions of the *Alexandre* with care to see if either of the editors comes up with a new explanation. Dana Nelson bases his "reconstrucción crítica" on the assumption that Berceo was the author and he sometimes corrects the text to correspond to a reading he finds in one of Berceo's known works. [22] Jesús Cañas Murillo is more moderate, [23] but he follows in the footsteps of Alarcos in Castilianizing the text. Both these editors use *P* as their base MS, but put in forms from *O* when it suits them to do so. The only interesting comment for the problem here under review is made by Nelson: he observes that st. 1548 corresponds more or less to the point where the poet has come to the end of Book V of the *Alexandreis* of Gautier de Châtillon and is about to embark on Book VI. [24] I had already noted this in my doctoral thesis of 1967, [25] but as with Nelson now, it did not then lead me to a solution of the enigma.

---

[22] Dana Arthur Nelson (ed.), Gonzalo de Berceo [*sic*], *El libro de Alexandre*, Madrid: Biblioteca Románica Hispánica, Gredos, 1978 (1979) .

[23] Anónimo, *Libro de Alexandre,* ed. Jesús Cañas Murillo, Madrid: Editora Nacional, 1978.

[24] It corresponds approximately only, because the Spanish poet altered the order of Gautier's account of Alexander's reception at Babylon and omitted the last dozen lines of his Book V, then he omitted the Argumentum and the opening lines of Book VI, again altering the order of the account that follows of Alexander's dispositions of his army, as well as inserting a Biblical reference to the marriage of Moses to Jethro's daughter.

[25] "The Treatment of Classical Themes in the *Libro de Alexandre*", Ph. D. thesis, University of Manchester, 1967; the section concerning the "enigma" was omitted from my book *The Treatment of Classical Material in the "Libro de Alexandre"*, Manchester: M.U.P., 1970.

I believe that a re-examination of the poet's references to himself, to the act of composition and to his source material can provide a solution. The anonymous poet makes occasional use of *abbreviatio* and similar *topoi* (sts. 294, 653, 1412, 1547, 1957, 2066, 2137, 2548, 2663), and in one instance refers to his own tiredness:

> Se quisiessemos todas las tierras ementar
> otro tamaño liuro podrie y entrar
> mas quiero ela cosa adestaio andar
> ca soe yo cansado querria me ya folgar
>
> (st. 2585, MS *O*)

As well as making mention of Homer (i.e. the *Ilias Latina*) at various points in the digression on the Trojan War (sts. 323*c*, 419*c*, 441*b*, 531*b*, 759*d*, 1504*d* and 2288*c*), and of Ovid (sts. 368*c*, 1874*d* and 2390*a*), he also refers to his main source, Gautier de Châtillon, usually in a quite personalized manner:

st. 247*c*

> *O:* cuemo diz Galente enel su uersificar
> *P:* como lo diz Galter en su versificar
> [refers to *Alexandreis*, I, 357].

st. 1501*c*

> *O:* Galter magar quiso nolas pudo conplir
> *P:* ca Galter non las pudo mager quiso conplir
> [refers to lack of this part of description of Babylon in *Alexandreis* (at V, 443), which is therefore supplemented from *Roman d'Alexandre, B* 7760-8049].

st. 1614*b*

> *O:* fue como galante dezie eutiçio lamado
> *P:* fue como Galter dize Cutiçio clamado
> [refers to *Alexandreis*, VI, 218: "Euctemon"].

The most interesting example is the reference to Gautier's "tiredness" in omitting the Wonders of the Orient at *Alexandreis*, IX, 282, which the Spanish poet supplements from the *Epistola de Situ Indiae* incorporated into a version of the *Historia de Preliis*:

st. 2098

> *O:*   Pero galter el bono en su uersificar
> seya ende cansado do querie destaiar
> dixo dela materia mucho eneste logar
> quando la el Rey dixo quiero lo yo cuntar
> *P:*   Pero Galter el bueno en su versificar
> sedia ende cansado e queria escasar
> dexo de la materia mucho en es logar
> quando lo el dexo quierolo yo contar.

A probable explanation of st. 1548, therefore, is not that it is a reference to the poet himself, nor to a sleepy member of a hypothetical audience listening to a recitation of the poem, but rather that it is another reference to Gautier de Châtillon's tiredness, made by the Spanish poet in a comic aside on reaching the end of Book V of Gautier's work, which he almost certainly had before him on his desk; he apostrophises the book as though Gautier himself were physically in front of him, so that the original may have read:

> Bien semeió en esso que fue de Dios amado:
> quando fue a su guisa el rrey soiornado,
> mandó mover las sennas [e] exir fuera al prado.
> —¡G[*alteri*]o, vé dormir, que assaz as velado! [26]

with "Go to sleep, Gautier, you've stayed up long enough!" as a witty filler for the fourth line. This joke was not understood either by the copyists or by later readers after the former had garbled the passage.

It remains to consider how the scribal corruption occurred. The most likely cause is a misreading of Gautier's name. The Latin form was *Gualtherius,* so we might expect to find in Spanish *Gualterio, Gualtero, Galterio* or *Galter.* [27] This last (Eastern) form we find in the text at the four points quoted above. There are already corrupted forms of the name

---

[26] The line-order in MS *O* is clearly preferable (*pace* Nelson), while the addition of *e dixo a* before *Gonçalo* in the same MS was a feeble and hypermetrical marginal insertion to make sense of an already garbled passage; the confusion is worse in MS *P:* "Go to sleep, Lorente, you will marry as a bridegroom[?]!" (*casarás velado* for *ca assaz as velado*).

[27] R. P. Gonzalo Díez Melcón, *Apellidos castellano-leoneses (siglos IX-XIII ambos inclusive),* Granada: Universidad de Granada, 1957, lists for the patronymic the following variants: *Goter, Gutier, Galter* (p. 64), *Gotiar, Gualterio* (p. 110), *Gutierrez, Gotierrez, Guterretz, Guterre, Guterrez* (pp. 150-51), *Guterriz, Guiteriz, Gualteriz, Gutieriz,* etc. (p. 177). Juan del Álamo, *Colección diplomática de San Salvador de Oña,* Madrid: CSIC, 1950, II, Index, p. 923, gives the following variants of the forename: *Guter, Guterio, Guterrio, Gutierrus, Guterrus, Gutier, Gutierre, Gutterius, Guttierrio.*

in MS *O: Galente* and *Galante*. It is not a big step from these forms to *Lorente*. Initial majuscule letters were frequently confused when written in Gothic script, especially when an abbreviation sign in the lower part of an initial could stand for *er, ar* or *or*. In addition, the initial majuscules at the start of lines of verse were sometimes omitted by the copyists to be inserted later in a different ink, so that an original reading $G^{a}l\tilde{\imath}(io)$ might be left as $l\tilde{\imath}(io)$ and then have been wrongly read as *lorent(io)*, given as *Lorente* by the Eastern scribe of MS *P*. It would have been even easier to misread $G^{a}l\tilde{\imath}io$ as $\tilde{G}l\varsigma uo$, giving rise to *Gonçaluo* (the older form) and then *Gonçalo* (or even more simple to misread G^{o}, as Brian Tate once suggested to me). [28] In each branch of the stemma, one would postulate two steps for the erroneous forms *Gonçalo* and *Lorente*, respectively, to be attained, and this is very likely considering the great divergence both in dialectal forms and other readings, in particular onomastic ones, between the two extant MSS, which is greater than the divergence we find in most other medieval Spanish stemmata (e.g. *Ovidio/Oraçio* in st. 1504*d*; *eutiçio/Cutiçio* for *Euctemon* in st. 1614*b*, etc.).

Elsewhere the *Alexandre* poet shows himself capable of quiet humour: in st. 2 he makes a joke of the fact that his *mester de clereçia* is *sen peccado;* in st. 5 he asks the public to regard him as a good scribe (*escribano*) if he succeeds in finishing the poem; later in st. 91 he thinks Lady Philosophy's belt given to Alexander is worth more than his own; in st. 1178 he declares he would not relish being on the journey through the desert to Ammon; in st. 1824 he comments that "we clerks are always going astray and full of vice". A mild joke to tell Gautier to go to bed when the Spanish poet is moving from Book V to Book VI of his main Latin source is entirely consistent with these other jocular comments, but the humour was thereafter consistently lost on copyists and readers of the work.

There only remains to be considered the discrepancy between the names given in the two MSS in the final stanza of the poem. Niall Ware

---

[28] Adriano Cappelli, *Dizionario di abbreviature latine ed italiane*, Milan: Manuali Hoepli, 1899, drawing on Latin and Italian MSS, gives the normal resolution of G^{o} as *Goffredus* (p. 137) and of *G.* as *Guidus, Gilinus, etc.* (p. 132); Auguste Pelzer, *Supplément au Dizionario ... de Adriano Cappelli*, Louvain: Publications Universitaires, 1964, adds *Godefridus* as a possible resolution of *G.*, but these names were very rare in Spain; Díez Melcón (*op. cit.,* pp. 109-110) lists only one example of *Guido* (s. XII) and one of *Joffre* (1248), whereas there are very numerous examples of *Gundisalvus, Gonçaluo*, which would be more credible as a resolution of *G.* or G^{o} in Spain.

(following T. A. Sánchez) made the interesting suggestion that this final
stanza is spurious, and its introducing phrase certainly smacks of many
other scribal explicits, cf. the following listed by Wattenbach: [29]

> Nomen scriptoris si tu cognoscere queris (followed by the copyist's name:
> p. 517)
> Nomen scriptoris si tu cognoscere velis (followed by the copyist's name;
> p. 518)

which are very close to st. 2675 in MS *O*: "Se quisierdes saber quien
escreuio este ditado", confirming one's impression that Juan Lorenzo de
Astorga was merely the scribe of an ancestor of MS *O*. [30] It might not
be too daring to suggest that this Juan Lorenzo was the person of that
name active at the monastery of Otero de las Dueñas between 1286 and
1297: *Johan Lorienço* (1286), *Johan Lorenço* (1295), *Johan Lorenzo*
(1297), since Díez Melcón [31] registers only one other occurrence of the
name: *Lorente so fillo Juan Lorente* (1248), quoting from Erik Staaff,
Etude sur l'ancien dialecte léonais, Uppsala, 1907. The final stanza in
MS *O* is highly ametric and confirms the impression that it did not
originate with the *Alexandre* poet. A better attempt was made in MS *P*
to produce a final stanza that is more or less metrically correct, but it
is so unlike Gonzalo de Berceo's usual method of revealing his identity
at the beginning and end of his hagiographical poems [32] that it must be

---

[29] Wilhelm Wattenbach, *Das Schriftwesen im Mittelalter*, 4th edn., Leipzig:
S. Hirzel, 1896 (1st edn. 1871), repr. Graz: Akademische Druck-u. Verlagsanstalt,
1958, cap. v.

[30] My opinion that Juan Lorenzo de Astorga was not the scribe of the extant
MS *O* is supported by the (second) scribal explicit in Latin: *Finito libro || reddatur
[s]ena magistro*, which should be read as *reddatur c[o]ena magistro*, i.e. "let the
master [of the scriptorium] reward me with supper", cf. Wattenbach, *op. cit.*, p. 499,
for other examples of this and similar requests for reward in scribal explicits.

[31] *Op. cit.*, pp. 99, 56 and 88, apart from *Juhan Lorentez*, 1245, Oña (p. 152),
and *Juan Laurenti*, 1032, Oviedo (p. 49). There is a further example of a landowner
called *Juhan Lorentez* cited in Juan del Álamo, *op. cit.*, II, pp. 613-14, doc. no.
501: *Reconocimiento de heredades en Tamayo por don Pedro IV, abad de Oña
(1245 febrero 3)*, who is probably one and the same as the man cited by Díez
Melcón, p. 152.

[32] Gonzalo de Berceo is assiduous in revealing his identity in these poems,
usually in the opening and closing stanzas and sometimes within the text. It is
very possible that the last stanza of *Alexandre* MS *P*, if it was a later spurious
addition made in the scriptorium of San Millán, was based on the last stanza of
La vida de San Millán de la Cogolla, MSS of which were preserved there:

> Gonzalvo fue so nomne qui fizo est tractado
> en Sant Millan de Suso fue de ninnez criado
> natural de Verceo, ond sant Millan fue nado
> Dios guarde la su alma del poder del Peccado.

> (ed. B. Dutton, st. 489).

treated with great caution, as must the biographical details it contains, if they were inserted as late as the fifteenth century. [33] It is not improbable that it was inserted by a member of the community at the monastery of San Millán when the *Libro de Alexandre* was being copied there in order to claim yet another Berceo poem for the greater glory of that house. This probably false addition to the original poem clearly was not connected in its perpetrator's mind to the proper name mentioned in st. 1548, which remained as the erroneous *Lorente*. The likely solution to the *Alexandre* "enigma" is, therefore, that the chiasmus does not exist except in the minds of modern critics of the poem. But the only chance of confirming this would be to discover one of the missing MSS of the work.

IAN MICHAEL

University of Oxford

---

[33] Isabel Uría Maqua (ed.), *Poema de Santa Oria,* Madrid: Clásicos Castalia, 1981, p. 11, also doubts the authenticity of the last stanza in MS *P* and the biographical details it contains. Francisco Rico, "La clerecía del Mester", *HR, 53* (1985), 1-23 and 127-50, at 136, thinks it a mistaken or deceitful attribution, but accepts the data it contains as authentic.

JORGE MANRIQUE Y LA MANIPULACIÓN
DE LA HISTORIA

N o siempre se quiere aceptar la auténtica realidad de la obra literaria. Por lo general, la crítica suele dejar de lado aspectos fundamentales del producto literario: sociedad, conciencia de clase, intenciones del autor, ideología implícita o explícita que en el texto aparece. Ocurre así que la lectura queda incompleta o bien se aborda de forma por lo menos ambigua. El caso que aquí me ocupa resulta bien sintomático: Jorge Manrique se ha convertido con sólo un poema, las *Coplas a la muerte de su padre,* en una de esas figuras imprescindibles del panorama literario en torno a la cual se ha montado un vastísimo edificio crítico, idealista, abstracto o, en el mejor de los casos, simplemente formalista. Y en más de una ocasión, el crítico se niega a aceptar la posibilidad de un verdadero entendimiento del poema de Manrique, como hiciera Azorín:

> Jorge Manrique es una cosa etérea, sutil, frágil, quebradiza [...] Jorge Manrique es una ráfaga que lleva nuestro espíritu allá hacia una lontananza ideal. La crítica no puede apoyar mucho sobre una de estas figuras; se nos antoja que examinarlas, descomponerlas, escrutarlas, es hacerlas perder su encanto. [1]

Tal vez porque las *Coplas* incluyen temas eternos y universales como tiempo, muerte, fama, tratados de forma extraordinaria y capaces de conmover al lector de cualquier época, la apreciación de los estudiosos se ha dirigido en una sola dirección, con referencia al hecho estético —inmutable, a lo que parece, al paso del tiempo— y olvidando el hecho social e ideológico, que hace de este poema una pertinaz y sutil defensa de unos intereses de clase bien particulares y delimitados. Como ha dicho Alberto del Monte, perdura pese a todo, en Manrique,

> in irresoluta perplesità il problema della posizione storico-umana del poeta, vale a dire della attualizzazione storica di quella tradizione culturale ch'egli, nell'accogliere, individualizza non solo come poeta ma anche come esponente di una realtà storico-sociale. [2]

---

[1] Azorín, *Al margen de los clásicos* (Madrid, 1915), p. 23.
[2] Alberto del Monte, "Chiosa alle *Coplas* di Jorge Manrique", en *La sera nello specchio* (Milán-Varese, 1971), pp. 7-8.

Teniendo en cuenta todo esto, que el objeto estético de las *Coplas* resulte magistral es algo que queda fuera de mi propósito en este momento. El cual no es otro, como he dicho, que poner al descubierto la ideología sobre la cual Manrique monta sus *Coplas* y el mecanismo de ese montaje.

No es extraño que las *Coplas* de Manrique representen, entre otras cosas, la literaturización de los intereses nobiliarios mediante una trama exterior que mejor puede ocultarlos: el tratamiento de unos tópicos poéticos que enmascaran el auténtico sentido de la obra. Conviene recordar lo dicho por Pedro Salinas:

> Un gran poema es una serie de repeticiones; repite las palabras de su idioma, dichas y escritas millones de veces; reitera los mecanismos sintácticos [...] Pero una misteriosa ley organizadora de todo esto [...] toca, como una varita mágica, los vocablos, las frases ordinarias, y el todo que ellos forman, el poema, aparece como novedad virginal e intacta, como nueva, nunca vista realidad. [3]

Es decir, como una realidad *natural*. Correlato, en este caso, de la *naturalidad* con que Manrique quiere imponer en sus *Coplas* la ideología de la clase dominante y de su propio clan familiar, formado por un importante grupo de poetas, soldados y políticos, así como oligarcas: Fernán Pérez de Guzmán, sobrino del canciller Ayala; el marqués de Santillana, sobrino del primero; Gómez Manrique, sobrino del marqués y tío de Jorge Manrique:

> Todo el clan mendocino, en sus diferentes ramas, respondiendo a la defensa de sus intereses aristocráticos, fue enemigo jurado de Álvaro de Luna y de su política, e intervino continua y activamente en las luchas civiles de la época. [4]

Y el poeta Manrique, "appartenente a una delle maggiori famiglie della feudalità castigliana, non poteva non partecipare all'ideologia di questa". [5]

Conviene comenzar por lo obvio, esto es, por el tratamiento de la figura de Rodrigo Manrique en virtud de la particular visión e intereses de la casta a que pertenece. La alabanza de las virtudes del caballero, su total idealización, constituye uno de los aspectos de la fama. El maestre Manrique, en efecto, puede aparecer tratado positivamente, como en los *Claros varones de Castilla* de Hernando del Pulgar:

---

[3] Pedro Salinas, *Jorge Manrique, o tradición y originalidad* (Barcelona, 1981, 2.ª edic.), p. 121.

[4] Julio Rodríguez Puértolas, Carlos Blanco Aguinaga e Iris M. Zavala, *Historia social de la literatura española,* I (Madrid: Castalia, 1981, 2.ª edic.), p. 139.

[5] Del Monte, *loc. cit.,* p. 14.

Esperaua con buen esfuerço los peligros, acometía las fazañas con grande osadía, e ningún trabajo de guerra a él ni a los suyos era nueuo [...] En las batallas e muchos rencuentros que ouo con moros e con cristianos, este cauallero fue el que mostrando grand esfuerço a los suyos, fería primero en los contrarios [...] porque boluer las espaldas al enemigo era tan ageno de su ánimo que elegía antes recebir la muerte peleando que saluar la vida huyendo. [6]

Pero puede aparecer de modo totalmente negativo, como en las anónimas *Coplas de la panadera:*

> Con lengua brava e parlera
> y el coraçón de alfeñique,
> el comendador Manrique
> escogió bestia ligera,
> y dio tan gran correndera
> fuyendo muy a deshora
> que seis leguas en un hora
> dexó tras sí la barrera. [7]

Podríamos pensar en una interpretación histórica en función de las adscripciones políticas de los cronistas. Mas un hecho no tiene vuelta de hoja: Rodrigo Manrique aprovechó los acontecimientos de su época en favor de sus propios intereses; no fue sino un protagonista más, aunque destacado, en los conflictos del momento entre nobleza y monarquía, como puede verse en los textos de la época y en la crítica subsiguiente. [8]

E. R. Curtius, citando a Hans Walter, disiente de éste cuando afirma que "en la Edad Media la personalidad individual quedaba casi totalmente pospuesta a la casta". [9] En Jorge Manrique se funden sabiamente los conceptos de *casta* y de *individualidad.* Perpetuar la memoria del padre era, al propio tiempo, perpetuar la casta, el linaje; por otro lado, el poeta afirmaba su propia individualidad a través de la misma creación literaria, con su fundamental componente ideológico. Pues, en efecto, como escribió J. Huizinga, "todo caso histórico o literario tiene la incli-

---

[6] Hernando del Pulgar, *Claros varones de Castilla,* ed. J. Domínguez Bordona, (Madrid: Clásicos Castellanos, 1969), pp. 91-92.

[7] Texto según mi *Poesía crítica y satírica del siglo XV* (Madrid, 1981), p. 134.

[8] Comp. lo que el propio Pulgar dice sobre las intrigas de Rodrigo Manrique para obtener el maestrazgo de Santiago, así como, por ejemplo, la introducción de Augusto Cortina a su edición de Manrique en Clásicos Castellanos. También la de Vicente Beltrán Pepió (Barcelona, 1981); el estudio de Antonio Serrano de Haro, *Personalidad y destino de Jorge Manrique* (Madrid, 1966) y el libro de Luis Suárez Fernández, *Nobleza y monarquía* (Valladolid, 1975).

[9] E. R. Curtius, *Literatura europea y edad media latina,* II (México, 1955), p. 719.

nación a cristalizarse en una parábola, en un ejemplo moral, en un número de una demostración". [10]

El contenido de las *Coplas* de Manrique ha servido para afirmar la idea de que es ésta una obra de transición hacia el Renacimiento. [11] Es indudable que en su fecha de composición comienza a apreciarse la ruptura de ciertos esquemas medievales, lógico producto del desarrollo social. En la disgregación del mundo medieval conviven las tendencias de los varios estamentos sociales, encaminados a la consecución de sus privilegios. Frente a la nueva cultura urbana y secularizadora, la nobleza mantiene su poder incluso después de haber visto mermada su significación. Jorge Manrique representa el famoso *equilibrio angustiado,* en el cual latía sin duda la consciencia de que los nuevos tiempos habían de ocasionar el deterioro de las prerrogativas de su casta. En las *Coplas* no aparecen alusiones de gran interés ni sobre el *pueblo llano* ni sobre la nueva clase burguesa ("los que biven por sus manos / y los ricos"; "los pobres pastores / de ganados"). [12] El protagonismo se centra, claro está, en "los buenos religiosos" y, de manera particular, en "los cavalleros famosos" (c. 36). Es obvio que el autor piensa en sólo dos estados, *oradores* y *defensores,* según la clásica división feudal.

El elemento religioso constituye una de las bases sobre las cuales se plantea la reflexión del poeta. Esta concepción teológica, sustentada por las invocaciones ("Aquel solo me encomiendo, / aquel solo invoco yo / de verdad"; c. 4), animada por el *acercamiento* de la historia religiosa ("y aún el hijo de Dios, / para sobirnos al cielo, / descendió / a nascer acá entre nós / y bivir en este suelo / do murió"; c. 6) y concretada en la actuación de la muerte, propicia —al menos inicialmente— la lectura del texto desde un punto de vista medieval. La religión es, además, la vía a través de la cual se encauza la lucha contra el infiel. Como ha dicho Américo Castro,

> Jorge Manrique imaginaba las vías conducentes a la eterna ventura de acuerdo con una idea ascético-guerrera, en la cual se armonizaban las ardientes plegarias con la matanza de moros. [13]

[10] J. Huizinga, *El otoño de la edad media* (Madrid, 1961, 5.ª edic.), p. 103.
[11] La bibliografía sobre la cuestión es abundante, y resulta inútil citarla aquí.
[12] Respectivamente, coplas 3 y 14. Sigo la edición citada de Beltrán Pepió.
[13] Américo Castro, "Cristianismo, Islam, poesía en Jorge Manrique", en *Los españoles: cómo llegaron a serlo* (Madrid, 1965), p. 182.

En este punto, no extraña la preocupación del poeta por la limpieza de sangre ("Pues la sangre de los godos, / el linage y la nobleza / tan crescida, / ¡por cuántas vías e modos / se sume su gran alteza / en esta vida!"; c. 10), o el hecho de que la casta se deteriore en la realización de empresas inadecuadas ("Unos, por poco valer, / ¡por cuán baxos y abatidos / que los tienen! / Otros que, por no tener, / con oficios no devidos / se sostienen"; c. 10). El dedo de Manrique llega así a tocar la verdadera llaga del siglo XV castellano desde su punto de vista oligárquico y clasista.

Estrechamente relacionado con el elemento religioso aparece el tema de la muerte. Frente a la aparente *serena aceptación* con que el maestre don Rodrigo parece disponerse a morir, los personajes de, por ejemplo, la *Dança de la Muerte* rechazan la llamada fúnebre. El maestre, en efecto, recibe a la muerte de modo resignado, conciliador y *natural*. Finaliza su perfecta existencia con un perfecto "Y consiento en mi morir / con voluntad plazentera / clara y pura, / que querer ombre bivir / cuando Dios quiere que muera, / es locura"; c. 38). La muerte es para el protagonista la consecuencia esperada de su trayectoria vital. Después de haber luchado contra el infiel, de haber luchado por la fe cristiana y de haber hecho gala de su perfección, el caballero tiene, irremediablemente, que aceptar la llamada de la muerte. Es el final lógico que exige la vida caballeresca; una reacción contraria significaría la ruptura de los esquemas de su condición social. Es la muerte de un perfecto cristiano que al mismo tiempo es un perfecto caballero, y ninguno, sin duda, sino el caballero, puede morir así. Por ello, y pese a que el fallecimiento de Rodrigo Manrique no debió de ser exactamente como su hijo nos cuenta, pues su enfermedad era nada menos que una úlcera cancerosa en el rostro, [14] en el poema

Manca dunque ogni fisicità della morte, rappresentata come un pacato dialogo fra un perfetto cristiano e l'inviata di Dio: come manca ogni riferimento al decadimento fisico nella vecchiezza, come manca, insomma, ogni pausa sulla miseria corporea della creatura umana. [15]

Las reflexiones manriqueñas acerca de la fugacidad de la vida y de los bienes terrenales adquieren valor únicamente en función de la muerte. El maravilloso final de don Rodrigo Manrique significa la justificación

---

[14] Comp., por ejemplo, Cortina, introducción a su *ed. cit.*, p. xxii.
[15] Del Monte, *loc. cit.*, p. 21.

para iniciar la plática acerca de las glorias pasadas, de las riquezas logra-
das o del ánimo austero del personaje. Y así, las *Coplas* se convierten en
una *danza de la vida*. [16] Luis Suñén ha observado que "la clave de la
originalidad de Jorge Manrique es justamente ese enaltecimiento gravemente exquisito de la vida en medio de la tradición cuatrocentista de la
muerte". [17] Ahora bien, ese "enaltecimiento gravemente exquisito" se
circunscribe al ámbito concreto de la nobleza, representada tanto en Jorge
Manrique como en su padre. El interés particularmente clasista del poeta
no debe confundirse con la actitud vitalista que el Renacimiento trae
consigo. Llegados a este punto quizá pueda rebatirse el argumento de
Pedro Salinas, según el cual, "una muerte, la de Don Rodrigo, bien
pudiera representar a todas las muertes". [18] Efectivamente, la muerte une
a todos los hombres, pero no *la forma* de morir, no el "aparato escénico"
de que se acompaña. De igual modo, es posible disentir de nuevo de
Salinas, cuando afirma:

> Si ahora don Jorge fatiga la figura de su padre con tanto ropaje encomiástico,
> es para que la muerte, en su enseñanza de humildad, de igualdad para todos, se
> los quite [...] con dos palabras. [19]

Pues el "ropaje encomiástico" no se impone por casualidad, sino que
pertenece al personaje, de la misma manera que pertenece también a otros
claros varones de la época. Es uno de los rasgos definidores de una clase
social. La alabanza del poeta pretende idealizar al personaje hasta extre-
mos insospechados, más allá incluso de la misma muerte. Jorge Manrique
perpetúa la figura del padre, y a la vez, acentúa su conciencia de clase.
Pues en efecto y además, resulta curioso cómo padre e hijo resultan difí-
ciles de distinguir a medida que progresa el poema. Me atrevo igualmente
a discrepar de otro juicio de Salinas:

> Esta muerte de este hombre, tan vívidamente representada, desemboca en el
> mar de todos los hombres muertos, y allí se borran los contornos del individuo,
> rendidos a la grandeza abrumadora de los sin nombre. [20]

---

[16] Stephen Gilman, "Tres retratos de la muerte en las coplas de Jorge Manrique", *NRFH*, XIII (1959), 308.
[17] Luis Suñén, *Jorge Manrique* (Madrid, 1980), p. 67.
[18] Salinas, *op. cit.*, p. 199.
[19] *Ibid.*, p. 171.
[20] *Ibid.*, p. 199.

El poeta se encarga de que la figura de su padre no desemboque "en el mar de todos los hombres muertos". Para conseguirlo recurre a un fino mecanismo de convicción, consistente en plantear primeramente de forma general y universalizada problemas que, como el paso inexorable del tiempo, afectan a todos los seres humanos. Es una trama sutilmente tejida: "Partimos cuando nascemos, / andamos cuando bivimos / y allegamos / al tiempo que fenescemos; / así que cuando morimos / descansamos" (c. 5). Desde la primera estrofa aparece la intención, sutil e inteligente, de imponer al lector un mensaje. Comienza Manrique su poema utilizando tres imperativos: *recuerde* (el alma dormida), *abive* (el seso) y *despierte* para contemplar "cómo se pasa la vida" y "cómo se viene la muerte" (c. 1). Un paso más, aún en la misma estrofa primera, y Manrique habla ya en nombre *de todos*: "cómo, a nuestro parescer, / cualquiera tiempo pasado / fue mejor". En efecto, el presente es fugaz; es preciso considerar el futuro como ya pasado. Y definitivamente, la opinión de Manrique, a modo de imperativo categórico, se alza ante el lector, al que no se deja ya de la mano: *no se engañe nadie, no* (c. 2). [21] Después, Jorge Manrique no tiene sino que concretar, apropiarse de las consecuencias del tiempo en los individuos de su casta: pérdida de riquezas, muerte de nobles famosos, recuerdos de hazañas y de virtudes, etc. Y tras esta imposición, otra: la absoluta idealización de la figura del padre. Estas consideraciones sirven para corroborar la idea de Américo Castro:

> ... *no es la doctrina* de la guerra santa lo ahora traído a primer plano, *sino la persona* del guerreador, dotada aquí de perfil, de volumen, de conducta y de voluntad, todo muy puesto de realce [...] Más importante poética y vitalmente que la guerra contra el infiel, es quien la hace. [22]

Conviene enlazar este punto con otro de los temas tópicos de las *Coplas,* el ideal de la fama, considerado como el "deseo de perduración personal por encima de la muerte, coincide con aspectos importantes de la ideología humanista y burguesa". [23] De igual modo, Huizinga, citando a Burckhardt, indica que "la ambición personal y el amor a la gloria [...] son cualidades características del hombre del Renacimiento". [24] No parece

---

[21] Véase Rodríguez Puértolas, Blanco Aguinaga, Zavala, *op. cit.,* I, pp. 154-55. Compárese la técnica de Manrique con la grosera imposición ideológica de Mateo Alemán en los prólogos a su *Guzmán de Alfarache.*

[22] Castro, *op. cit.,* pp. 188-89.

[23] Rodríguez Puértolas, Blanco Aguinaga, Zavala, *op. cit.,* I, p. 133.

[24] Huizinga, *op. cit.,* p. 94.

tan claro que el tema de la fama sea un rasgo definidor de la modernidad en el caso concreto de las *Coplas:* primero, porque "esta vida de honor / tampoco no es eternal, / verdadera" (c. 35); segundo, porque esa fama puede sin grandes problemas insertarse como un componente más en el armazón construido por Jorge Manrique en defensa de sus intereses de clase. Se trata, de cualquier forma, de utilizar un caso histórico con fines bien concretos, unos fines que bien pueden definirse, sin escándalo, como *propagandísticos,* si por propaganda entendemos aquí una visión del mundo y de la sociedad que el poema pretende imponer a los lectores. Cosa que, por otro lado, intenta todo producto literario, bien de modo inteligente y sutil, bien de modo grosero. Las pretensiones del poeta Manrique de hacer perdurable la figura de su padre más allá de la muerte, significan desviar la realidad histórica para después manipularla, es decir, utilizar la Historia como pretexto para una aparente des-realización y des-historización, para montar una nueva "Historia" que, al tiempo de exaltar al individuo-héroe (Rodrigo Manrique), exalta también y necesariamente el clan oligárquico al que aquél —y el poeta— pertenecen, justo en un momento tanto de crisis personal y familiar como social. [25] De este modo, y como dice María Rosa Lida, Rodrigo Manrique es

> convenientemente exaltado del noble adocenado e intrigante que fue en vida, a la imagen esquemática del reconquistador devoto que el pueblo castellano estaba hecho a venerar [...]. La acomodación de la turbulenta biografía a la vida ejemplar de "caballero famoso" equiparable a Fernán González o al Cid queda cumplida con sutil perfección. [26]

Resulta claro así que sólo los personajes de las clases altas de la sociedad están en condiciones de alcanzar la *fama,* esto es, la perfección; por el contrario, las clases populares participan sólo de modo anecdótico de las hazañas de los héroes. El "montaje escénico" —del cual, como se ha dicho antes, es parte fundamental la forma de morir, coronación lógica de una vida de perfección— preparado por el poeta, responde, por lo tanto, a unos esquemas medievales de exaltación del héroe (*Poema de Mío Cid, Libro de Alexandre, Poema de Fernán González, Poema de Alfonso XI,* etc.), mas en el caso de Jorge Manrique el ideal de la fama

---

[25] Sobre la crisis familiar de los Manrique —incluida la del poeta—, cf. Beltrán Pepió, introducción a su *ed. cit.,* pp. lxxx-lxxxi y lxxxiv. Y sobre la crisis social, comp., por ejemplo, Salvador de Moxó *et al., La sociedad castellana de la baja edad media* (Madrid, 1969).

[26] Lida, *La idea de la fama en la edad media castellana* (México, 1952), p. 292 y nota.

sólo sirve para mantener el *status* social del clan. Lo dicho por Antonio Serrano de Haro confirma el especial interés del poeta:

> Se diría, en efecto, que la sangre de los godos, la nobleza y el linaje jugaron pobremente en favor de don Jorge. La ilustre estirpe de los Manrique, comprometida en la pugna política de la nobleza y los Trastámara, había perdido su primer rango. Brillaban otras casas tradicionales, y de una segunda nobleza y el estado llano emergían los verdaderos poderosos del momento. [27]

Y así, el poema se sustenta sobre unas bases temporales claramente inmovilistas. Ya en la segunda copla se nos ofrece una particular visión del tiempo: "Y pues vemos lo presente / cómo en un punto es ido / y acabado, / si juzgamos sabiamente, / daremos lo no venido / por pasado". Esta concepción estática justifica la ideología medieval del poeta. La inmovilidad temporal favorece el recuerdo del pasado, en el cual la casta representada por los Manrique ha logrado sus hazañas. Y al propio tiempo se anula cualquier posibilidad de evolución al negar el futuro, que ya aparece como pasado y sin valor: "No se engañe nadie, no, / pensando ha de durar / lo que espera / más que duró lo que vio, / porque todo ha de pasar / por tal manera" (c. 2). [28]

La preocupación de Jorge Manrique por mantener el nivel de convicción que sostenga el interés propagandístico del poema se cumple, parcialmente, en las quince primeras coplas, en las cuales el juicio y la reflexión sobre la fugacidad del tiempo es una extraordinaria generalización abstracta y una impresionante ejemplificación de lo que Karl Marx llamaba "falacia ideológica". [29] Sin embargo, el entramado estructural se va desgajando progresivamente cuando aparecen los primeros protagonistas: Juan II, infantes de Aragón, Álvaro de Luna, etc., y se desmorona definitivamente al incorporarse a la acción la figura central, Rodrigo Manrique. El poeta no consigue ya mantener una línea coherente de acuerdo con sus aseveraciones previas, y surgen así las contradicciones, acaso de acuerdo con lo que se ha llamado "mentalidad de contrastes que constituye profundo rasgo común de los caballeros del siglo xv" [30] —indicación, a su vez, de una sociedad en crisis.

---

[27] Serrano de Haro, *op. cit.*, pp. 35-36.
[28] Comp. la concepción histórico-temporal del aristócrata Manrique con la de un intelectual como Juan de Mena en su *Laberinto de Fortuna*, estrofas 56-59, ed. José Manuel Blecua (Madrid: Clásicos Castellanos, 1960).
[29] Comp. Ist007ván Mészáros, *Marx's Theory of Alienation* (Nueva York, 1972), p. 163.
[30] Serrano de Haro, *op. cit.*, p. 337.

Así, la renuncia al mundo pagano y al espíritu y a la forma del humanismo, presente en la copla 4 ("Dexo las invocaciones / de los famosos poetas / y oradores; / no curo de sus ficiones, / que trayen yervas secretas / sus sabores") encuentra su contradicción en las coplas 27 y 28, donde aparecen quince personajes de la Antigüedad con quienes es comparado Rodrigo Manrique, dentro del famoso *canon imperial* clásico. [31] De igual modo, en la copla 25 el poeta considera innecesario alabar las virtudes de su padre ("sus grandes hechos y claros / no cumple que los alabe"), pero nos las presenta en las ocho coplas siguientes en extraordinario catálogo de perfecciones. La tercera contradicción, en fin, la hallamos en la copla 34 ("Y pues de vida y salud / hezistes tan poca cuenta / por la fama"), que es preciso entender correctamente no sólo en sentido literal, sino también en lo que realmente significa: poder. Y así, el poeta habla de las hazañas del padre, pero sin que dejen de deslizarse las realidades ocultas: "hizo guerra a los moros / ganando sus fortalezas / y sus villas / [...] / y en este oficio ganó / las rentas y los vasallos / que le dieron" (c. 29); "hizo tratos tan honrosos / que le dieron muy más tierra / que tenía" (c. 30); "alcançó la dignidad / de la gran cavallería / de la espada" (c. 31).

Mas pese a contradicciones, a cierta incoherencia textual, a ese "equilibrio angustiado", Jorge Manrique y su poema permanecen en todo momento fieles a los intereses oligárquicos del clan. Como dijera Américo Castro, Manrique

> sintió heridas su mente y su alma de castellano por la idea de la muerte. Pero su "isla" humana estaba afirmada sobre una vividura ya muy consciente de su valor; el saberse ser castellano y de casta dominante, hacia 1470, incluía la tendencia a exhibir y valorar la conciencia de estar existiendo como tal. [32]

De este modo, las intenciones de Jorge Manrique, encaminadas al mantenimiento de sus intereses de clase, descansan sobre unas bases claramente medievales. Inmovilismo, religión, muerte, son cuestiones que el poeta manipula a su favor, así como la Historia. Sin embargo, los cambios sociales que se van desarrollando durante el siglo xv se reflejan en el poema, aun a pesar de la misma actitud tradicional del autor. Las contradicciones o posibles incoherencias del texto reflejan la imposibilidad de

---

[31] Comp. E. R. Curtius, "Jorge Manrique und der Kaisergedanke", *ZRPh*, LII (1932), 129-51.
[32] Castro, *op. cit.*, p. 192.

someter la razón a unos presupuestos desacordes con la auténtica realidad social. En cualquier caso, no deben confundirnos los atisbos de modernidad presuntamente inmersos en las *Coplas*. Son la consecuencia lógica de la época, pero no parecen operar voluntariamente en el poeta, obstinado desde la primera copla en la defensa del estamento social al que pertenece: la oligarquía nobiliaria castellana. Para Antonio Machado, la poesía de Manrique no era otra cosa que la palabra en el tiempo. Sin duda. Pero un tiempo sutil, inteligentemente manipulado, en el cual las hermosas palabras ocultan una ideología bien determinada y concreta.

JULIO RODRÍGUEZ PUÉRTOLAS

Universidad Autónoma de Madrid

FIFTEENTH-CENTURY GUADALUPE: THE PARADOXES OF PARADISE

O N E Saturday afternoon in the early spring of 1435 the Castilian king Juan II, his son Enrique, and an escort of some thirty knights came riding over the last of the low mountain ridges which separate the Tagus valley from the narrow upland dale of Guadalupe in Extremadura. At the point where the turrets of the Hieronymite monastery come into view a cross had been erected by the wayside. Here the king and his followers dismounted from their mules — horses were little use in that rough and rocky terrain — and, bearing green branches in their hands, walked the last mile or two down to the monastery gates. The monks of Guadalupe, one hundred and twenty strong, were waiting in line to receive them. The king stayed for almost a fortnight; he was joined after a few days by his wife, Queen María. There were solemn services in the monastery chapel, feasts in the refectory, and visits to the community's country estates. One of these outings was to the artificial lake, bounded by a dam some 200 feet long and 45 feet high, which the monks had built to power their mills and provide trout for their table. Before the king himself was rowed in state upon its waters, two boatloads of royal pages were issued with a supply of oranges and a sham fight was waged for a couple of hours, much to Juan's delight and, no doubt, to that of his ten-year-old son as well. [1]

The king's falconer, describing these events in his chronicle, refers to the visit as a "pilgrimage" — and so indeed it was. Juan was paying homage to the miraculous Virgin of Guadalupe, who had appeared in a vision to a wandering cattleman on the banks of a remote mountain stream rather more than a century earlier. The vision had led to the discovery of a statue; the name of Our Lady of Guadalupe had been invoked

---

[1] Pedro Carrillo de Huete, *Crónica del Halconero de Juan II*, ed. Juan de Mata Carriazo, Madrid, 1946, pp. 195-96; Lope Barrientos, *Refundición de la Crónica del Halconero*, ed. Juan de Mata Carriazo, Madrid, 1946, pp. 172-73; also (with minor differences) José de Sigüenza, *Historia de la Orden de San Jerónimo*, ed. Juan Catalina García, 2 vols., Madrid, 1907-9, I, p. 424. Dimensions of dam in Germán Rubio, *Historia de Nuestra Señora de Guadalupe*, Barcelona, 1926, pp. 84-85.

by Alfonso XI, Juan's great-great-grandfather, at the crucial battle of
El Salado against the Moors. There had been a number of royal visits
to her shrine in the intervening years, most recently by Juan himself in
1430. His well-attested taste for serious theological discussion with men
of piety and learning may have been an additional motive for repeating
the visit now. [2] He may well have felt, too, as his queen certainly did,
that Guadalupe, besides being a shrine of national importance, was the
home of an authentic contemporary saint. Its prior, Fray Pedro de Caba-
ñuelas, was an ascetic whose clothing consisted chiefly of patches, a
dispenser of personal charity on a heroic scale, a mystic who saw visions
while celebrating Mass, a man soon to be so renowned for holiness that
sailors in peril would call upon God to hear his prayers on their behalf.
Perhaps most remarkably of all, he was a monastic superior of whom
his fellow monks could find nothing but good to say. There was, said
Queen María, no-one in Castile to compare with him in point of saint-
liness. From the 1435 visit to his death in 1441, Fray Pedro was to be
her confessor and her confidant, and she gave orders that when she died
her body should be buried close to his — "a great honour in her eyes",
as the monks were to recall. [3] All this is of a piece with the king's humble
descent into the valley, the ceremonial, the solemn Masses. And, of
course, any monastery honoured by a visit from the king would do its
best to welcome him in style. But certain details — the multi-purpose
mill-dam, and the boys pelting one another with oranges — add to this
picture in unexpected ways. The first of these items suggests a community which, by the standards of that time, enjoyed an unusually self-
confident and enterprising mastery over its own material environment.
The second expresses a human warmth and naturalness which one might
not automatically associate with the public image of a great medieval
religious house. Both phenomena are reminders of the very remarkable

---

[2] Foundation stories: Albert A. Sicroff, "The Jeronymite Monastery of Guadalupe in 14th and 15th Century Spain" (hereafter *JM*) in *Collected Studies in
Honour of Américo Castro's Eightieth Year*, Oxford, 1965, pp. 397-99; Sigüenza, I,
pp. 77-83; cf. also Peter Lineham, "The beginnings of Santa María de Guadalupe
and the direction of fourteenth-century Castile", in *JEH*, 36 (1985), 284-304. The
1430 visit: Rubio, p. 87; Sigüenza, I, p. 428. Juan's theological interests: Rodrigo
Sánchez de Arévalo, *Historia Hispánica*, IV, p. 34, in *Rerum Hispanarum Scriptores
Aliquot*, Frankfurt, 1579, p. 422.
[3] Sicroff, *JM*, p. 413, following Gabriel de Talavera, *Historia de Nuestra
Señora de Guadalupe* (Toledo, 1597), fols. 65-74; Sigüenza, I, pp. 418-26; J. R. L.
Highfield, "The Jeronymites in Spain, their Patrons and Successes, 1373-1516", *JEH*,
34 (1983), 524.

institution which the Hieronymite monastery of Guadalupe in this period was.

The spiritual profile of Hieronymite Guadalupe in its early years was outlined some two decades ago by Albert A. Sicroff in a manner which it would still be hard to better or to displace. The present essay, whose indebtedness to Sicroff will be everywhere apparent, seeks to do neither, but rather to furnish that earlier characterization with a context in which aspects of the monastery's material development are given more prominence. [4] Yet the topic of Hieronymite spirituality is not thereby relegated to a secondary plane. As Sicroff very clearly demonstrated, the distinctiveness of Guadalupe was rooted in the unique interaction there of both material and spiritual concerns.

The shrine, of course, went back further in time than the Hieronymite Order itself. The cowherd's vision, the finding of the statue, the first miracles and pilgrimages, belonged to a prehistory which is still, in much of its detail, obscure, but which was evidently, to a degree, anarchic. Medieval pilgrim-centres were never very stable communities at the best of times, and Guadalupe presented certain special problems of its own. The place was hardly off the map, for through it there ran the so-called "Guadalupe trail", one of the great transhumant sheep-routes of the Castilian wool-guild. But it lay an arduous two-day journey away from Talavera, the nearest town of any size, and further still from Toledo, the ecclesiastical capital of the area. The people of the township which soon grew up about the shrine, finding in the steady flow of pilgrims the basis of a thriving tourist trade, set about running it with an essentially secular set of priorities. Guadalupe, moreover, was one of those small Castilian towns — common enough before the last years of the fourteenth century brought in a new period of communal strife — where Christians and Jews carried on their daily activities side by side, with a certain blurring of clear-cut boundaries. Exemplary as this coexistence might now seem, it was deeply disturbing to religious purists at the time. The Castilian Crown was aware that the independent and somewhat *ad hoc* community of monks which served the shrine lacked the institutional

---

[4] Sicroff, *JM,* pp. 395-422, and "Clandestine Judaism in the Hieronymite Monastery of Nuestra Señora de Guadalupe" in *Studies in Honor of M. J. Benardete,* New York, 1965), pp. 89-125 applies, very cogently, the approach of Américo Castro, *Aspectos del vivir hispánico* (Santiago de Chile, 1949); cf. revised edn., Madrid, 1970, pp. 74-97. Many of the material data presented here are from Rubio who, though he seldom names sources, usually turns out to be reliable where these can be identified.

strength to deal with all this. Anxious to regularize the affairs of both town and monastery, King Juan I in 1389 called in the Order of St Jerome. [5]

The founder of the Hieronymites, Brother Thomas of Siena, had visited Spain around 1350 and had left disciples there. These had lived as hermits until 1373, when their rule of life received papal approval; thereafter, several Hieronymite communities had been founded in Castile, of which the most important was San Bartolomé de Lupiana. It was a party of monks from Lupiana who took over Guadalupe by royal command in October 1389. Though the origins of their Order were eremitic, world-renouncing, and even, to an extent, anti-intellectual, the Hieronymites were already launched upon an evolution which was to make them a less single-minded fraternity, but in some ways a more radical one. The character which their movement assumed was perhaps best expressed by a future Prior of Guadalupe, Juan Serrano the Younger. In 1428 Serrano appeared before the Pope to oppose the demand for a radically ascetic reform of the Order's rule, as canvassed by Fray Lope de Olmedo, its former head in Castile. Serrano's case, as Hieronymite tradition recalled it, rested on the assertion that members of the Order were never intended to live "as angels or as beasts", but rather as men. Their life, indeed, was one of work and discipline, but not of especially severe physical privation. Reading and study, on the whole discouraged in their original statutes, were now recognized activities for them. And in a whole variety of ways Hieronymite foundations, with Guadalupe foremost among them, had come to be both economically active and materially rich. All this, it is true, might suggest nothing more remarkable than a slide into worldliness, but this was not how Juan Serrano saw matters. He was able to emphasize the firm liturgical basis of the Hieronymite rule and the Order's record of practical charity. He also drew

---

[5] Sicroff, *JM*, pp. 399-401, following Sigüenza, I, pp. 83-7; Highfield, p. 523. For the "senda de Guadalupe", see *Crónica del Halconero*, p. 50; J. A. García de Cortázar, *La época medieval*, Madrid, 1973, p. 238. Journey-time from Talavera: Nicholas G. Round, "La correspondencia del Arcediano de Niebla en el Archivo del Real Monasterio de Santa María de Guadalupe", *HID*, 7 (1981), 246; from Toledo: Guy Beaujouan, *Médecine humaine et vétérinaire à la fin du Moyen Age*, Geneva, 1966; difficult access: Sigüenza, p. 317; Ildefonso M. Gómez, "Monasterios y monjes jerónimos en los viajeros Ponz, Jovellanos y el barón Davillier", in *Studia Hieronymiana*, 2 vols., Madrid, 1973, II, p. 90 (hereafter *SH*); cf. also the building of the fourteenth-century Puente del Arzobispo to enable pilgrims to Guadalupe to cross the Tagus, Jean-Pierre Molenat, "Les communications en Nouvelle Castille au XVe siècle et au début du XVIe siècle", in *Les communications dans la Péninsule Ibérique au Moyen-Age*, Paris, 1981, p. 158.

attention to the success of even their remoter houses as centres of pilgrimage and popular devotion. And despite Olmedo's personal ties with Pope Martin V, the latter essentially accepted Serrano's defence. Fray Lope went his own way and the Hieronymites were allowed to go theirs. [6]

What they were doing was not to lapse into a comfortably secular existence; rather, they were developing a strenuous "this-worldly spirituality" of their own. That, indeed, had its monastic precedents. But it is arguably closest in character to certain features of other religious developments associated with the very end of the Middle Ages. If the Guadalupe Hieronymites' almost exact contemporaries, the Dutch "Brethren of the Common Life", were contrasted with them in their renunciation of academic achievement and their rejection of any formal rule at all, the two movements shared a strongly positive attitude to work, and a similar efficiency in its organization. If the Erasmians, a century later, were no friends to monks or friars, their pursuit of the inner religious life and their way of making themselves useful in the world seem to carry Hieronymite echoes too. [7]

It may be assumed of the Hieronymites, as of other religious orders before them, that they evolved as they did because the society which sustained them needed and fostered that line of evolution. But it is far easier to suggest how this process may have worked to promote the Order's material advance than it is to trace the social connections of Hieronymite spirituality. The Order at large, and more particularly in Guadalupe, became rich in the first instance because the patronage of kings and magnates made it so. Even before the Hieronymites took over, the list of property belonging to the shrine was beginning to be impressive. Holdings of land, it is true, were first concentrated around Guadalupe itself, but the steady rate of land purchase bears witness to

---

[6] Highfield, 513-21; also, in *SH*, I: Justo Pérez de Urbel, "El monaquismo al aparecer los jerónimos españoles", pp. 51-56; Ignacio de Madrid, "La bula fundamental de la Orden de San Jerónimo, pp. 59-74; Baldomero Jiménez Duque, "Fuentes de la espiritualidad jerónima", pp. 107-21. On the 1428 dispute, Sicroff, *JM*, pp. 409-12, 419n, follows Sigüenza's literary versions of Serrano's and Olmedo's speeches. These may have a basis in actual records; the curial decision still survives (see L. de la Cuadra, *Catálogo-Inventario de los documentos del Monasterio de Guadalupe*, Madrid, 1973, p. 84).

[7] Sigüenza, I, p. 318, has Serrano quote, aptly, from St Jerome: "A ti busca Dios, que no tus riquezas". See R. W. Southern, *Western Society and the Church in the Middle Ages*, Harmondsworth, 1970, pp. 334-58; Sicroff, *JM*, p. 422, following Castro and Bataillon; Melquíades Andrés Martín, "Tradición conversa y alumbramiento (1480-1487): una veta de los alumbrados de 1525", in *SH*, I, pp. 385-94.

the healthy state of the institution's finances. After 1389 further acquisitions of land, along with donations of vassals, taxes and various local privileges in Guadalupe, Talavera, Trujillo and elsewhere, continued to build up the monastery's economic base. Exemptions from royal taxation, together with the many spiritual privileges granted by the papacy, contributed less directly but still effectively to the same purpose. It was a time of Hieronymite advance in Castile generally, but the record of Guadalupe was unique. [8] Yet the most remarkable aspect of all this was not the wealth which accrued to the Hieronymites from such sources, it was what they then made of it.

That they should become sheep-farmers in a large way of business might, of course, have been foreseen. The change in their pattern of landholding between the late fourteenth and the early fifteenth centuries — from a predominance of arable holdings to a massive preponderance of grazing lands — reflected the conventional economic priorities of that age. Sheep-rearing was the way in which every large landowner in Castile turned his domains to profitable account; the "Guadalupe trail" itself was a reminder of that. The scale of the development is, none the less, arresting. In 1389 Guadalupe had owned just 1260 head of sheep; by the 1460s the monastery's flocks approached 13,000, and by the late 1470s they probably surpassed, a tax-exempt limit of 15,000. But these flocks were pastured on only nine of the thirty-three parcels of grazing land which the monastery owned; the rest were leased to other graziers. [9] Against this background, the range and scope of Guadalupe's other activities emerges as yet more surprising.

Cattle-raising, for example, was an important subsidiary interest. Though numbers were subject to fluctuation, and never remotely approached those for sheep, the Guadalupe herds multiplied fivefold in the

---

[8] Sicroff, *JM*, pp. 401-2 on tax exemptions; see also La Cuadra, *passim*, especially, pp. 66 and 72-3 for the *alcabala* (sales tax) and the *servicio y montazgo*, levied on flocks and herds; pp. 404-6 on spiritual privileges; Highfield, pp. 323-7 on royal favour; Carlos Vizuete Mendoza, "El patrimonio del monasterio de Santa María de Guadalupe (1340-1785)", in *En la España medieval: Estudios dedicados al profesor D. Julio González González*, Madrid, 1980, pp. 595-602, on gifts and purchases. See also Consuelo González Flórez, "Documentos sobre la Orden Jerónima en la sección de Clero del Archivo Histórico Nacional", in *SH*, II, pp. 679-729 (134 Guadalupe-related documents out of 182 Castilian items prior to 1450).

[9] Vizuete Mendoza, pp. 596 and 600, generally confirms Rubio, p. 284 (7 grazing *dehesas* and 48 other parcels in 1389; 33 *dehesas*, of which 24 rented out, by later fifteenth century). Totals for sheep: Vizuete Mendoza, p. 602 (1389; in post-1479 period, 16,000); Rubio, p. 286 (in 1462, 12,796); Sicroff, *JM*, p. 402 (tax-limit, 1460).

century or so following the Hieronymite takeover, to reach the respectable total of some 2400 head. Local manufactures of both cloth and leather were established. The monastery produced salt for its own flocks and herds; its non-pastoral landholdings yielded corn, wine and honey. The great dam had its associated mills, and the monks' supplies of timber were cut with a water-powered saw. The picture is one of comprehensive demesne exploitation. In Biblical terms, the Hieronymites were making the wilderness blossom as the rose; in a more modern idiom, they were promoting development in an underdeveloped area. For this was what Extremadura was: a region of low wages, its economy badly distorted by the dominance of large-scale sheep-raising. As major graziers themselves, the Hieronymites were very much a part of the problem. But on the scale of their local activities, they offered a notable model for its solution. [10]

To an extent, the process, once launched, was self-generating. Sheep and cattle in large numbers, for example, provided the basis for textile and leather industries. Other developments had a logic which may well have been the result of planning. From its early days the monastery had owned a number of bee-farms, the mountain flora of the surrounding region proving especially suitable for this. By the fifteenth century Guadalupe owned 3000 hives. But their usefulness was not confined to providing honey for the monastery table; honey was also an important ingredient in electuaries compounded for Guadalupe's hospitals. [11] Beeswax, moreover, could be used to make candles, which were in constant ceremonial use in the monastery, of a finer quality than tallow. As the shrine grew more important as a place of pilgrimage, these could also be sold to pilgrims. Elements of this particular economic nexus may antedate the Hieronymites' arrival, but the dam was all their own work. It ran the corn-mills and the salt-mill and the fulling-mill and the saw-mill; it farmed fish for fast days and for Lent, and it served on occasion, as in 1435, as a tourist attraction in its own right. Clearly it was a piece of

---

[10] Vizuete Mendoza, p. 602 (437 cattle in 1389; post-1479: 2400); Rubio, p. 286 (in 1462: 3489); p. 283 (fulling mill; therefore cloth manufacture); p. 298 (leather); p. 85 (salt); p. 289 (honey); p. 297 (grain); Vizuete Mendoza, pp. 596 and 601 (grain and wine); Round, p. 262 (wine). On the dam and its mills, see Rubio, pp. 84-5 and 283. See also José Luis Martín, *Economía y sociedad en los reinos hispánicos de la baja edad media*, 2 vols., Barcelona, 1983, II, pp. 390-5.

[11] Vizuete Mendoza, p. 598n; Rubio, p. 289; Marcelino V. Amasuno, *Un texto médico-astrológico del siglo XV: "Eclipsi del sol" del licenciado Diego de Torres*, Salamanca, 1972, p. 128.

developmental planning on the grand scale. Water-powered mills had long been a crucial energy source for the medieval economy, and the state of the technology in the fifteenth century was advanced enough in the West to attract the admiration of Byzantine visitors. The monks of Guadalupe were evidently aware of the economic importance of mills, for they made something of a speciality of owning them, over a wide area. [12] But the dam and its associated complex pose in especially dramatic terms the question which is prompted by the more general phenomenon of Guadalupe's economic expansion: how and why did all this come about?

In the first place, certainly, such a range of enterprises responded to the immediate needs of a remote monastery, whose geographical setting and spiritual traditions alike made self-sufficiency a necessary goal. The monks of Guadalupe were farmers because they had to feed themselves; they set up manufactures because they had to clothe themselves; they commissioned building works to make a house for themselves and for Our Lady of Guadalupe whom they served; they became the proprietors of a string of pack-mules because it took two days to get to Talavera. [13] Theirs was, moreover, an expanding community. Thirty-two Hieronymites had migrated from Lupiana in 1389. By the early 1420s the numbers in Guadalupe had passed the hundred mark; in the mid-fifteenth century they stood at about 120 or 130. But the totals for lay brothers and secular helpers — herdsmen, muleteers, labourers and craftsmen of all kinds — multiplied that figure several times. When patients in the monastery's hospitals, pilgrims and guests were added, Guadalupe in the early 1460s expected to provide meals for over 800 persons every day. To meet only these and other basic needs a formidable effort of production was called for. It is still not wholly clear, even so, how that effort came to be so comprehensively effectual. [14]

Initially, its success was very far from certain. In the generation after the arrival of the Hieronymites, the rate of acquisition of land and property, measured by the number of transactions, was lower than it had

---

[12] Rubio, pp. 84-5; Fernand Braudel, *The Structures of Everyday Life,* London, 1981, pp. 353-9; Lynn White, Jr., *Medieval Technology and Social Change,* Oxford, 1962, p. 129n; Vizuete Mendoza, p. 602.

[13] For minor manufactures, see Round, pp. 224, 247 and 261 (articles ordered by the Archdeacon of Niebla: footwear, sacking, knives, wooden trenchers, storage-jars); pp. 246 and 261, and Rubio, p. 253 (mules and muleteers).

[14] For numbers of monks see Sigüenza, I, p. 87; Rubio, p. 305 (in 1424: over 100; in 1462: 130); Beaujouan, p. 373 (in 1442: over 120). For daily meals in 1462, Rubio, p. 290: the 130 monks; up to 170 other residents; well over 200 guests; 50 hospital staff; the rest being patients, recipients of charity etc.

been since the shrine was founded, or was to be again for at least a century. And if the first decades of the fifteenth century saw important new building works, they also saw a period of tension between the monastery and the townsfolk of Guadalupe. [15] The crucial period for economic development seems to have been the Priorate of Gonzalo de Ocaña, who governed the monastery from 1415 to 1429. The year following his accession was the beginning of a long spell of acute water shortage in Extremadura, and Guadalupe found itself at times alarmingly short of both grain and ready money. Yet these crises were always overcome by one means or another. The traditions speak sometimes of the prayers and penances of the monks, sometimes of the generosity of friends and patrons, and there is consistent praise of Ocaña's chief financial officer, the *mayordomo* Fray Juan del Corral. As a charitable centre which had not been incapacitated by famine, Guadalupe attracted many refugees from elsewhere. These in their turn had to be fed. It was a logical step, then, to bring more of the monastery lands under the plough, and this is known to have been Ocaña's policy. Great upland tracts of wood and waste were cleared and planted; former grazing lands were also cultivated — a notable departure from the tendency then prevailing for the monastery to add to its pastoral rather than its arable holdings. Grain yields were high, possibly because this agriculture went beyond the customary methods of "slash and burn"; periodically the lands were given over to grazing again to renew their fertility. In the shorter term, however, the expanding farms of Guadalupe enjoyed what must have seemed to their proprietors like providential favour. The rainfall of 1418 was abundant and the harvest of 1419 a record. It was not very long before the public works of Guadalupe included a grain silo, capable of feeding much of the surrounding region in time of dearth. But the immediate undertaking to which Prior Ocaña's monks now turned their minds and efforts was the great dam, built — perhaps with the labour of those same refugees whom Guadalupe had fed in the recent drought — in the early 1420s. [16]

---

[15] Acquisitions, 1340-89: under 1.5 per year; 1390-1420: under 0.5 per year, Vizuete Mendoza, pp. 596 and 601. The monastery church completed in 1412, Jocelyn Hillgarth, *The Spanish Kingdoms 1250-1516*, 2 vols., Oxford, 1976-8, I, p. 200. Anti-Hieronymite unrest in the town in 1405, 1406 and 1409, Rubio, pp. 76 and 78-9.

[16] Sigüenza, I, pp. 415-8 (Ocaña) dates the beginning of the drought in 1412, cf. Angus MacKay, "Popular Movements and Pogroms in Fifteenth-century Castile", *P&P*, 55 (1972), 56, who notes that 1412-14 was a time of drought, dearth and

Some of the chronology of these events is still conjectural. It is not
certain, for example, whether agricultural expansion was primarily a
response to the climatic crisis or whether it was Ocaña's policy in any case,
for reasons unknown to us now. Nor is it clear how the larger crisis of
subsistence which affected the whole of Castile in 1412-14 interacted
with the local difficulties of the Guadalupe region a couple of years later.
Yet there is some corroboration of the account given above to be found
in the record of the monastery's acquisitions of land and property. In
the period from 1420 to 1435, these transactions were three times as
numerous as they had been in the whole of the preceding thirty years.
And the great majority of these acquisitions came by way of purchase.
Clearly, something very dramatic had happened to Guadalupe's prosperity. [17] It does look very much as if the crisis of 1416-19 and the
Hieronymite response to it provided the springboard for Guadalupe's
economic triumphs. A rhythm was established of bold enterprise and
expansion which could look confidently forward to their providential
reward. The link thus generated between resourceful practical enterprise
and a buoyant sense of divine favour seems fundamental to the achievements of Guadalupe over the next few decades.

It is also necessary, of course, to take into account the initial dispo-
sition of the wider Castilian society to accept what Guadalupe had to
offer. This is most obviously the case in relation to the monastery's financial dealings with the world beyond its doors. Owners of money and
valuables were in the habit of depositing sums — often very large sums —
for safe-keeping in Guadalupe. Such deposits might be used to meet the
Hieronymites' own short-term needs, in which case the owners seem to
have received some return on their investments. On other occasions the
monks themselves made loans to magnates in need, or to the Crown. We
still need to know a good deal more about these transactions: the con-
ditions, rates of return and so forth, and the comparative importance of
Guadalupe in this field, both among other Hieronymite houses and among
monasteries generally. But it is clear enough that what was in question

---

plague. Rubio, pp. 83-86 has the drought beginning in 1416. In general, the account
of famine successfully resisted rings true, perhaps with some exaggeration of miraculous deliverances. For pasture and marginal land reclaimed, see Sigüenza, I, p. 417;
Rubio, pp. 84 and 297. The grain silo (*ibid.*, p. 297) belongs to the mid fifteenth
century (Sigüenza, II, pp. 207-8). The dam, dated 1420-25 by Rubio, p. 84, was in
being by 1427 (Round, p. 241).

[17] Acquisitions, 1420-35: almost 2.5 per year (a rate not bettered in the next
seventy-five years), nearly two-thirds by purchase (Vizuete Mendoza, p. 601).

was an embryonic banking system. There were some obvious links between its development and aspects of the religious life of Guadalupe. Deposits could be regarded as secure because any attack on such a shrine would be an unthinkable sacrilege, because the monks were wholly to be trusted and because they were politically neutral. Outgoing loans made powerful friends for the monastery; incoming investment helped to fuel the process of economic expansion to which the Hieronymites felt themselves called. But Hieronymite involvement in banking is hardly to be explained in terms of spirituality alone; it responds, rather, to Castile's demand for institutions which could play such a role. That demand was to be reflected in the economic life of Guadalupe well into the sixteenth century. [18]

Yet in a sense, the willingness of the monks to make all these matters their business did have its roots in a total outlook on life which was spiritually distinctive. What went on in their farms and workshops and in their business transactions was of a piece with what was going on in the monastery itself. By the mid 1390s it had its own grammar school; twenty years later there were the beginnings of a library; before very long the chapel of Guadalupe was becoming known as an important musical centre. And if these things were only what might be expected of any great monastic house, other features of life in Guadalupe outran that expectation. A Hieronymite experienced in public affairs like Juan Serrano did not renounce that experience, but drew upon it to act as a consultant to persons of importance — even, on occasion, to the king himself. Monks who had trained as lawyers were allowed to practice on the monastery's behalf and on behalf of all those who placed themselves under the protection of its prior. Others, who had studied medicine, tended the sick in Guadalupe's several hospitals around which there grew up, as the fifteenth century advanced, a medical library and school of much distinction. In part, no doubt, such things were made possible by the successful recruitment of monks from privileged and educated backgrounds, the sons of royal officials and wealthy gentry. But something else was at work too — the conviction that every talent which the Hiero-

---

[18] Rubio, p. 294 (banking); Sicroff, *JM*, p. 403 (loans to Crown pre-1389). Some typical transactions in the Archdeacon of Niebla's letters: deposit (Round, p. 225); withdrawal, p. 246; speculative activity, p. 231; charges against current account, pp. 260, 262; for a very large deposit in kind, security for the Archdeacon's loan to the Queen of Aragon, see pp. 230-1 and 233. See also Rubio, pp. 96-7, for a follower of Álvaro de Luna as a client, despite difficult financial relations with Luna himself, p. 99.

nymites possessed was there, as was every resource which their estates could furnish, to be exploited for the greater glory of God and the furtherance of the Order's purposes. Such a sense of inclusiveness is implicit in Serrano's apologia for the Hieronymites, as Sigüenza reports it. The guiding impulse of Guadalupe in the days of its greatness was an attitude of religious humanism. [19]

Not all the manifestations of this inclusiveness were equally attractive. There is, for example, room for much unease about the way in which the Hieronymites ruled the town of Guadalupe. Its people were, of course, their vassals, and the relationship between the two communities was sometimes tense. There were several anti-Hieronymite disturbances in the town in the decade after 1400, though tempers cooled thereafter — aided, presumably, by the improvements which the monks were making in the material environment and by the prosperity which pilgrims and distinguished visitors brought to the place. No further serious outbreak occurred until the mid 1440s, when an enterprising prior tried to recoup the money spent on an over-ambitious waterwork scheme by levying a tax on the townsfolk. They, for their part, had long held the view that the tax-exempt status of their Hieronymite overlords also applied to them. After a sharp reminder from an angry crowd, the prior too was happy to acquiesce in this traditional state of affairs. But if, as this episode showed, there were limits to what the Hieronymites could do in Guadalupe, they were still able, in most respects, to run it as a company town. Their code of local laws, issued in 1424 under Prior Ocaña, was administered by one of their own number, acting as chief magistrate. No aspect of life was left out: the monks had taken thought for public health, for wage-rates, for strikes — these last were strictly forbidden, and involvement in a third offence meant expulsion from the town. There were laws prescribing

---

[19] Rubio, pp. 307-8 (school), p. 274 (library), p. 264 (music); Beaujouan, p. 387 (school), p. 385 (library), pp. 369-457 (hospitals and medical school — the definitive account); Sicroff, *JM*, p. 405 (legal practice). On Juan Serrano see Talavera, fols. 63r-64r; Sigüenza, I, pp. 426-28; Sicroff, *JM*, p. 405. Educated recruits: Diego de Sevilla, "gran letrado", son of royal treasurer (Rubio, pp. 275-6; Beaujouan, p. 386); Gómez González de Cuéllar, Doctor of Laws and papal chaplain (Ildefonso M. Gómez, "Jerónimos y cartujos", *SH*, II, p. 411); Licenciados Juan de Vargas, Bartolomé de Córdoba (Rubio, p. 276), Juan Vázquez (Round, p. 236); Juan de Sevilla, Latinist (*ibid.*); Fray Pedro, son of Chancellor of Aragon p. 228. For aristocratic recruitment, see Highfield, p. 530 (Conde de Belalcázar), Sigüenza, II, p. 209 (Rodrigo de Medina, son of *Mariscal*); a possible propaganda exercise to attract such recruits is the handsomely written *Carta de consejos para un caballero que despreciase este mundo, enbiada por un fraile desta casa*, in *Legajo* 71 of the Guadalupe archive.

modesty in dress, laws regulating the number of guests at weddings, laws forbidding all-night parties. Guadalupe's three inns were all owned, needless to say, by the monastery; the law told customers how much they could have to drink in them and how long they could stay there drinking it. The system was still less than perfect in its working. One thing which the monks found they had to provide was a system of orphanages for a rather large number of foundling and illegitimate children. Not even this commendably enlightened charity, though, can alter the somewhat chilling character of the overall pattern. If, in other ways, Hieronymite practical spirituality looks forward to the Christian humanism of the Erasmians, its application here prefigures the drab rigidities and godly gin-shops of Calvin's Geneva. [20]

The most obvious comment to be made is that the Hieronymites were being Utopian. Utopia — itself the product of an Erasmian imagination — was the perfect polity, but not a place where most people would choose to dwell. Its very inclusiveness seems to rule out any form of spontaneity and the creativity that goes with it. The trouble, however, with any account in these terms is that it ignores the actual relationships through which the episode was lived out. Queen Isabel the Catholic, a frequent visitor to Guadalupe in the later fifteenth century, did more justice to these. Her deep personal attachment to the place was never in doubt; she called it "my Paradise". But she was also heard to remark that anyone who wanted to put a fence around the whole of Castile ought to hand it over to the Hieronymites — they being, by implication, the people who knew all about erecting fences. Etymologically, the Queen was being quite consistent: a Paradise was, in its early meaning a park or pleasance, and the term was derived from an Old Persian word meaning an enclosure. Of that, Isabel was almost certainly unaware; what she does seem to have registered is the paradox of what the Hieronymites had achieved. [21] They had made Guadalupe into a pleasant place — pleasanter, certainly, than they had found it; arguably nearer to Eden than anything the secular

---

[20] See above, n. 14 (earlier revolts); Rubio, pp. 92-94, 97 and 336 (the 1446 outbreak); pp. 346-49 (regulations governing the town); La Cuadra, p. 86 (nomination of Fray Bartolomé de Córdoba as *vicario de la Puebla* with full powers over civil, canonical and matrimonial cases, February 1428); Rubio, p. 351 (orphanage).

[21] Miguel Ángel Ladero Quesada, *España en 1492*, Madrid, 1978, p. 241 (Paradise); the enclosure story (from Melchor de Santa Cruz de Dueñas, *Floresta española*, II, 1, p. 23) in Américo Castro, *The Spaniards: An Introduction to their History*, Berkeley, 1971, p. 359. Cf. *NED*, s.v. "paradise".

world could show. But its making necessarily involved an exercise of power and an extension of ownership, the issue of laws and the drawing of boundaries. Paradisal it might be to the monks and the queen; those who found themselves constrained to obey the laws and observe the boundaries might have perceived it rather differently.

The constraints, and the difference which they made, were never more tragically evident than in 1485, when the Hieronymites of Guadalupe, under pressure from Inquisitorial activity in their town, set themselves to repair their own doctrinal fences within the monastery. Those monks who were secret Judaizers, and the much larger number who had lived ambiguously between religions, suffered punishment. The general body of Jewish-descended New Christians were henceforth excluded by statute from membership of the Order. It is impossible not to see this episode, with Sicroff, as one of loss for the Hieronymites: loss of innocence, perhaps, but certainly loss of a richer plurality and vitality. Sicroff may well be correct too in arguing that, but for this clash with Old Christian prejudices, the Hieronymite example might have influenced Spain towards a much earlier capitalist development than actually took place there. Yet, in another sense, what happened over the Hieronymite *conversos* is ominously of a piece with that development. The saddest irony of the events of 1485 is that New Christians were present in strength in Guadalupe because the Order had, in the first place, made them welcome. The most disturbing aspect of the purge is that the Hieronymites actually conducted it for themselves. [22] Their dealings with the *conversos* can be seen as an extreme and poignant instance of their sometimes uneasy dialectic of enhanced openness and assertive social discipline.

In this, as in much else, the Hieronymites seem to prefigure an age not yet begun. On a far ampler scale than that of a single monastery and its domains, that age would see an inclusive sense of this-worldly human potential first given legitimacy in spiritual terms, and then applied wholeheartedly to the business of producing wealth. In its own secular idiom the capitalist phase of European development was to promise a kind of Paradise. But the Paradise of some was to be the fenced and

---

[22] Sicroff, "Clandestine Judaism...", pp. 89-125; also *JM*, p. 422, and his *Les controverses des statuts de "pureté de sang" en Espagne du XVe au XVIIe siècle*, Paris, 1960, pp. 76-87. Further references in Highfield, p. 532, who notes that, institutionally at least, the Order was to recover from these events.

regulated enclosure of others and the theme of liberation was to be accompanied in that vaster development, as in the local instance of Guadalupe, by the elaboration of new forms of social control.

NICHOLAS G. ROUND

University of Glasgow

WHITE KINGS ON BLACK KINGS: RUI DE PINA AND THE PROBLEM OF BLACK AFRICAN SOVEREIGNTY

T H E work of Rui de Pina (c. 1450-1522) is of special interest to historians of the maritime expansion of Europe because Pina, in his *Crónica de Dom João II*, [1] was the first Portuguese chronicler-royal who had to include in his biographical brief the task of depicting his former royal master functioning as self-proclaimed Lord of Guinea. At least in theory the assumption of this title involved a vast expansion of the territorial and political possessions of the Portuguese crown for the term "Guinea" then included the whole of the Atlantic littoral of Black Africa as far south as the continent might prove to run. Pina was well placed to carry out his task. As secretary of John II, he had observed and no doubt participated in the king's handling of the affairs of Guinea at first hand. Though the *Crónica* was not finished until some years after John's death, we know that Pina had already been entrusted by the king in 1490 with the task of recording "os feitos famosos asy nossos como de nossos regnos". [2] He began to do so right away: it has been established that the seven chapters of the chronicle dealing with the affairs of the kingdom of the Kongo were originally drafted about 1492. [3]

The following are the occasions on which Pina describes John's interventions in Black Africa: (i) Construction in 1482 of the castle of São Jorge da Mina, on the Mina [later Gold] Coast (cap. II); (ii) Assumption by the king in 1485 of the title "Senhor de Guiné" (cap. XIX); (iii) An

---

[1] Rui de Pina, *Crónica de El-Rei D. João II*, ed. Alberto Martins de Carvalho (Coimbra, 1950); the page references in the present article refer to this edition *(CDJII)*. Garcia de Resende, who also was employed in the household of John II, wrote a chronicle with the same title. Resende frequently copies Pina more or less verbatim. For Resende's chronicle I have used the Biblioteca de Clásicos Portugueses edition (Lisbon, 1902); there is a modern one edited by J. Veríssimo Serrão (Lisbon, 1973). Resende got his chronicle into print in 1545; Pina's remained unpublished until 1792.

[2] See *CDJII*, p. xxiv and *Crónicas de Rui de Pina*, ed. M. Lopes de Almeida (Oporto 1977), pp. xvi-xvii.

[3] See Francisco Leite de Faria, "Uma relação de Rui de Pina sobre o Congo escrito em 1492", *Studia*, 19 (1966), pp. 223-303. This account survives only in a contemporary Italian translation. Pina got his 1492 material from the "libro del chapitano della nave" which had brought back from the Kongo in 1492 the expedition of Rui de Sousa.

account of the discovery of the kingdom of Benin and of John's attempts to persuade the Oba to convert to Christianity. The brevity of this account is no doubt due to Pina's characteristic unwillingness to dwell on a royal failure (cap. XXIV); (iv) A long description of the arrival in Portugal of the Wolof king "Bemoim" and of his conversion to Christianity (cap. XXXVII); (v) Pina's account, referred to above, of the discovery of the kingdom of the Kongo by Diogo Cão in 1482 [4] and the conversion of the Manikongo — the title of the Kongo ruler (caps. LVII-LXIII). Pina, judging by the exceptional amount of space he devotes to it and the trouble he went to in order to secure his information, evidently rated the conversion of the Kongo as the most spectacular achievement of John II's reign as far as Black Africa is concerned.

It is indicative of his attitude to the affairs of Guinea that the chronicler makes no attempt to treat them in a separate section of his narrative. What he wishes to record about them is inserted rather awkwardly into the main narrative as and when his annalistic scheme calls for it. His principal concern is overwhelmingly with the king's doings as ruler of metropolitan Portugal. Nor does he seem to visualise Black Africa politically or ethnographically in general terms: he presents Portuguese contacts there as relationships with a number of different rulers and states each to be dealt with in isolation as separate political entities. There is no discussion of the general problems and situations that confronted the Portuguese king in his role as Lord of Guinea. Nor is there any attempt to communicate a sense of Portugal's imperial destiny. Pina presents the king's dramatic interventions in Guinea in what seems today to be a rather provincial way, seeing them simply as an extension of the history of metropolitan Portugal which was not going to change anything fundamentally.

Pina has been much criticized for his undoubted failure to supply fuller details of the discoveries made in John's time. Such criticism does not take into account Pina's view of the historian's task. He repeatedly, in all the chronicles he wrote or revised, makes it plain that he believes, as medieval chroniclers usually did, in the exemplary theory of history. In the prologue to his account of the reign of Duarte I he makes his position entirely clear:

---

[4] The account included by Pina in the *Crónica* reproduces, with few changes, the 1492 *relação*.

... a doutrina hystorial, polo grande provimento dos verdadeiros enxemplos passados que consigo tem, hé assi doce e conforme a toda a humanidade, que até os maaos, que per lição ou per ouvida com ella partecipam, torna logo boõs, ou com desejo de o seer; e os boõs muyto melhores. [5]

His account of John II, accordingly, will always primarily concern itself with showing those aspects of John's reign that, in Pina's view, most provide moral example and inspiration for posterity. As much as with recording the doings of John as an individual monarch, the chronicler is concerned with showing his readers, through these, how kingship should be exercised. This view of royal biography necessarily limits the kind of matters he thinks it appropriate to dwell on. Details about the Guinea trades, in which John II was personally much interested, will be excluded because they would, as Pina sees it, trivialize the portrait he wants to paint. Other matters will not be recorded because their presence might detract from the moral inspiration he aimed at. There is thus no mention of Diogo Cão's mistaken claim that he had reached the Cape of Good Hope — a claim which humiliated the king by causing him to disseminate a false report of a great success to his brother monarchs and to the Pope. Chroniclers like Pina were well aware of the historian's other duty — to tell the truth. But they did not think that historical truth necessarily depended solely on recording all the facts. When these and exemplariness did not entirely coincide, the latter aim usually won the day. Pina's approach to the affairs of Guinea reveals all these qualities at work.

In this paper I propose to examine the chronicler's account of the visit to Portugal of the Wolof king Pina calls "Bemoim" — a name that possibly derives from the Wolof word *bumi*, "heir". This affair seems to have attracted scant interest among modern historians though it was the only occasion on which John II actually received in Portugal one of the Black African sovereigns whose suzerain he considered himself to be. The existence of an alternative account of the affair written well into the sixteenth century by João de Barros, who makes use of additional information about it obtained from a Portuguese official who was familiar with the Wolof kingdom's affairs at the period in question, provides an unusual chance to compare two versions of the same events. In addition we also have a foreign eyewitness's account of Bemoim's

---

[5] See Pina's prologue to the *Crónica de El-Rei D. Duarte* in *Cronicas de Rui de Pina,* ed. M. Lopes de Almeida (Oporto, 1977), p. 487.

visit to Portugal. This is contained in a letter home written from Lisbon in November 1488 by a Florentine merchant, Paolo d'Olivieri. [6]

John II, as is well known, was the first Portuguese king to give serious personal attention to the affairs of Guinea. One new aspect of his policy there was his decision to try to give some tangible backing to the Portuguese attempt to persuade the rest of Europe that they were actively engaged in evangelizing work in Black Africa. The famous bull, *Romanus pontifex,* granted by Nicholas V in 1455, [7] conceded to the Portuguese their monopoly over all navigation and trade in the African Atlantic. The Pope, using, as the bull is at pains to stress, his temporal authority over the whole world, discovered or undiscovered, *(cuncta mundi climata omniumque nationum illis degentium qualitates),* also granted to the Portuguese crown full and unfettered rights to conquer all the lands, rulers and peoples to be found in Guinea and to enjoy full *dominium* over all three. Pina was thus perfectly correct when he asserted (*CDJII,* 64) that the title "Lord of Guinea" had been available to the crown for the taking before John's time, though his suggestion that it perhaps had not been adopted previously because, until John came along, "foy Guinee cousa muy pequena, e de pouca estima" is plainly motivated by his desire to aggrandize that king's reputation even at the expense of downgrading the achievements sponsored by Henry the Navigator and Afonso V.

There was, of course, a price to be paid for placing the Portuguese maritime expansion under papal authority: the Portuguese crown for its part committed itself to bringing about, by force or by other means, the conversion of the peoples of Guinea to Christianity. Without this commitment the papal grant would lack any validity and the monopoly be void.

In fact the crusading posture *Romanus pontifex* attributes to the intentions of the Portuguese in Guinea had already been quietly dropped ten years before the bull was issued; since 1444, as a result of defeats

---

[6] João de Barros, *Asia, Primeira década,* ed. Antonio Baião (Coimbra, 1932), pp. 92-102. Paolo d'Olivieri's letter (MS Riccardiano, 1186c) is printed in Zelina Zafarana, "Per la storia religiosa di Firenze nell Quattrocento", *Studi Medievali,* IX (1968), 1109-10. I am grateful to Dr Alison Brown for making this important reference known to me.

[7] The best text of this often reprinted bull is now that in *Monumenta henricina,* XII (Coimbra, 1971), pp. 72-9. For a discussion of it see C.-M. de Witte, "Les bulles pontificales et l'expansion portugaise au XVe siècle", *RHE,* 51 (1956), pp. 413 *et seq. Romanus pontifex* and the successor bulls issued by later popes nevertheless still await a detailed analysis, specially in the light of contemporary arguments about papal power.

suffered by the soldiers and sailors aboard the caravels at the hands of the black warriors of Senegambia, Prince Henry had decreed that crusading there was to be replaced by peaceful trading. As for attempts at evangelizing in Guinea, all the evidence suggests that, until John's time, this was not really attempted at all, despite assurances to Rome that the work was proceeding apace. It was John II who, for the first time, seriously set about trying to give some semblance of reality to the Portuguese commitment. How far simple Christian piety played its part in shaping his new policy we cannot tell. Political motives certainly did. Between 1475 and 1479, during the war between Portugal and Castile, Castilian royal fleets and private merchant adventurers, paying no attention to *Romanus pontifex,* had successfully broken the Guinea monopoly, trading on the Mina Coast and penetrating as far as modern Nigeria. [8] The construction of the castle of São Jorge da Mina and the assumption of the title "Senhor de Guiné" represented part of the rethinking of Portuguese policy undertaken by John as a result of this ominous experience. A display of missionary zeal in Black Africa was another consequence. The king, a skilled politician, was evidently aware of the vulnerability of the Portuguese because of their failure in this respect. There was also the point that, as a Christian king, the newly proclaimed Lord of Guinea could hardly avoid seeking to change the infidel or pagan status of those rulers whose suzerain he now claimed to be. Converts or not, it would not enhance John's reputation to suggest that these Black African rulers were a group of barbarians. This consideration explains why Pina, when describing Bemoim, or the Akan ruler at São Jorge da Mina, or the Manikongo, is always at pains to tell his readers how truly regal their demeanour and behaviour was.

Pina describes the Wolof king as having arrived in Portugal in 1488, when the court was in Setubal. It was there in September and October so that we can probably place the arrival then. Paolo d'Olivieri's letter, written on 20 November, places the arrival of "Benmui" in Portugal "circha d'uno mese fa". The chronicler implies that Bemoim's contacts with John II began in 1487 when one Gonçalo Coelho was trading on the Senegal coast on John's behalf. [9] Pina, characteristically losing no

---

[8] For an account of Castilian penetration of the Portuguese Guinea monopoly during the war see P. E. Russell, "Fontes documentais castelhanas para a história da expansão portuguesa na Guiné nos últimos anos de D. Afonso V", *Do tempo e da história,* 4 (1971), pp. 5-33.

[9] A remarkable description of the Wolofs and their society in 1454 is supplied by the Venetian merchant Alvise da Ca da Mosto [the Cadamosto of Por-

opportunity to stress the king's fame and virtues, declares that Bemoim, "sendo enformado pelas lingoas [the native interpreters who accompanied Coelho] da Real perfeiçam, e muytas vertudes d'El Rey" (90) sent him presents of gold, a hundred young slaves and an embassy whose purpose was to ask for arms and ships. The reality was that Bemoim, hard-pressed by one of the civil wars in which the rulers of the Wolofs frequently found themselves involved because of that kingdom's complex succession arrangements, turned to the Portuguese king because he saw in him an ally who would help him to crush his enemies at home. According to the information given to Barros by Gonçalo Coelho, he had good relations with the Portuguese court well before the political crisis referred to. Trading relations between all the coastal kingdoms of Senegal and the Portuguese had, in fact, flourished since the 1450s when the Venetian merchant, Ca da Mosto, visiting the region under Prince Henry's auspices, had recorded his remarkably detailed account of its characteristics and customs and been impressed by the regal state of the ruler he met. [10] None of this is mentioned by Pina, who implies that serious contacts with the Wolof royal house only began in John's time.

The Portuguese king rejected the request for help, explaining that canon law prohibited him from supplying arms to a non-Christian ruler but declaring that all would be changed if the Wolof king abandoned Islam. In 1488 Bemoim, "por traiçam lançado fora do Regno" according to Pina, put himself in a Portuguese trading caravel together with some of his relatives and arrived in Portugal to plead his case in person; the Florentine letter says that the Wolof king's retinue numbered forty and included a son, many other relatives as well as slaves (*servi*). Barros's well-informed account explains that matters were a great deal more complicated than Pina suggests. John, it seems, had for some time been pressing Bemoim to accept conversion and had used the latter's un-

---

tuguese historians] who made voyages to Senegambia in 1454 and 1455 under Prince Henry's auspices; see *Le navigazioni atlantiche del veneziano Alvise da Mosto,* a cura di Tullia Gasparrini Leporace (Rome, 1966), pp. 39-73; English translation, *The Voyages of Cadamosto,* trans. and ed. G. R. Crone (London: The Hakluyt Society, Second Series, No. LXXX, 1937), pp. 29-51.

[10] Ca da Mosto (*Navigazioni,* pp. 52-53) made much of the fact that the public demeanour and state of the Wolof kings and the extreme respect accorded them by their subjects showed that, though black, they were true kings ("se pono chiamar segnori veramente, come altro signor paro"). Contrast this with the insistence on the barbarity of the pagans and infidels of Africa in some of the papal bulls relating to the condition of the unredeemed people of Black Africa.

comfortable political position to further this aim. The Wolof king rightly concluded that a conversion to Christianity in the middle of a civil war would hardly help his cause and therefore kept promising to become a Christian but continually put off doing so while, at the same time, keeping Portuguese agents and merchants hanging about his court in order to make his enemies believe that he had the support of the Portuguese king (*Asia*, I, 94). Coelho eventually reported to John that he and the Portuguese with him were wasting their time and they all received orders to return home, to Bemoim's chagrin. The latter was then speedily defeated and overthrown by a rival claimant to his throne.

Pina's account of the reception of Bemoim in Portugal deals with events that Pina himself must have witnessed. Barros therefore follows the latter's account for the most part but, since he wrote a generation later and belonged to a more sophisticated historical tradition, he criticizes Pina for being too short on essential details of the affair. He also complains, not without reason from a modern point of view, that Pina overdoes the amount of praise of the Portuguese king he puts in Bemoim's mouth and overstresses the latter's supposed expressions of astonishment at the splendour of John's royal state. Barros, who knew Guinea and its rulers at first hand, recognized the sheer implausibility of the elegantly rhetorical, Europeanized, speeches placed by his predecessor in the mouth of the Wolof ruler who, on the chronicler's own admission, could only communicate with his host through native interpreters.

The first thing was to kit out Bemoim and his retinue so that they conformed to Portuguese ideas of how a king and his courtiers should be dressed and equipped. In their dealings with the peoples of Black Africa the Portuguese of this period seem to show a firm belief that a change of dress also changed the inner man. John presented the visitors with clothing appropriate to their rank, with silver plate for their table and a suitable number of servants. When this had been done Bemoim was formally received at court with all the customary ceremonial reserved for any visiting prince. The chronicler noted that, as a special courtesy, John did not remain seated during his first audience with Bemoim but rose and moved forward a few paces from his throne. Bemoim and his retinue threw themselves on the ground signalling their wish to cast earth on their heads "em synal de sogeiçam, e senhorio". John, however, courteously helped the Wolof refugee to rise and invited him, through the interpreters, to state his case.

If we are to believe the chronicler, Bemoim was well able to play his part; he was, says Pina, fortyish, big of stature, well proportioned, with a very long beard, very black and "com muy graciosa presença" (91). In his praising of the excellence of the Wolof exile's speeches, however, the chronicler seems unwittingly to disclose the existence of a much less favourable general view of black Africans among his fellow-countrymen than such passages suggest. For example, he comments, in a moment of rhetorical excess, that Bemoim put his case so impressively and with such notable oratorical skill that his words "...nom pareciam de Negro bárbaro, mas de Príncepe Grego criado en Athenas" (92)! Barros, some three decades later, seems to reflect similar surprised racial prejudice when, rewording Pina's comment, he says of Bemoim: "representaua nam homem de suas cores, mas hũ príncipe a quem se deuia todo acatamento" (*Asia,* I, 95). The whole speech is, as Barros complains, turned into an exaggerated eulogy of the Portuguese king during which, if the chronicler is to be believed, Bemoim claimed that, as John was Lord of Guinea and he was therefore his vassal, he had a right to receive aid, justice and sympathy from him. He also announced that he now wished to receive baptism, though denying that this desire was motivated merely by his recent misfortunes. Paolo d'Olivieri's reporting of these events is as unsceptical as that of Pina himself. He gives as the only reason for the African king's journey his wish that "llui chon tutti gli suoi vogliono essere christiani".

Bullfights, dancing and other general demonstrations of rejoicing over this religious triumph were arranged. Bemoim, we are told, received instruction in the faith from theologians and lawyers. The conversion went according to plan. When attending a royal mass to see what it was like, the Wolof king was, not unexpectedly, so moved at the elevation of the Host that he became instantly certain of the Christian truth. On 3 November 1488 he and six of the nobles of his retinue were baptised late one night in the queen's bedchamber. The hour chosen for this event seems curious. Was it one recommended by the royal astrologers as propitious or had the king become worried about unfavourable popular reactions to the red-carpet reception accorded to Bemoim? John II himself, the queen and the heir to the throne served as his godparents at the ceremony. The royal convert, unsurprisingly, chose "John" as his Christian name. Another of his godparents was a papal commissioner who conveniently happened to be visiting the Portuguese court at the time; it is possible that a desire to impress the commissioner contributed to the exceptional fuss that was made of Bemoim's conversion. Pina reports without comment that the new convert sent a letter in Latin to the pope reporting what had happened (94-5). In it, says the chronicler, he praised the Portuguese king and expressed his devotion to him. Pina, as royal secretary, may well have written the document. As happened in the case of correspondence from the Manikongo, the Portuguese did not hesitate to overcome language problems on such occasions by writing on behalf of African rulers letters containing the sentiments they felt sure the nominal originator would have wished to use had he personally been capable of handling such correspondence.

The king now proceeded to make good his promises that, once any African ruler became a member of the Christian community (the *communitas fidelium*), he would be treated just like any other Christian prince allied to the Portuguese crown. Four days after Bemoim's baptism he was dubbed a knight by his suzerain and provided with a coat of arms consisting of a golden cross on red ground, the borders being edged with the *quinas* of Portugal. He then paid formal homage to the Portuguese king as the latter's vassal. How could the papal commissioner fail to report on his return to Rome that he had seen with his own eyes the success with which John II was carrying out his commitment to convert the infidel rulers of Guinea to Christianity?

To prove that he was as good as his word John now informed Bemoim that a fleet of twenty caravels carrying soldiers and military equipment would convey him to the mouth of the Senegal River and see that he recovered his usurped throne. The Florentine merchant's letter refers to "ben dodici navili" and states that the Portuguese force consisted of 300 men, as well as friars and priests. Though he does not mention any purposes other than a missionary one, its size clearly confirms the chronicler's statement that military action was also planned. The fleet was placed under the command of a general called Pero Vaz da Cunha. To help in the conversion of the Wolofs, ready-worked stone, wood and other materials, Bemoim was told, would be carried by the caravels to enable a church to be constructed in a suitable place. The caravels would also carry a number of missionary priests to Senegal to undertake the conversion of Bemoim's kingdom (95).

It now became apparent that all the honours showered on Bemoim had a political and strategic purpose as well as a religious one. The

prepared stone and other materials the fleet carried were not just intended to build a church — if they were really intended at all for that
end. As had happened at São Jorge da Mina in 1482, the purpose of
carrying these building materials by sea to Guinea was to make it
possible for the Portuguese to start building a fortress rapidly on a site
in the estuary of the Senegal. Pero Vaz was directed to make sure that
the fortress, when built, was, like those at Arguim and São Jorge, held
extraterritorially by him as captain in the king of Portugal's name. A
permanent trading factory was to be associated with the fortress. Pina
explains that the Portuguese king, believing [wrongly, of course] that
the great gold markets at Timbuktu and elsewhere in the far interior
were located on the upper reaches of the Senegal River, expected to gain
access to these from the new factory at the river's mouth.

John II's plans collapsed ignominiously, after the expedition had
reached its destination, when Pero Vaz, apparently in collusion with
others, personally killed Bemoim with his sword, alleging that he had
evidence that the Wolof prince was planning treachery. Pina, who must
have had first-hand knowledge of what had really happened, treats this
ignominious finale with extreme succinctness, no doubt because the
matter could not be manipulated in any way that convincingly showed
the king in a creditable light. He confines himself to saying that many
believed the truth to be that the Portuguese general wanted to return
to Portugal and had killed Bemoim to make this possible. The king, he
reports, was extremely angry but refrained from taking any action against
Pero Vaz "por nom dar a elle grave pena, e a outros muitos, que por
o mesmo caso a mereciam" (96). This suggestion that John's inaction was
due to dislike of capital punishment is plainly an unconvincing attempt
to make the best of a bad job. The chronicler himself, more truthfully,
elsewhere describes the king as "mui amigo de justiça, e nas exuquções
della mais riguroso, e severo, que piedoso" (203). In any case, as Pina
points out, if the general really had grounds for suspecting Bemoim of
treason, it was his duty to bring him back to Portugal for the king to
judge his royal vassal. Barros, perhaps again relying on the information
supplied to him by Gonçalo Coelho, reports that the building of the
fortress was already under way at the time of Bemoim's murder and that
it was badly sited in a place liable to flooding (*Asia* I, 101-2). Barros
also suggests that the real reason for the murder was that Pero Vaz
took fright at the amount of fever suffered by his men and, having

therefore no stomach for the task of acting as governor of the castle
when it was finished, wished to make sure that the whole project had
to be abandoned (*Asia,* I, p. 101). It seems quite unlikely that Bemoim,
who still had a civil war to win with Portuguese aid, would have planned
any betrayal of his protectors, even if we allow for the possibility that
he was far less delighted with aspects of his stay in Portugal than Pina's
account suggests.

So ended an attempt to repeat, in the land of the Wolofs, the success
the Portuguese were having at this time in turning the Kongo into a
nominally Christian kingdom. So, too, ended John's plan to establish, as
he had done on the Mina Coast, a fortress and factory to defend Senegal
from foreign interlopers and to try to divert the Saharan caravan trade
in gold and other rare materials towards yet another point on the
African coast. The sordid nature of Bemoim's death and the king's
failure to take any action against his murderer necessarily compels us
to ask how far the spectacular events that marked the Wolof prince's
visit to Portugal corresponded to realities acceptable to John and his
subjects and how far they simply represented a piece of elaborate play-
acting by the king for political and economic reasons. It is not possible
at this distance to attempt to reach a firm conclusion on this point.
When religion and economic gain go hand-in-hand it is always difficult
to be sure which is the conscious dominant motive. Excessive scepticism
would be out-of-place for Paolo d'Olivieri was convinced that he had
witnessed a remarkable religious event which, if all went well, would lead
to the general conversion of "tutta quella setta negra". He added ap-
provingly "e chi non vorrà, morrà" and stressed the fame the event
would bring to Portugal.

What seems to be beyond dispute is that most of John's subjects
were unable to accept the egalitarianism implicit in the doctrine of the
communitas fidelium when this required them to defer to Black African
kings and nobles who had accepted Christian baptism. Pero Vaz's murder
of Bemoim, if any of the recent ceremonies in Portugal meant anything, was
an act of regicide. Clearly the general himself did not see the situation in
that light at all and John's failure to punish it can only have given the
impression that the regality of these Christianized Black African rulers
need not be taken too seriously. Resende, whose account of these
matters is largely lifted directly from Pina, can, like him, do no more than
attempt to turn the king's inaction into an edifying example of virtue:

"El-Rei fez soffrer isto, porque havendo de dar castigo, cumpria que matasse muitos que d'isso foram culpados, o que por sua virtude dissimulou". [11] Both chroniclers are at pains to avoid directly stating the embarrassing truth that the king's leniency was due to his awareness that Bemoim's murder represented a point at which ideology had to give way to the realities that ruled in Portuguese society: his people would not tolerate the execution of a white Portuguese of noble rank for killing a black African, king or not. The feelings that lay behind this attitude were what would always undermine the attempts of John II and his successors to extend to Guinea the concept of the *communitas fidelium*. Portugal was by now a society where most people were only conscious of black Africans as slaves relegated to the lowest social level. In consequence, whatever the demands of high policy, it would always prove impossible to persuade them to recognize a distinction between blacks who were slaves and those who were persons of rank and importance in their own lands. Documents relating to the behaviour of Portuguese officials and missionaries in Guinea itself or those which disclose the attitude of ordinary people in metropolitan Portugal to the African princes and nobles they were expected to defer to, amply demonstrate the point. [12] The first king of the Kongo to be converted in John's time soon apostatised, disappointed not only by the behaviour of the Christians when he had to deal with them at close quarters but even more, it seems, by the attempt of the missionary friars to impose monogamy in a land whose agricultural system depended entirely on the practice of polygamy. His successor, Afonso I, appears to have been more enthusiastic a practising Christian than most of his Portuguese mentors but he, too, made many complaints to King Manuel about the lack of respect with which the latter's subjects in his country treated him. Thus, in 1514, he reported that the Portuguese officials who were supposed to reside in his palace at São Salvador refused to do so, one declaring that, even if offered all the treasure the Kongo king possessed, "he would not live with us since he has no intention of sharing a dwelling with a black man". [13] Another complaint was that the captain of the island of

---

[11] Resende, *op. cit.*, II, pp. 18-19.
[12] See, for example, *Monumenta missionária africana (Africa Ocidental)*, ed. António Brasio, I (Lisbon, 1952), no. 83. This document is a long letter of complaint written by Alfonso I of the Kongo to Manuel I in 1514 listing all the offences committed by Portuguese officials, merchants, missionaries and teachers in his kingdom over the years.
[13] *Ibid.*, no. 83, p. 319.

São Tomé — a regular port-of-call on the Lisbon-Kongo route — was accustomed to refer to him as "that infidel dog". [14] A Kongolese ambassador to the Portuguese court protested, in 1514, that he had been insulted by the royal stabler who, directed by the king to provide him with a mount during his stay in Lisbon, had told him a broken-down mule was all he was going to get. This was, said the ambassador, to treat him as if he was a low peasant who did not understand the proper respect due to a knight. [15] Things were no better at São Jorge da Mina; another Portuguese king, in 1523, upbraided the castle's governor severely for refusing to treat with the respect due to their rank the black Christian *cavaleiros* ("vasalos nosos") living in the adjacent Portuguese "city". [16] Though very few documents of this kind survive to illustrate attitudes in John II's time, the case of Bemoim seems to show that, despite the king's efforts, where Black Africa was concerned the inevitable prejudices of a society that accepted slavery as part of the natural order usually proved stronger even then than the theories of theologians and canonists or the demands of state policy.

P. E. RUSSELL

University of Oxford

---

[14] *Ibid.*, pp. 305 and 311.

[15] *Ibid.*, no. 95, pp. 349-350. Here "low peasant" is to be understood as code for "black slave".

[16] J. D. M. Ford, *The Letters of John III, King of Portugal* (Cambridge, Mass., 1931), no. 1.

INTROSPECTION IN AUSIÀS MARCH

F O R some time now, there has been a tendency to speak of Ausiàs March's "powers of introspection", usually without much attempt to explain what such a process might involve for a poet writing in the fifteenth century. Pere Bohigas, for example, discusses "introspection" and "analysis" as a single concept with two aspects, one personal, the other theoretical: "El primer [i.e. the personal] pot remarcar-se en la prolixitat amb què l'autor descriu certs estats psicològics que atribueix a l'amador, en els quals es reflecteix una experiència humana que ha pogut formar-se al marge de la psicologia amorosa". [1] More recently, Pere Ramírez i Molas has distinguished between "introversion" and "extroversion" in connection with one of March's most characteristic devices, the extended metaphor or small-scale allegory:

> Sabem que Ausiàs March és un home introvertit, almenys en la seva poesia... El procés d'introversió, però, és lent i culmina en les obres tardanes. La comparança *sí com... ne pren a mi* és, de fet, una porta oberta a l'extroversió: el poeta no pot expressar la seva vivència sinó per mitjà d'un *analogon* del món exterior. La introspecció és incapaç de traduir-se en una mera anàlisi psicològica sense el mirall del món objectiu. [2]

I shall return later to the last part of this statement, with its implied evaluation of the inner at the expense of the outer. At this point, however, it may be more helpful to look at the particular example of introspection which Bohigas goes on to quote:

> Coratge meu, a pendre esforç molt tard,
> no piadós de tots los qui et sostenen,
> l'arma i lo cos a departir-se vénen,
> per tu ser flac lo cos de viure és fart,
> mos ulls no són lliberts fer son ofici,
> mon pas és tolt, ma llengua no em profita
> e d'açò la vergonya es delita
> com só plagat de tan vergonyós vici!

---

[1] Ausiàs March, *Poesies,* ed. Bohigas, 5 vols. (Barcelona, 1952-59), I, p. 56.
[2] Pere Ramírez i Molas, *La poesia d'Ausiàs March: anàlisi textual, cronologia, elements filosòfics* (Basle, 1970), p. 251.

Paor me sent. Gran suor me comença.
Surtint, mon cor lo pits me cuida rompre.
No em trop esforç per vergonya corrompre.
Ésser no pot ma esperança por vença.
No puc mostrar lo secret de ma pensa
e vanament he por de la resposta.
Lo meu dubtar major dubte m'acosta.
Femenil gest ardiment me defensa.
    Alguns han dit que vergonya no es troba,
mas jo en pusc fer, d'aquella, testimoni
(de vista, no: semblant és al dimoni):
part de mos senys e parlar me derroba;
dóna a sentir de si alguns forts actes,
segons de molts havem oïdes gestes,
creent-los tals qui descolen les festes;
senyor és meu: amor ferma els contractes.

(XLIII, vv. 1-24) [3]

Bohigas's comment on this passage runs as follows:

Aquest tòpic [i.e. the timidity of the lover] tan utilitzat per la poesia medieval dóna peu al nostre poeta per a fer descripcions precises, ... on sembla no haver oblidat cap de les torbacions del tímid quan es troba en presència de la persona que ocasiona la timidesa. Però això, que podria semblar anàlisi freda, pren relleu per obra d'algun vers espars que de sobte suggereix vigorosament tot el drama que el poeta està descrivint, i eleva la descripció i li dóna vida. Aleshores és quan Ausiàs March ens apareix no com un home del seu temps, sinó com un home del nostre. [4]

Leaving aside for the moment the large issues raised by the final sentence, we can probably agree with this as far as it goes. Two additional features, however, should be noted: one is that the long description of the physical effects of timidity is conventional to the extent that the details of the individual symptoms might be taken directly from almost any medieval treatise on the passions; the other is the persistent presence of the first-person singular forms which thrust their way through the entire poem, energizing not merely "a few scattered verses", but the whole pattern of argument.

The combined result is not so much "introspection" in the modern sense of the word as the creation of an "I" which gives focus and power to what Paul Zumthor has called a "registral commonplace". In earlier

---

[3] The text of all passages quoted is taken from *Les poesies d'Ausiàs March,* ed. Joan Ferraté (Barcelona, 1979).

[4] Bohigas, *op. cit.,* I, pp. 86-87.

troubadour poetry, as Zumthor goes on to claim, the acceptance of such a "register" or network of commonplaces more often than not serves to empty the "I" of any personal content: "Ce qui pendant assez long-temps encore restera étranger au discours poétique 'courtois' c'est son investissement par un sujet concret, riche de ses expériences et lourd de ses secrets". [5] This, one might argue, is precisely the stage which Ausiàs March has reached: time and again in his poems, a powerful ego — what Joan Fuster calls "un jo hipertrofiat" [6] — seems on the point of bursting through the schemes of analysis which the poet himself has brought into play and without which the presentation of such an ego would be im-possible. This, clearly, is one of the things which set March apart from many of the troubadour poets: where, for the latter, the "I" and the "you" are often no more than fixed counters in a formal game, in March the "I" is possessed of an energy which draws the still nebulous "you" into its orbit in such a way that the whole question of love is subordinated to the quest for self-definition.

The crucial question here is the nature of the self which is displayed in the poems. This self, as Marie-Claire Zimmermann rightly says, is essentially unstable: [7] compared with his immediate predecessors — for example Pere March, Andreu Febrer or Jordi de Sant Jordi — March, except in a small number of didactic poems, never speaks from a fixed point of view; the "I" of the poems, in other words, is never taken for granted, but has to be constructed each time in terms of the poetic discourse itself. At the same time, there is no question of role-playing: though the nature of the self is constantly at issue, there is a consistency of performance which makes it possible to speak, as Zimmermann does, of an "essential I" which has nothing to do with the "I of narrative". This "essential I", one should add, is not to be confused with the soul. Orthodox Christianity, of course, presupposes the existence of a soul or central self; yet although March speaks continually of the body and the soul and at times is concerned as a suffering individual with questions of damnation and salvation, there is no point at which he comes to rest on spiritual certainties. By comparison, the nature of the self which can

---

[5] Paul Zumthor, *Langue, texte, énigme* (Paris, 1975), p. 188.
[6] Ausiàs March, *Antologia poètica*, ed. Joan Fuster (Barcelona, 1959), p. 39.
[7] Marie-Claire Zimmermann, "Metàfora i destrucció del món en Ausiàs March", in *Actes del Vè Col·loqui Internacional de Llengua i Literatura Catalanes*, ed. J. Bruguera and J. Massot i Muntaner (Montserrat, 1980), pp. 124-50. The references in this and the following sentence are to pp. 126 and 137, respectively.

be deduced from March's poems is both less orthodox and more elusive. In its simplest terms, the self is the point of reference of the "I", the entity — however defined — which determines personal identity. The difficulties begin when one attempts to locate this self; as a contemporary philosopher puts it: "the self is not the body, nor the brain, nor a construction from certain psychological relations". [8] Nor, one might add, can self-awareness be identified with the awareness of one's own mental states; though the latter can be analysed up to a point — a point which will vary according to the conceptual theories available at the time — the self finally eludes immediate introspection if only because self and awareness of self are too close together for any genuinely introspective act to take place.

One consequence of this is that the idea of the self tends to be determined by convention. The same is true to some extent of the inner life in general: it is not so much that certain cultural phases (e.g. the Romantic period) place a greater value on the inner life as that the actual notion of an inner life and its relations with external reality differ according to the preconceptions of the age in which one lives. The self which March presents in his poems, one might say, manipulates existing conventions to a quite unconventional degree. If, in Joan Fuster's brilliant phrase, he is "un senyor feudal amb un problema de consciència", [9] it is important to recognize that his moral conscience is subject to the fluctuations of a self whose contours he attempts to define in terms familiar to any educated fifteenth-century reader. The strategies he employs in order to create a sense of self include several which appear, though usually less forcefully, in earlier troubadour poetry: contrast, hyperbole and, more generally, the admission of obstacles, both concrete and emotional, whose resistance reinforces one's awareness of the speaker's identity. And one of the things which give conviction to such strategies, as has often been observed, is March's decision to write in a Catalan almost entirely free from Provençalisms — a clear break with tradition which at the same time insists on the truthfulness of the "I" who speaks.

---

[8] Colin McGinn, *The Character of Mind* (Oxford, 1982), p. 115. Elsewhere, McGinn describes the self as "a simple mental substance whose identity over time is primitive and irreducible" (p. 122). For a sharp critique of current notions of introspection, see Gilbert Ryle, *The Concept of Mind* (Harmondsworth, 1966), pp. 156-60.

[9] Fuster, *op. cit.*, p. 12.

At other times, the sense of self is conveyed by negative means: the self is something which one can become alienated from or otherwise lose. Thus, in Poem LXXVIII, the lover's thoughts and pleasures are said to be entirely dependent on the woman:

> Mon pensament és en vós més que en mi
> e mon delit per vós passa primer;
> jamés aquell ans que vós jo sentí:
> ma voluntat a mi troba derrer.
> Jo son content si veig contenta vós
> e tant en mi aquest desig és gran
> que el sentiment és perdut de mon cos
> fins que el voler vostre es va sadollant.

(vv. 17-24)

March's characteristic word for this is "transport" ("Per molt amar en altre mi tresport / sí que ésser pens tot la persona aquella", LIV, vv. 21-22), and, as this last example shows, the philosophical implications may go beyond the actual love situation. Elsewhere, the alienation from self may come from other causes, for example death and the consequent defeat of reason:

> En altre món a mi par que jo sia
> i els propis fets estranys a mi aparen,
> semblant d'aquells que mos juís lloaren:
> lo fals par ver, la veritat falsia.
> (XCII, vv. 131-34)

In all such cases, the self has either been totally absorbed by another self or has been rendered unrecognizable by the loss of one of its principal powers, though in the process the speaker, by virtue of his own analysis of the situation, is made all too aware of what it is which has been overthrown.

For the most part, however, March's powers of self-analysis are concerned with more positive states of mind, and it is here that one sees most clearly both the nature of the conceptual framework he uses and the extraordinary subtlety with which he deploys it. The framework itself, as is well known, derives both from medieval scholasticism and, though the two things are by no means separate, from the vocabulary of *fin'amors*. [10] The combination of terms which these provide — the soul-

---

[10] There is also a considerable influence of the philosophy, and at times the vocabulary, of Ramon Llull; see Ramírez i Molas, *op. cit.*, pp. 313-87.

body distinction, the divisions of the faculties, the sins and vices, as well
as the more detailed *topoi* of courtly love — forms a system for judging
human experience which, however rigid it might seem in theory, in
practice can be used to create an almost endless number of new configurations. These configurations are for the most part composed of
abstractions which easily lend themselves to personification or allegory.
At the same time, the actual weight given to abstractions may vary
considerably within a particular poem; as Stephen Medcalf points out,
certain nouns, "though not outright allegories, seem to do more work
in the sentence, to be more solid than if they were mere abstractions", [11]
and unless one is alert to such nuances, one may underestimate the degree
of flexibility which a poet like March is capable of achieving.

Take for example the opening stanza of Poem xxxiv:

> Tots los desigs escampats en lo món
> entre les gents, segons for de cascú,
> ab trencat peu, a pas, van detràs u,
> qui és lo meu, e llong temps ha que fon.
> Sí com los puigs poran fugir al vent,
> ma voluntat d'ell poria campar;
> en un lloc ferm li cové d'esperar:
> no el pot minvar, aquell mal pensament.

(vv. 1-8)

Here, the controlling structure — the movement which leads directly
into the rest of the poem — consists of a carefully graded progression:
"*All* desires... *my* desire... my will". Yet what strikes one immediately
is the way these abstractions are made to form a spatial pattern. Thus
the "desires" are not only personified, but also first scattered ("escampats") and then brought together ("van detràs u") in a state of subjection
("ab trencat peu, a pas"), like defeated troops in a triumphal procession.
However, if there is a sense of triumph here, it is clearly dispelled by the
second half of the stanza. Here, the speaker's desire is identified as a
"mal pensament" from which his will would like to flee but cannot.
(There is a nice symmetry between "campar" (v. 6) and "escampats"
(v. 1); the will would like to "decamp" from the desire to which the
other, "scattered" desires have become subject.) Again, the situation is
defined in terms of space: the will must remain in a fixed place (like the

---

[11] Stephen Medcalf, "Inner and outer", in *The Later Middle Ages,* ed. S. Medcalf (London, 1981), pp. 108-71, at p. 134.

mountains) to await the onslaught of desire — "lloc ferm" perhaps suggesting the "firm ground" where one makes a stand in a battle. And finally the explicit comparison (mountain-wind: will-desire) is reinforced by a verb ("minvar") which can apply to both sets of terms: neither thoughts nor winds can be "diminished" at will — a fact which knits the comparison still more closely to the main argument.

In this instance, flexibility is achieved through a combination of personification, metaphor and simile which together create a penumbra of meanings which qualify and enrich an otherwise simple statement. Later in the same poem, however, the allegorical drama is presented more starkly:

> L'enteniment e qualitat s'acorden
> amar a vós, en qui és llur semblança,
> e los volers han gran desacordança:
> contra raó en tanta part discorden.
>
> (vv. 37-40)

This comes at the end of a long explanation of the speaker's inability to translate his thoughts of love into action; the self here is imagined as a group of warring entities which align themselves vis-à-vis one another with geometrical precision. Nevertheless, if this particular configuration is relatively rigid, the difference between this and the earlier more "flexible" passage is mainly one of degree; however much the essential abstractions are qualified, they remain abstractions and thus constitute a limit to introspection. Though abstractions may be personified, they have no inner complexity such as a character in fiction might possess; as John Burrow observes: "personifications are not themselves suitable subjects for analysis, but represent precisely the point at which, in any given text, a writer has chosen to *stop* in the almost endless process of breaking human behaviour into its constituents". [12] Given the nature of the conventions at his disposal, one may wonder whether a writer really has a choice in the matter. However one interprets his presentation of the self, it seems clear that for March, as for other late medieval writers, the essence of analysis is to make the invisible visible. Allegory, of course, is the principal means by which the inner may be described in terms of the outer; what is more difficult to grasp is the sense in which medieval conceptions of inner and outer differ from modern ones. And this in turn

---

12 J. A. Burrow, *Medieval writers and their work* (Oxford, 1982), p. 91.

has to do with the rules by which one distinguishes between subjective and objective. As Stephen Medcalf puts it:

> Among the medieval philosophers, *subjective* does not have our connotation of 'imaginary', nor *objective* of 'existing as it would do if we were not conscious of it'; rather, *subjective* means 'existing in itself' and *objective* 'presentational', with no sense of consciousness as a film between the two, or as something projected on reality. [13]

This difference of emphasis is nowhere more evident than in medieval theories of the imagination. Though the role of the imagination in Ausiàs March is too complex to go into here, it is worth pointing out how close he comes at times to the idea of the imagination as a neutral creator of images which embody the kind of mental archetypes on which the understanding feeds. Thus the image does not so much imitate reality as provide the reason with raw material for ideas which are conveyed to the reader through other images. Consequently, when March writes that "Sobresdolor m'ha tolt l'imaginar" (xxvii, v. 1), what he has lost is his power of creating images in this sense. And the reason for this is given in the same stanza: "... ma dolor és tanta / que mon voler en parts ne tinc partit" (vv. 5-6). In other words, if the imagination represents visually the idea which gives unity to what is materially diverse, then it cannot function if one of the faculties — in this instance, will — is divided.

This, however, is not the only kind of division which may affect the imagination. Though the latter, in the first place, is dependent on the senses for its impressions of external objects, the senses, insofar as they are also the instruments of desire, may also be at cross-purposes with the idealizing tendencies of the imagination. In March's later poems, the distance between the imagination and the senses often takes the form of an opposition between the contemplation and practice of love, as in the long opening passage of Poem cxvii. It is this distance which, as Douglas Kelly argues, "[separates] the authorial ego from realizing the qualities in the Image" [14] and at the same time reinforces the impression of a self which is attempting to define itself in the course of externalizing its inner divisions. In another late poem, cxix, the emphasis falls, not so much on the ideal, as on the work which the imagination performs in going beyond sensual content to find pleasure in more spiritual qualities:

---

[13] Medcalf, *loc. cit.,* p. 115.
[14] Douglas Kelly, *Medieval Imagination* (Wisconsin, 1978), p. 56.

Lo toc per si molt no s'hi adelita:
quan pren delit, l'imaginar lo hi porta,
pel gest, que tal pensament me reporta
que, tot mi ensems, per ella tota em cita.

(vv. 51-54)

Yet the important thing, as always with the notion of "gest", is that the superior qualities should be made visible. Lovers, as March claims more than once, cannot see into one another's minds: "No imagín de mi us puscau altar, / car dintre meu jo creu que no veeu" (LXXVIII, vv. 33-34); hence, in this same poem, the fear of the timid lover that his rival will outdo him in practice.

Though to a modern eye March may often seem to be stressing the inner at the expense of the outer — hence the claim that he excludes or "destroys" external reality [15] — his analysis of inward states, even when it breaks down, attempts a kind of clarification which can be expressed in public terms. This is why it seems misleading to speak, as Ramírez i Molas does in the comment I quoted earlier, of "introversion" and "extroversion". His point here is that the extended metaphor characteristic of much of March's verse — clearly an externalizing device — appears much less in the later poems, which consequently have a greater "inwardness": "Això vol dir que el recurs de la comparança anirà esdevenint superflu a mesura que es va enriquint i fent autònoma la contemplació interior". [16]

The function of such allegories, as Robert Archer has recently pointed out, is to create a picture in the mind of the reader which, whatever its emotional effect, can be linked heuristically to the kind of mental schema which is central to March's whole understanding of the imagination. [17] Though, as Archer makes clear, the balance between the primary and secondary subjects of the allegory may vary according to the amount of explanation given in the context, the essential mechanism remains entirely compatible with the kind of analysis used elsewhere to describe mental states. In view of this, the implied contrast between externalizing allegory and an increasing inwardness which can dispense with allegory seems misplaced: allegory is rather a natural extension of

---

[15] See the essay by Marie-Claire Zimmermann referred to in n. 7 above.
[16] Ramírez i Molas, op. cit., pp. 251-52.
[17] Robert Archer, "The Workings of Allegory in Ausiàs March", MLN, 98 (1983), 169-88.

the process by which any sense of an inner life must be conveyed through the medium of abstractions.

All this might be of little more than academic interest if it were not related to the extraordinary energy one associates with March's finest poetry. This energy, as I have said, is partly a matter of compression and of the directness which comes of using a language relatively free from convention. In a less tangible way, however, the sense of presence this entails has also to do with the way in which the reader himself is involved in the creation of meaning and, by extension, in the actual process by which the "I" of the speaker is constructed within the poem. Poem LXI, for instance — one of the "Llir entre cards" cycle — begins by addressing "fort dolor": pain wishes the speaker to die, but the woman he loves will not permit this; therefore he will surrender his understanding to pain and preserve his body from death. The second stanza goes on:

> La que jo am mi no consent morir.
> Dóna'm a tu, llançat a ton voler,
> e sap que tu no em seràs mercener:
> no em desempars fins a vida finir
> e, en aquell punt, hages compassió
> d'aquella que jamés de mi l'haurà.
> Com l'esperit del cos eixir volrà,
> oblida mi, membre't de la qui só.

> (vv. 9-16)

The sense of the first four lines is clear: "no em desempars fins a vida finir" takes up the earlier plea of stanza 1 ("no em despulls dels teus dons", v. 4) and relates it to the speaker's imagined death. The next four lines, however, are denser, not only in texture but because of the kind of questions they provoke in the reader. What would it mean for pain to "take pity" on a "pitiless" mistress? If pain is to "forget" the speaker when he is at the point of death, what would be the result of its "re-membering" the woman? Any possible answers can scarcely be clear-cut; the point, however, is that, by enforcing this kind of speculation on the reader, March ensures that the latter will give the poem some of its energy by the sheer act of reading it. What happens here, in other words, is that by inventing an imaginary plot in which abstractions and human agents are held in mutual tension, March puts the reader through something approaching the experience which the poem itself is trying to bring into focus. In other poems, this kind of immediacy is compounded by the admission that self-knowledge is necessarily deficient: "Al grau

primer, bo, del pecant me trobe, / que del mal fet ha coneixença fosca"
(CXVII, vv. 21-22). In such instances, the impression of self is all the
more powerful since the edges of self-analysis are deliberately blurred.
At the same time, the "coneixença fosca" of which March speaks, though
perhaps the best kind of knowledge he can hope to achieve, more often
than not appears as a stage on the way towards greater clarity — a
movement from inner confusion to visible order. This is particularly
apparent in two of March's most ambitious poems, LXXXVII and XCII,
where the relations between inner and outer are expressed in remarkably
similar terms.

Poem LXXXVII, a didactic poem with a more personal second half,
begins with a reflection on the difficulty of defining *amor mixtus* ("No es
pot bé dir com arma i cos pratiquen / aquest voler..." vv. 101-02), which
leads into a description of spiritual love (vv. 141-50), followed by a
contrast, frequent in March's later poetry, between contemplation and
action (v. 176). Shortly after this point (v. 185), the more personal part
of the poem begins, with a notable increase in the use of metaphor and
simile. Two passages of this are especially interesting for the present
discussion. In the first (vv. 195-220), the struggle between body and
spirit is expressed in terms of a brilliantly sustained prison metaphor, at
the core of which lies a striking contrast between blindness and half-
seeing:

> Tant com lo cos sa passió gran lleixa,
> de l'esperit, és sa presó pus ampla
> e ses virtuts e potences eixampla
> sí que no veu tras paret, mas per reixa.
>
> (vv. 195-98)

The second (vv. 231-40) is even more remarkable, in that it imagines an
ideal woman — one who would correspond to the kind of spiritual love
described earlier in the poem:

> Mon esperit contemplant se contenta
> e dintre si una persona forja.
> D'ella no pens braços, peus, mans ne gorja,
> car tot semblant altre semblant presenta.
> Solament vull d'ella tan clara pensa
> que res de mi no el fos cosa secreta,
> apta i sabent, e d'amor fos estreta,
> lo contrafer prengués en gran ofensa,
> de son voler volgués ésser celosa
> e que per mi vers mort fos animosa.

Here, clearly, perfect correspondence transcends the physical level, thus removing the obstacles (such as the inability to see into another's mind) which are overwhelmingly present in other poems. In the rest of the poem, however, this imagined figure is recognized as the pure product of contemplation, in sharp contrast to the realities of practice (vv. 267-70). Nevertheless, just before the end, the meditation turns to the subject of death (vv. 301-10) and the possible survival of lovers' souls, a theme which clearly looks ahead to the first of the "Cants de la mort".

This (XCII), like other poems in the group, relies heavily on images of purification and refinement; the general sense is that the death of the loved one has brought about the one kind of circumstance in which love can exist in a pure state. Significantly, several of these images involve the notion of "bringing to light". Just as in Poem LXXXVII the imprisoned soul was able to look through bars, so here the "amor d'amistança pura" which follows the death of the beloved gives partial sight to the blind will:

> Lo voler cec del tot ella il·lumena,
> mas no en tant que lleve el cataracte,
> e, si posqués fer sens empatx son acte,
> no fóra al món ull ab gota serena.
>
> (vv. 35-38)

Full sight, perhaps it is implied, is scarcely possible, given the fallen nature of humanity; nevertheless, the effect of death is to clarify the inner life of the lover by externalizing it: "Tots los volers que en mi confusos eren / se mostren clar per llur obra forana" (vv. 21-22). Elsewhere, in Poem XCIV, the same situation is described in terms which suggest even more forcibly the movement from the invisible to the visible:

> De tots aquests passions m'atengueren
> mescladament, sí com mesclats jaïen,
> mas bé distints són aprés de son opte
> e separats los sent, quasi visibles.
>
> (vv. 53-56)

This is perhaps the clearest expression of a process which, in one way or another, determines the whole thrust of March's self-analysis. In Poem XCII, as in other poems, the source of pain is imagined in spatial terms which, taken together, form a kind of geography of the self:

> Lo lloc on jau la dolor gran que passe
> no és del tot fora de mes natures
> ne del tot és fora de llurs clausures:
> lo moviment creu que per elles passe.
>
> (vv. 71-74)

Again, the terms of the description are conventional; yet they are brought to life partly by the casual reference to the speaker's own experience (*"creu* que per elles passe") and by the characteristic way in which he rounds off the argument by claiming the superiority of his own know-ledge: "Opinió falsa per tots és dita, / que fora nós e dintre nós habita!" (vv. 79-80).

It is at moments like these that March's poems speak most powerfully to a modern reader, by creating the sense of a "presence" which has little to do with biographical fact. What matters, of course, is the "I" of the poems — a voice which exists only within the poems and which convinces us precisely because of the doubts and tensions it involves. Yet however compelling we feel this to be, to praise March for his "moder-nity", as critics have often done, is to risk misunderstanding the kind of imagination which is at work in his poems. The intention of this essay has not been to make the poetry seem more remote, still less to invoke the kind of false historicism which claims to read an author "in his own terms". As Hans Robert Jauss has argued, the true "modernity" of medieval literature, as opposed to that which merely finds confirmation for contemporary interests in the past, "means the recognition of a significance in medieval literature which is only to be obtained by a reflective passage through its alterity". [18] If reflection on the nature of March's self-analysis makes him seem a less "original" poet in the post-Romantic sense of the word, a greater awareness of the resources on which he draws and of the way he moulds these to his purpose can only confirm one's sense of the coherence of his work as a whole and increase one's admiration for the tenacity and intelligence with which, in poem after poem, he stakes out the limits of an experience which constantly escapes definition.

ARTHUR TERRY

University of Essex

---

[18] Hans Robert Jauss, "The Alterity and Modernity of Medieval Literature", *NLH*, 10 (1979), 181-229, at 198.

LIST OF SUBSCRIBERS

Rafael Alemany Ferrer
Peter R. Beardsell
University of Belfast
University of Bristol
Richard A. Cardwell
Guillermo Carnero
Trevor Dadson
Alan Deyermond
John England
Exeter University
José Luis Gotor
Nigel Griffin
Calouste Gulbenkian Foundation
John Hall
Derek Harris
L. P. Harvey
Albert G. Hauf
J. R. L. Highfield
F. W. Hodcroft
David Hook
B. W. Ife
Lynn Ingamells
Instituto de España, London
John Alan Jones
Ronald G. Keightley
J. N. H. Lawrance
University of Liverpool
D. W. Lomax
Westfield College, London
C. A. Longhurst
Angus MacKay
Malveena McKendrick
David Mackenzie
Ian Macpherson

Elizabeth Matthews
Ian Michael
Ministério da Educaçao Instituto de
    Cultura e Lingua Portuguesa
G. B. Gybbon-Monypenny
University of Nottingham
Taylor Institution, Oxford
Magdalen College, Oxford
Oriel College, Oxford
D. G. Pattison
Frank Pierce
C. J. Pountain
J. M. Ruiz Veintemilla
Nicholas G. Round
Peter E. Russell
University of St. Andrews
Joseph Seniff
Harvey L. Sharrer
Donald L. Shaw
University of Sheffield
Joseph Snow
Luís de Sousa Rebelo
Strathclyde University
Arthur Terry
Alan S. Trueblood
R. W. Truman
Geoffrey J. Walker
Roger M. Walker
Bruce W. Wardropper
Julian Weiss
Keith Whinnom
Clive Willis
Christine J. Whitbourn